Mastering Apache Cassandra

Get comfortable with the fastest NoSQL database, its architecture, key programming patterns, infrastructure management, and more!

Nishant Neeraj

open source*

community experience distilled

PUBLISHING

BIRMINGHAM - MUMBAI

Mastering Apache Cassandra

First published: October 2013

Production Reference: 1181013

Published by Packt Publishing Ltd.
Livery Place
35 Livery Street
Birmingham B3 2PB, UK.

ISBN 978-1-78216-268-1

www.packtpub.com

Cover Image by Tanmay Vora (tanmay.vora@gmail.com)

Credits

Author
Nishant Neeraj

Reviewers
Peter Larsson

Ravi Saraswathi

Paul Weinstein

Acquisition Editor
Owen Roberts

Lead Technical Editor
Anila Vincent

Technical Editors
Tanvi Bhatt

Jalasha D'costa

Kapil Hemnani

Proshonjit Mitra

Copy Editors
Tanvi Gaitonde

Dipti Kapadia

Sayanee Mukherjee

Kirti Pai

Adithi Shetty

Project Coordinator
Anugya Khurana

Proofreader
Jonathan Todd

Indexer
Monica Ajmera Mehta

Graphics
Ronak Dhruv

Yuvraj Mannari

Production Coordinator
Nitesh Thakur

Cover Work
Nitesh Thakur

About the Author

Nishant Neeraj (`http://naishe.in`) is a software engineer at the BrightContext corporation. He builds software that can handle massive in-stream data, process it, and store it reliably, efficiently, and most importantly, quickly. He also manages the cloud infrastructure and makes sure that things stay up no matter what hit the data center in the middle of hardware failures and sudden surges of data inflow.

He has six years of experience in building web applications in Java as a backend engineer. He has been using Cassandra in production-ready web applications since Version 0.6 in 2010. His interests lie in building scalable applications for large data sets. He works with Java, MySQL, Cassandra, Twitter Storm, Amazon Web Services, JavaScript, and Linux on a daily basis, and he has recently developed an interest in Machine Learning, Data Analysis, and Data Science in general.

Acknowledgments

It would have been difficult for me to complete this book without the support of a large number of people.

First, I would like to thank the people at BrightContext (`http://www.brightcontext.com`) for giving me the opportunity to do a lot of experiments with distributed computing and cloud infrastructure, and especially Leo Scott, Arunn Rajagopalan, and Steven Fusco for their technical suggestions.

A lot of credit goes to the online resources that helped me learn about the various technologies in this book. In the context of this book, I would like to acknowledge the people at Cassandra's mailing list, Jonathan Ellis and Christian Hasker of DataStax (`http://www.datastax.com/`), Aaron Morton of The Last Pickle (`http://thelastpickle.com/about.html`), Julian Browne (`http://www.julianbrowne.com/`) for one of the most excellent articles on the CAP theorem, Dave Gardner (`http://www.davegardner.me.uk/`), and DataStax for their exhaustive documentation.

On a more personal note, my siblings Rashmi, Deepshikha, and Rajat have provided invaluable support during the writing process, tolerating my highs and lows as I put together the final draft on top of an already busy schedule. Thanks to my friends Nihar and Tauseef, who kept me motivated, and thanks to my nieces Pariwa and Kittoo, without whom this book would have been completed a month earlier, but with a lot less fun. Lastly, thanks to my parents for their inspiration.

I'd like to express my gratitude to everyone at Packt Publishing involved in development and production of this book. I'd like to thank Anugya Khurana for keeping me on my toes to make sure things happen as they were scheduled, Anila Vincent, Peter Larsson, and Paul Weinstein for patiently going through the first draft and providing valuable feedbacks.

I am indebted to the FOSS (`http://en.wikipedia.org/wiki/Free_and_open-source_software`) community for providing excellent tools that are at par with their commercial counterparts. Cassandra is one of the greatest examples of the success of open source. Until the final draft, this book was written using only free and open source software such as Ubuntu, LibreOffice Writer, LibreOffice Draw, Git, VIM, Cassandra, PyCassa, Hadoop, Nagios, and others.

About the Reviewers

Peter Larsson is a passionate software engineer and an open source evangelist. He has spent 28 years of his career creating software and commercially successful software products. And at all times, he has had the privilege to work with state-of-the-art technology in collaboration with very talented fellow workers. His special skills are in the fields of systems architecture and high-level design, and he views technology from a holistic perspective. Back in the 90s, he pioneered agile ways of working and used Java in large-scale product development organizations. Peter has a wide range of experience from different business domains, but with emphasis on telecom and high volume transaction systems.

> I would like to thank my great colleagues at Callista Enterprise, for making every day a learning experience.

Ravi Saraswathi is an IT executive with more than 20 years of global professional experience. Ravi has expertise in aligning business and IT, SOA implementation, IT strategy, cloud infrastructure design, IT operations, security, architecture, and performance tuning. He has a proven track record of successfully delivering large-scale technical projects and solutions. He is an expert in open source and vendor-based middleware products. From his experience, Ravi gained a solid understanding of the tools and technologies needed to create large-scale web-based software and services.

He currently heads the middleware engineering group for a highly reputed Fortune 500 financial company. He has spoken at several international conferences such as Apache, WebLogic conferences, and Java User Group meetings. His professional focus is on technical management, SOA, middleware architecture, and infrastructure design. He is the author of the book titled *Oracle SOA BPEL Process Manager 11gR1 – A Hands-on Tutorial*.

He holds a Master's degree in Technology Management from George Mason University and has a Bachelor of Engineering degree in Electronics and Communication Engineering from Karnataka University. He holds a CIO University Certificate from Federal CIO University, General Services Administration, United States. He also has extensive experience in architecting and designing solutions using various Oracle fusion and open source middleware products.

He is an aspiring leader and entrepreneur. He has founded a successful IT consulting company. He has trained many associates in Fusion Middleware 11g to gain the skills for developing and designing solutions using Oracle SOA Suite and Service Bus. He actively contributes to the online community for open source and commercial middleware products, SOA, cloud, BPM, and infrastructure architecture technologies.

He holds various IT certifications such as TOGAF, Java, ITIL, Oracle, and WebLogic. His interests include open source containers, Java, infrastructure architecture, troubleshooting methodologies, and software design. He blogs at www.ravisaraswathi.com.

I would like to thank my family for supporting my efforts in reviewing this book.

Paul Weinstein started working in the computer industry when he learned his first programming language. He has yet to look back, as the wondering road delivered his personal understanding of technology to a wide variety of locations, from public elementary schools and political campaigns to pioneering open source companies and local businesses.

At Orbit Media Studios, Paul works alongside Orbit's team of developers. His focus is on optimizing Orbit's development and operations and connecting the codebase with the server infrastructure.

www.PacktPub.com

Support files, eBooks, discount offers and more

You might want to visit www.PacktPub.com for support files and downloads related to your book.

Did you know that Packt offers eBook versions of every book published, with PDF and ePub files available? You can upgrade to the eBook version at www.PacktPub.com and as a print book customer, you are entitled to a discount on the eBook copy. Get in touch with us at service@packtpub.com for more details.

At www.PacktPub.com, you can also read a collection of free technical articles, sign up for a range of free newsletters and receive exclusive discounts and offers on Packt books and eBooks.

http://PacktLib.PacktPub.com

Do you need instant solutions to your IT questions? PacktLib is Packt's online digital book library. Here, you can access, read and search across Packt's entire library of books.

Why Subscribe?

- Fully searchable across every book published by Packt
- Copy and paste, print and bookmark content
- On demand and accessible via web browser

Free Access for Packt account holders

If you have an account with Packt at www.PacktPub.com, you can use this to access PacktLib today and view nine entirely free books. Simply use your login credentials for immediate access.

To my parents

Dr Sushila Devi & Ratan Kumar who are like most of the parents – caring and worried. They are unorthodox and inspiring, but above all, if I am a computer, they authored the kernel.

Table of Contents

Preface

Back in 2007, Twitter users experienced the fail whale, occasionally captioned with "Too many tweets...". On August 3, 2013, Twitter posted a new record of high tweets rate of 143,199 per second, and we rarely see the fail whale. Many things changed since 2007. People and things connected to the Internet have increased exponentially. Cloud computing and hardware on demand has become cheap and easily available. Distributed computing and the NoSQL paradigm has taken off with a plethora of freely available, robust, proven, and open source projects to store large data sets and then process and visualize the data. Big data has become a cliché. With massive amounts of data that get generated at a very high speed via people or machines, our capability to store and analyze the data has increased. Cassandra is one of the most successful data stores that scales linearly, is easy to deploy and manage, and is blazing fast.

This book is about Cassandra and its ecosystem. The aim of this book is to take you through the basics of Apache Cassandra to understand what goes on under the hood. The book has three broad goals: the first is to help you to make the right design decisions and understand the patterns and anti-patterns, the second is to enable you to manage infrastructure and rainy days, and the third is to introduce you to some of the tools that work with Cassandra to monitor and manage Cassandra and to analyze the big data that you have inside it.

The book does not take a purist approach, rather a practical one. You will come to know proprietary tools, GitHub projects, shell scripts, third-party monitoring tools, and enough references to go beyond this book and dive deeper if you want.

What this book covers

Chapter 1, Quick Start, is about getting excited and gaining instant gratification. If you have no prior experience with Cassandra, you leave this chapter with enough information to get yourself started on the next big project.

Chapter 2, Cassandra Architecture, covers design decisions and Cassandra's internal plumbing. If you have never worked with a distributed system, this chapter has a lot of useful distributed design concepts. This chapter will be helpful for the rest of the book when we look at patterns and infrastructure management. It will also help you to understand the discussion of the Cassandra mailing list and JIRA. It is a theoretical chapter; you may skip it and come back later.

Chapter 3, Design Patterns, discusses various design decisions and their pros and cons. You will learn about Cassandra limitations and capabilities. If you are planning to write a program that uses Cassandra, this is the chapter for you. Do not miss *Chapter 9, Introduction to CQL 3 and Cassandra 1.2* for CQL.

Chapter 4, Deploying a Cluster, is a full chapter about how to deploy a cluster correctly. Once you have gone through the chapter, you will realize it is not really hard to deploy a cluster. It is probably one of the simplest distributed systems.

Chapter 5, Performance Tuning, explains how to get the most out of the hardware the cluster is deployed on. Usually you will not need to rotate lots of knobs and the default is just fine.

Chapter 6, Managing a Cluster, is about the daily DevOps drills. For example, scaling up a cluster, shrinking it down, replacing a dead node, and balancing the data load across the cluster.

Chapter 7, Monitoring, talks about the various tools that you can use to monitor Cassandra. If you already have a monitoring system, you would probably want to plug Cassandra health monitoring to it, or you may choose to use dedicated Cassandra monitoring tools.

Chapter 8, Integration, Shows how to integrate Cassandra with other tools. Cassandra is about large data sets, fast writes, and reads terabytes of data. What is the use of data if you can't analyze it? Cassandra can be smoothly integrated with various Hadoop projects, and integrating with tools such as Spark and Twitter Storm is just as easy. This chapter gives you an introduction to get you started with setting up Cassandra and Hadoop setup.

Chapter 9, Introduction to CQL 3 and Cassandra 1.2, fills the version gap. At the time of writing this book, Cassandra's latest version was 1.1.11. The complete book uses that version and the Thrift API to connect to Cassandra. Cassandra 1.2 was released later and Cassandra 2.0 is also expected to be released anytime now. CQL 3 is the preferred way to query Cassandra, and Cassandra 1.2 has some interesting upgrades.

What you need for this book

If you have any development experience, this book should be easy to follow. A beginner level knowledge of Unix commands, Python, and some Java is good to speed up the understanding, but they are not absolute requirements.

In terms of software and hardware, a machine with 1 GB RAM and a dual core processor is the minimum requirement. For all practical purposes, any modern machine (your laptop from 2007 or newer) is good. You should have the following software installed: Python, Java development kit 6 (JDK), Cassandra 1.1.x, and Hadoop 1.1.x. The examples in this book are done in Ubuntu 11.10/13.04 and CentOS 5.5. So, if you have a Linux/Unix/OS X machine, that would be hugely beneficial. You may need to look for a Windows equivalent if it is your environment.

Who this book is for

This book is for anyone who is curious about Cassandra. A beginner can start from *Chapter 1*, *Quick Start*, and learn all the way up to advanced topics. If you have an intermediate level of experience, that is, you have worked on a toy project or better with Cassandra, you may skip to *Chapter 2*, *Cassandra Architecture*.

A DevOps engineer is probably the best job title who needs to read the book end to end. If you wear multiple hats during the day (very common in startups) — writing code, managing infrastructure, working on analytics, and evangelizing your product— you may find this book extremely useful.

Conventions

In this book, you will find a number of styles of text that distinguish between different kinds of information. Here are some examples of these styles, and an explanation of their meaning.

Code words in text are shown as follows: "Fire up your shell and type in `$CASSANDRA_HOME/bin/cassandra -f`."

A block of code is set as follows:

```
[default@unknown] USE crud;
Authenticated to keyspace: crud
[default@crud] CREATE COLUMN FAMILY test_cf
... WITH
... DEFAULT_VALIDATION_CLASS = UTF8Type AND
... KEY_VALIDATION_CLASS = LongType AND
... COMPARATOR = UTF8Type;
```

When we wish to draw your attention to a particular part of a code block, the relevant lines or items are set in bold:

```
[default@unknown] USE crud;
Authenticated to keyspace: crud
[default@crud] CREATE COLUMN FAMILY test_cf
... WITH
... DEFAULT_VALIDATION_CLASS = UTF8Type AND
... KEY_VALIDATION_CLASS = LongType AND
... COMPARATOR = UTF8Type;
```

New terms and **important words** are shown in bold.

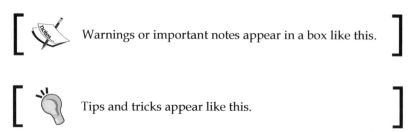

Warnings or important notes appear in a box like this.

Tips and tricks appear like this.

Reader feedback

Feedback from our readers is always welcome. Let us know what you think about this book—what you liked or may have disliked. Reader feedback is important for us to develop titles that you really get the most out of.

To send us general feedback, simply send an e-mail to feedback@packtpub.com, and mention the book title via the subject of your message. If there is a topic that you have expertise in and you are interested in either writing or contributing to a book, see our author guide on www.packtpub.com/authors.

Customer support

Now that you are the proud owner of a Packt book, we have a number of things to help you to get the most from your purchase.

Downloading the example code

You can download the example code files for all Packt books you have purchased from your account at http://www.packtpub.com. If you purchased this book elsewhere, you can visit http://www.packtpub.com/support and register to have the files e-mailed directly to you. You may also clone authors GitHub page for this book at https://github.com/naishe/mastering_cassandra.

Errata

Although we have taken every care to ensure the accuracy of our content, mistakes do happen. If you find a mistake in one of our books—maybe a mistake in the text or the code—we would be grateful if you would report this to us. By doing so, you can save other readers from frustration and help us improve subsequent versions of this book. If you find any errata, please report them by visiting http://www.packtpub.com/submit-errata, selecting your book, clicking on the **errata submission form** link, and entering the details of your errata. Once your errata are verified, your submission will be accepted and the errata will be uploaded on our website, or added to any list of existing errata, under the Errata section of that title. Any existing errata can be viewed by selecting your title from http://www.packtpub.com/support.

Piracy

Piracy of copyright material on the Internet is an ongoing problem across all media. At Packt, we take the protection of our copyright and licenses very seriously. If you come across any illegal copies of our works, in any form, on the Internet, please provide us with the location address or website name immediately so that we can pursue a remedy.

Please contact us at `copyright@packtpub.com` with a link to the suspected pirated material.

We appreciate your help in protecting our authors, and our ability to bring you valuable content.

Questions

You can contact us at `questions@packtpub.com` if you are having a problem with any aspect of the book, and we will do our best to address it.

1
Quick Start

Welcome to Cassandra and congratulations for choosing a database that beats most of the NoSQL databases in performance. Cassandra is a powerful database based on solid fundamentals and well tested by companies such as Facebook, Twitter, and Netflix. This chapter is an introduction to Cassandra. The aim is to get you through with a proof-of-concept project to set the right state of mind for the rest of the book.

In the following sections, we will see a simple **Create**, **Read**, **Update**, and **Delete** **(CRUD)** operation in Cassandra's **command-line interface (CLI)**. After that, we will model, program, and execute a simple blogging application to see Cassandra in action. If you have a beginner-level experience with Cassandra, you may opt to skip this chapter.

Introduction to Cassandra

Quoting from Wikipedia:

> *Apache Cassandra is an open source distributed database management system designed to handle large amounts of data across many commodity servers, providing high availability with no single point of failure. Cassandra offers robust support for clusters spanning multiple datacenters, with asynchronous masterless replication allowing low latency operations for all clients.*

It may be too complicated to digest as a one-liner. Let's break it into pieces and see what it means.

Distributed database

In computing, distributed means something spread across more than one machine — it may be data or processes. In the context of Cassandra, it means that the data is distributed across multiple machines. So, why does it matter? This relates to many things: it means that no single node (a machine in a cluster is usually called a **node**) holds all the data, but just a chunk of it. It means that you are not limited by the storage and processing capabilities of a single machine. If data gets larger, add more machines. Need more parallelism, add more machines. This means that a node going down does not mean that all the data is lost (we will cover this issue soon).

If a distributed mechanism is well designed, it will scale with a number of nodes. Cassandra is one of the best examples of such a system. It scales almost linearly with regard to performance, when we add new nodes. This means Cassandra can handle the behemoth of data without wincing.

 Check out an excellent paper on the NoSQL database comparison titled *Solving Big Data Challenges for Enterprise Application Performance Management* at http://vldb.org/pvldb/vol5/p1724_tilmannrabl_vldb2012.pdf.

High availability

We will discuss availability in the next chapter. For now, assume availability is the probability that we query and the system just works. A high availability system is the one that is ready to serve any request at any time. High availability is usually achieved by adding redundancies. So, if one part fails, the other part of the system can serve the request. To a client, it seems as if everything worked fine.

Cassandra is a robust software. Nodes joining and leaving are automatically taken care of. With proper settings, Cassandra can be made failure resistant. That means that if some of the servers fail, the data loss will be zero. So, you can just deploy Cassandra over cheap commodity hardware or a cloud environment, where hardware or infrastructure failures may occur.

Replication

Continuing from the last two points, Cassandra has a pretty powerful replication mechanism (we will see more details in the next chapter). Cassandra treats every node in the same manner. Data need not be written on a specific server (master) and you need not wait until the data is written to all the nodes that replicate this data (slaves).

So, there is no master or slave in Cassandra and replication happens asynchronously. This means that the client can be returned with success as a response as soon as the data is written on at least one server. We will see how we can tweak these settings to ensure the number of servers we want to have data written on before the client returns.

We can derive a couple of things from this: when there is no master or slave, we can write to any node for any operation. Since we have the ability to choose how many nodes to read from or write to, we can tweak it to achieve very low latency (read or write from one server).

Multiple data centers

Expanding from a single machine to a single data center cluster or multiple data center is very trivial. We will see later in this book that we can use this data center setting to make a real-time replicating system across data centers. We can use each data center to perform different tasks without overloading the other data centers. This is a powerful support when you do not have to worry about whether the users in Japan with a data center in Tokyo and the users in the US with a data center in Virginia are in sync or not.

These are just broad strokes of Cassandra's capabilities. We will explore more in the upcoming chapters. This chapter is about getting excited.

A brief introduction to a data model

Cassandra has three containers, one within another. The outermost container is **Keyspace**. You can think of Keyspace as a database in the RDBMS land. Next, you will see the column family, which is like a table. Within a column family are columns, and columns live under rows. Each row is identified by a unique row key, which is like the primary key in RDBMS.

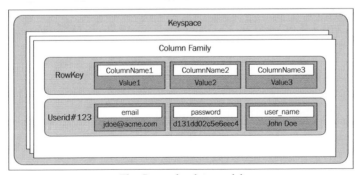

The Cassandra data model

Things were pretty monotonous until now, as you already knew everything that we talked about from RDBMS. The difference is in the way Cassandra treats this data. Column families, unlike tables, can be schema free (schema optional). This means you can have different column names for different rows within the same column family. There may be a row that has user_name, age, phone_office, and phone_ home, while another row can have user_name, age, phone_office, office_address, and email. You can store about two billion columns per row. This means it can be very handy to store time series data, such as tweets or comments on a blog post. The column name can be a timestamp of these events. In a row, these columns are sorted by natural order; therefore, we can access the time series data in a chronological or reverse chronological order, unlike RDBMS, where each row just takes the space as per the number of columns in it. The other difference is, unlike RDBMS, Cassandra does not have relations. This means relational logic will be needed to be handled at the application level. This means we may want to denormalize things because there is no join.

Rows are identified by a row key. These row keys act as partitioners. Rows are distributed across the cluster, creating effective auto-shading. Each server holds a range(s) of keys. So, if balanced, a server with more nodes will have a fewer number of rows per node. All these concepts will be repeated in detail in the later chapters.

Installing Cassandra locally

Installing Cassandra in your local machine for experimental or development purposes is as easy as downloading and unzipping the tarball (the .tar compressed file). For development purposes, Cassandra does not have any extreme requirements. Any modern computer with 1 GB of RAM and a dual core processor is good to test the water. Anything higher than that is great. All the examples in this chapter are done on a laptop with 4 GB of RAM, a dual core processor, and the Ubuntu 13.04 operating system. Cassandra is supported on all major platforms; after all, it's Java. Here are the steps to install Cassandra locally:

1. Install Oracle Java 1.6 (Java 6) or higher. Installing the JVM is sufficient, but you may need the **Java Development Kit (JDK)** if you are planning to code in Java.

 Hadoop examples in the later part of this book use Java code.

```
# Check if you have Java
~$ java -version
java version "1.7.0_21"
```

```
Java(TM) SE Runtime Environment (build 1.7.0_21-b11)
Java HotSpot(TM) 64-Bit Server VM (build 23.21-b01, mixed mode)
```

If you do not have Java, you may want to follow the installation details for your machine from the Oracle Java website (`http://www.oracle.com/technetwork/java/javase/downloads/index.html`).

2. Download Cassandra 1.1.x version from the Cassandra website, `http://archive.apache.org/dist/cassandra/`. This book uses Cassandra 1.1.11, which was the latest at the time of writing this book.

 By the time you read this book, you might have version 1.2.x or Cassandra 2.0, which have some differences. So, better stick to the 1.1.x version. We will see how to work with later versions and the new stuff that they offer in a later chapter.

Uncompress this file to a suitable directory.

```
# Download Cassandra
$ wget http://archive.apache.org/dist/cassandra/1.1.11/apache-
cassandra-1.1.11-bin.tar.gz
# Untar to /home/nishant/apps/
$ tar xvzf apache-cassandra-1.1.11-bin.tar.gz -C /home/nishant/
apps/
```

The unzipped file location is `/home/nishant/apps/apache-cassandra-1.1.11`. Let's call this location `CASSANDRA_HOME`. Wherever we refer to `CASSANDRA_HOME` in this book, always assume it to be the location where Cassandra is installed.

3. Configure a directory where Cassandra will store all the data. Edit `$CASSANDRA_HOME/conf/cassandra.yaml`.

4. Set a cluster name using the following code:

```
cluster_name: 'nishant_sandbox'
```

5. Set the data directory using the following code:

```
data_file_directories:
    - /home/nishant/apps/data/cassandra/data
```

6. Set the commit log directory:

```
commitlog_directory: /home/nishant/apps/data/cassandra/commitlog
```

7. Set the saved caches directory:

```
saved_caches_directory: /home/nishant/apps/data/cassandra/saved_
caches
```

8. Set the logging location. Edit $CASSANDRA_HOME/conf/log4j-server. properties:

```
log4j.appender.R.File=/tmp/cassandra.log
```

With this, you are ready to start Cassandra. Fire up your shell, and type in $CASSANDRA_HOME/bin/cassandra -f. In this command, -f stands for foreground. You can keep viewing the logs and *Ctrl + C* to shut the server down. If you want to run it in the background, do not use the -f option. The server is ready when you see Bootstrap/Replace/Move completed! Now serving reads in the startup log as shown:

```
$ /home/nishant/apps/apache-cassandra-1.1.11/bin/cassandra -f
xss =  -ea -javaagent:/home/nishant/apps/apache-cassandra-1.1.11/
bin/../lib/jamm-0.2.5.jar -XX:+UseThreadPriorities
-XX:ThreadPriorityPolicy=42 -Xms1024M -Xmx1024M -Xmn200M
-XX:+HeapDumpOnOutOfMemoryError -Xss180k
 INFO 20:16:02,297 Logging initialized
[-- snip --]
 INFO 20:16:08,386 Node localhost/127.0.0.1 state jump to normal
 INFO 20:16:08,394 Bootstrap/Replace/Move completed! Now serving
reads.
```

CRUD with cassandra-cli

Cassandra is up and running. Let's test the waters. Just do a complete **CRUD** (**create**, **retrieve**, **update**, and **delete**) operation in cassandra-cli. The following snippet shows the complete operation. cassandra-cli can be accessed from $CASSANDRA_HOME/bin/ cassandra-cli. It is the Cassandra command-line interface. You can learn more about it in the Appendix.

```
# Log into cassandra-cli
$ /home/nishant/apps/apache-cassandra-1.1.11/bin/cassandra-cli -h
localhost
Connected to: "nishant_sandbox" on localhost/9160
Welcome to Cassandra CLI version 1.1.11

Type 'help;' or '?' for help.
Type 'quit;' or 'exit;' to quit.
```

Create a keyspace named `crud`. Note that we are not using a lot of the options that we may set to a Keyspace during its creation. We are just using the defaults. We will learn about those options in the *Keyspaces* section in *Chapter 3, Design Patterns*.

```
[default@unknown] CREATE KEYSPACE crud;
e9f103f5-9fb8-38c9-aac8-8e6e58f91148
Waiting for schema agreement...
... schemas agree across the cluster
```

Create a column family `test_cf`. Again, we are using just the default settings. The advanced settings will come later in this book. The ellipses in the preceding command are not a part of the command. It gets added by cassandra-cli as a notation of continuation from the previous line. Here, DEFAULT_VALIDATION_CLASS is the default type of value you are going to store in the columns, KEY_VALIDATION_CLASS is the type of row key (the primary key), and COMPARATOR is the type of column name. Now, you must be thinking why we call it comparator and not something like COLUMN_NAME_VALIDATION_CLASS like other attributes. The reason is column names perform an important task—sorting. Columns are validated and sorted by the class that we mention as comparator. We will see this property in a couple of paragraphs. The important thing is that you can write your own comparator and create data to be stored and fetched in custom order. We will see how to create a custom comparator in the *Writing a custion comparator* section in *Chapter 3, Design Patterns*.

```
[default@unknown] USE crud;
Authenticated to keyspace: crud
[default@crud] CREATE COLUMN FAMILY test_cf
...WITH
...DEFAULT_VALIDATION_CLASS = UTF8Type AND
...KEY_VALIDATION_CLASS = LongType AND
...COMPARATOR = UTF8Type;
256297f8-1d96-3ba9-9061-7964684c932a
Waiting for schema agreement...
... schemas agree across the cluster
```

It is fairly easy to insert the data. The pattern is COLUMN_FAMILY[ROW_KEY][COLUMN_NAME] = COLUMN_VALUE.

```
[default@crud] SET test_cf[1]['first_column_name'] = 'first value';
Value inserted.
Elapsed time: 71 msec(s).
[default@crud] SET test_cf[1]['2nd_column_name'] = 'some text value';
Value inserted.
Elapsed time: 2.59 msec(s).
```

Retrieval is as easy, with a couple of ways to get data. To retrieve all the columns in a row, perform GET COLUMN_FAMILY_NAME[ROW_KEY]; to get a particular column, do GET COLUMN_FAMILY_NAME[ROW_KEY][COLUMN_NAME]. To get *N* rows, perform LIST with the LIMIT operation using the following pattern:

```
[default@crud] GET test_cf[1];
=> (column=2nd_column_name, value=some text value,
timestamp=1376234991712000)
=> (column=first_column_name, value=first value,
timestamp=1376234969488000)
Returned 2 results.
Elapsed time: 92 msec(s).
```

Did you notice how columns are printed in an alphabetical order and not in the order of the insertion?

Deleting a row or column is just specifying the column or the row to the DEL command:

```
# Delete a column
[default@crud] DEL test_cf[1]['2nd_column_name'];
column removed.


# column is deleted
[default@crud] GET test_cf[1];
=> (column=first_column_name, value=first value,
timestamp=1376234969488000)
Returned 1 results.
Elapsed time: 3.38 msec(s).
```

Updating a column in a row is nothing but inserting the new value in that column. Insert in Cassandra is like upsert that some RDBMS vendors offer:

```
[default@crud] SET test_cf[1]['first_column_name'] = 'insert is
basically upsert :)';
Value inserted.
Elapsed time: 2.44 msec(s).


# the column is updated.
[default@crud] GET test_cf[1];
=> (column=first_column_name, value=insert is basically upsert :),
timestamp=1376235103158000)
Returned 1 results.
Elapsed time: 3.31 msec(s).
```

To view a schema, you may use the SHOW SCHEMA command. It shows the details of the specified schema. In fact, it prints the command to create the keyspace and all the column families in it with all available options. Since we did not set any option, we see all the default values for the options:

```
[default@crud] SHOW SCHEMA crud;
create keyspace crud
  with placement_strategy = 'NetworkTopologyStrategy'
  and strategy_options = {datacenter1 : 1}
  and durable_writes = true;

use crud;

create column family test_cf
  with column_type = 'Standard'
  and comparator = 'UTF8Type'
  and default_validation_class = 'UTF8Type'
  and key_validation_class = 'LongType'
  and read_repair_chance = 0.1
  and dclocal_read_repair_chance = 0.0
  and gc_grace = 864000
  and min_compaction_threshold = 4
  and max_compaction_threshold = 32
  and replicate_on_write = true
  and compaction_strategy = 'org.apache.cassandra.db.compaction.
SizeTieredCompactionStrategy'
  and caching = 'KEYS_ONLY'
  and compression_options = {'sstable_compression' : 'org.apache.
cassandra.io.compress.SnappyCompressor'};
```

Another thing that one might want to do, which is pretty common when learning Cassandra, is the ability to wipe all the data in a column family. TRUNCATE is the command to do that for us:

```
# clean test_cf
[default@crud] TRUNCATE test_cf;
test_cf truncated.

# list all the data in test_cf
[default@crud] LIST test_cf;
Using default limit of 100
Using default column limit of 100

0 Row Returned.
Elapsed time: 41 msec(s).
```

Dropping column family or keyspace is as easy as mentioning the entity type and name after the DROP command. Here is a demonstration:

```
# Drop test_cf
[default@crud] drop column family  test_cf;
29d44ab2-e4ab-3e22-a8ab-19de0c40aaa5
Waiting for schema agreement...
... schemas agree across the cluster


# No more test_cf in the schema
[default@crud] show schema crud;
create keyspace crud
  with placement_strategy = 'NetworkTopologyStrategy'
  and strategy_options = {datacenter1 : 1}
  and durable_writes = true;

use crud;

# Drop keyspace
[default@crud] drop keyspace crud;
45583a34-0cde-3d7d-a754-b7536d7dd3af
Waiting for schema agreement...
... schemas agree across the cluster


# No such schema
[default@unknown] show schema crud;
Keyspace 'crud' not found.


# Exit from cassandra-cli
[default@unknown] exit;
```

 Notice that all the commands must end with a semicolon.

Cassandra in action

There is no better way to learn a technology than doing a proof of concept with it. This section will work on a very simple application to get you familiarized with Cassandra. We will build the backend of a simple blogging application where a user can:

- Create a blogging account
- Publish posts

- Have people comment on those posts
- Have people upvote or downvote a post or a comment

Modeling data

In the RDBMS world, you would glance over the entities and think about relations while modeling the application. Then you will join tables to get the required data. There is no join in Cassandra. So, we will have to denormalize things. Looking at the previously mentioned specifications, we can say that:

- We need a blog metadata column family to store the blog name and other global information, such as the blogger's username and password.

- We will have to pull posts for the blog. Ideally, sorted in reverse chronological order.

- We will also have to pull all the comments for each post when we are seeing the post page.

- We will also have to have counters for the upvotes and downvotes for posts and comments.

So, we can have a blog metadata column family for fixed user attributes. With posts, we can do many things, such as the following:

- We can have a dynamic column family of super type (super column family—a super column is a column that holds columns), where a row key is the same as a user ID. The column names are timestamps for when the post was published, and the columns under the super column hold attributes of the post, which include the title, text, author's name, time of publication, and so on. But this is a bad idea. I recommend that you don't use super columns. We will see super columns and why it is not preferred in the *Avoid super columns* section in Chapter 3, *Design Patterns*.

- We can use **composite columns** in place of super columns. You can think of a composite column as a row partitioned in chunks by a key. For example, we take a column family that has CompositeType columns, where the two types that make a composite column are LongType (for timestamp) and UTF8Type (for attributes). We can pull posts grouped by the timestamp, which will have all the attributes.

See the following figure. If it is too confusing as of now, do not worry; we will cover this in detail later.

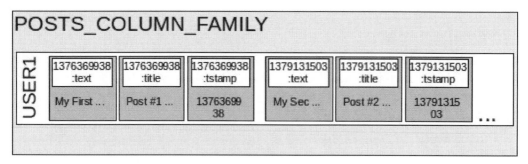

Writing time series grouped data using composite columns

- Although a composite column family does the job of storing posts, it is not ideal. A couple of things to remember:
    - A row can have a maximum of two billion columns. If each post is denoted by three attributes, a user can post a maximum of two-thirds of a billion posts, which might be OK. And if it is not, we still have solutions.
    - We can bucket the posts. For example, we just store the posts made in a month, in one row. We will cover the concept of bucketing later.

The other problem with this approach is that an entire row lives on one machine. The disk must be large enough to store the data.

In this particular case, we need not be worried about this. The problem is something else. Let's say a user has very popular posts and is responsible for 40 percent of the total traffic. Since we have all the data in a single row, and a single row lives on a single machine (and the replicas), those machines will be queried 40 percent of the time. So, if you have a replication factor of two, and there are 20 Cassandra servers, the two servers that hold the particular blog will be serving more than 40 percent of the reads. This is called a **hotspot**.

It would be a good idea to share the posts across all the machines. This means we need to have one post per row (because rows are shared). This will make sure that the data is distributed across all the machines, and hence avoid hotspots and the fear of getting your disk out of space. We wouldn't be limited by a two-billion limit either.

But, now we know that the rows are not sorted. We need our posts to be arranged by time. So, we need a row that can hold the row keys of the posts in a sorted order. This again brings the hotspot and the limit of two billion. We may have to avoid it by some sort of bucketing, depending on what the demand of the application is.

So, we have landed somewhere similar to what we would have in a RDBMS posts column family. It's not necessary that we always end up like this. You need to consider what the application's demand is and accordingly design the things around that.

Similar to the post, we have comment. Unlike posts, comments are associated with posts and not the user. Then we have upvotes and downvotes. We may have two counter column families for post votes and comment votes, each holding the upvotes and downvotes columns.

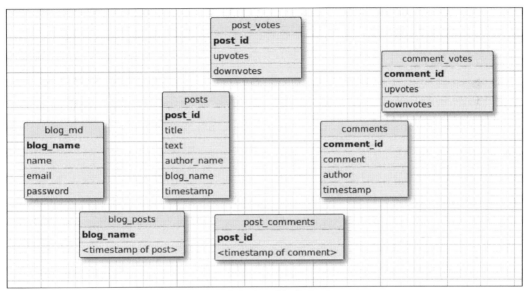

Schema based on the discussion

The bold letters in the preceding diagram refer to the row keys. You can think of a row key as the primary key in a database. There are two dynamic or wide row column families: blog_posts and post_comments. They hold the relationship between a blog and its posts, and a post with its comments, respectively. These column families have column names as timestamps and the values that these columns store is the row key to the posts and comments column families, respectively.

Writing code

Time to start something tangible! In this section, we will see how to get a working code for the preceding schema. Our main goal is to be able to create a user, write a post, post a comment, upvote and downvote them, and to fetch the posts. The code in this section and in many parts of this book is in Python—the reason being Python's conciseness, readability, and easy-to-understand approach (*XKCD – Python*, http://xkcd.com/353/). Python is an executable pseudocode (Thinking in Python – Python is executable pseudocode. Perl is executable line noise. http://mindview. net/Books/Python/ThinkingInPython.html). Even if you have never worked in Python or do not want to use Python, the code should be easy to understand. So, we will use **Pycassa**, a Python client for Cassandra. In this example, we will not use CQL 3, as it is still in beta in Cassandra 1.1.11. You may learn about CQL3 in *Chapter 9, Introduction to CQL 3* and *Cassandra 1.2*, and about Pycassa from its GitHub repository at http://pycassa.github.io/pycassa/.

Setting up

Setting up involves creating a keyspace and a column family. It can be done via cassandra-cli or cqlsh or the Cassandra client library. We will see how this is done using cassandra-cli later in this book, so let's see how we do it programmatically using Pycassa. For brevity, the trivial parts of the code are not included.

SystemManager is responsible for altering schema. You connect to a Cassandra node, and perform schema tweaks.

```
from pycassa.system_manager import *
sys = SystemManager('localhost:9160')
```

Creating a keyspace requires some options to be passed on. Do not worry about them at this point. For now, think about the following code, as it sets the simplest configurations for a single node cluster that is good for a developer laptop:

```
sys.create_keyspace('blog_ks', SIMPLE_STRATEGY,
{'replication_factor': '1'})
```

Creating a column family requires you to pass a keyspace and column family name; the rest are set to default. For static column families (the ones having a fixed number of columns), we will set column names. Other important parameters are row key type, column name type, and column value types. So, here is how we will create all the column families:

```
# Blog metadata column family (static)
sys.create_column_family('blog_ks', 'blog_md', comparator_type=UTF8_
TYPE, key_validation_class=UTF8_TYPE)
sys.alter_column('blog_ks', 'blog_md', 'name', UTF8_TYPE)
sys.alter_column('blog_ks', 'blog_md', 'email', UTF8_TYPE)
sys.alter_column('blog_ks', 'blog_md', 'password', UTF8_TYPE)

# avoiding keystrokes by storing some parameters in a variable
cf_kwargs0 = {'key_validation_class': TIME_UUID_TYPE, 'comparator_
type':UTF8_TYPE}

# Posts column family (static)
sys.create_column_family('blog_ks', 'posts', **cf_kwargs0)
sys.alter_column('blog_ks', 'posts', 'title', UTF8_TYPE)
sys.alter_column('blog_ks', 'posts', 'text', UTF8_TYPE)
sys.alter_column('blog_ks', 'posts', 'blog_name', UTF8_TYPE)
sys.alter_column('blog_ks', 'posts', 'author_name', UTF8_TYPE)
sys.alter_column('blog_ks', 'posts', 'timestamp', DATE_TYPE)

# Comments column family (static)
sys.create_column_family('blog_ks', 'comments', **cf_kwargs0)
sys.alter_column('blog_ks', 'comments', 'comment', UTF8_TYPE)
sys.alter_column('blog_ks', 'comments', 'author', UTF8_TYPE)
sys.alter_column('blog_ks', 'comments', 'timestamp', DATE_TYPE)

# Create a time series wide column family to keep comments
# and posts in chronological order
cf_kwargs1 = {'comparator_type': LONG_TYPE, 'default_validation_
class': TIME_UUID_TYPE, 'key_validation_class': UTF8_TYPE}

cf_kwargs2 = {'comparator_type': LONG_TYPE, 'default_validation_
class': TIME_UUID_TYPE, 'key_validation_class': TIME_UUID_TYPE}

sys.create_column_family('blog_ks', 'blog_posts', **cf_kwargs1)
sys.create_column_family('blog_ks', 'post_comments', **cf_kwargs2)

# Counters for votes (static)
```

```
cf_kwargs = {'default_validation_class':COUNTER_COLUMN_TYPE,
'comparator_type': UTF8_TYPE, 'key_validation_class':TIME_UUID_TYPE }

# Blog vote counters
sys.create_column_family('blog_ks', 'post_votes', **cf_kwargs)
sys.alter_column('blog_ks', 'post_votes', 'upvotes', COUNTER_COLUMN_
TYPE)
sys.alter_column('blog_ks', 'post_votes', 'downvotes', COUNTER_COLUMN_
TYPE)

# Comments votes counter
sys.create_column_family('blog_ks', 'comment_votes', **cf_kwargs)
sys.alter_column('blog_ks', 'comment_votes', 'upvotes', COUNTER_
COLUMN_TYPE)
sys.alter_column('blog_ks', 'comment_votes', 'downvotes', COUNTER_
COLUMN_TYPE)
```

We are done with setting up. A couple of things to remember:

- A static column family does not restrict you to storing arbitrary columns.

- As long as the validation satisfies, you can store and fetch data.

- Wouldn't it be nice if you could have the votes column sitting next to the posts column and the comments column? Unfortunately, counter columns do not mix with any other types. So, we need to have a separate column family.

Application

This section discusses a very basic blog application. The code sample included here will show you the basic functionality. It is quite easy to take it from here and start building an application of your own. In a typical application, you'd initialize a connection pool at the start of the application. Use it for the lifetime of the application and close it when your application shuts down. Here is some initialization code:

```
from pycassa.pool import ConnectionPool
from pycassa.columnfamily import ColumnFamily
from pycassa.cassandra.ttypes import NotFoundException
import uuid, time
from Markov import Markov
from random import randint, choice

cpool = ConnectionPool(keyspace='blog_ks', server_
list=['localhost:9160'])
blog_metadata = ColumnFamily(cpool, 'blog_md')
```

```
posts = ColumnFamily(cpool, 'posts')
comments = ColumnFamily(cpool, 'comments')
blog_posts = ColumnFamily(cpool, 'blog_posts')
post_comments = ColumnFamily(cpool, 'post_comments')
post_votes = ColumnFamily(cpool, 'post_votes')
comment_votes = ColumnFamily(cpool, 'comment_votes')
```

Create a new blog using the following code:

```
def add_blog(blog_name, author_name, email, passwd):
    blog_metadata.insert(blog_name, {'name': author_name, 'email':
email, 'password': passwd})
```

Insert a new post and comment using the following code:

```
def add_post(title, text, blog_name, author_name):
    post_id = uuid.uuid1()
    timestamp = int(time.time() * 1e6 )
    posts.insert(post_id, {'title':title, 'text': text, 'blog_name':
blog_name, 'author_name': author_name, 'timestamp':int(time.time())})
    blog_posts.insert(blog_name, {timestamp: post_id})
    return post_id


def add_comment(post_id, comment, comment_auth):
    comment_id = uuid.uuid1()
    timestamp = int(time.time() * 1e6)
    comments.insert(comment_id, {'comment': comment, 'author':
comment_auth, 'timestamp': int(time.time())})
    post_comments.insert(post_id, {timestamp: comment_id})
    return comment_id
```

Not having a relational setup in Cassandra, you have to manage relationships on your own. We insert the data in a posts or comments column family and then add this entry's key to another column family that has the row key as a blog name and the data sorted by their timestamp. This does two things: one, we can read all the posts for a blog if we know the blog name. The other fringe benefit of this is that we have post IDs sorted in a chronological order. So, we can pull posts ordered by the date of creation.

Updating vote counters is as easy as mentioned in the following code:

```
def vote_post(post_id, downvote = False):
    if(downvote):
            post_votes.add(post_id, 'downvotes')
    else:
            post_votes.add(post_id, 'upvotes')
```

```
def vote_comment(comment_id, downvote = False):
    if(downvote):
            comment_votes.add(comment_id, 'downvotes')
    else:
            comment_votes.add(comment_id, 'upvotes')
```

With all this done, we are able to do all the creation-related stuff. We can create a blog, add a post, comment on it, and upvote or downvote posts or comments. Now, a user visiting the blog may want to see the list of posts. So, we need to pull out the latest 10 posts and show them to the user. However, it is not very encouraging to a visitor if you just list 10 blog posts spanning a really lengthy page to scroll. We want to keep it short, interesting, and a bit revealing. If we just show the title and a small part of the post, we have fixed the scroll issue. The next thing is making it interesting. If we show the number of upvotes and downvotes to a post, a visitor can quickly decide whether to read the post, based on the votes. The other important piece is the number of comments that each post has received. It is an interesting property that states that the more comments, the more interesting a post is.

Ultimately, we have the date when the article was written. A recent article is more attractive than an older one on the same topic. So, we need to write a getter method that pulls a list with all this information. Here is how we go about it:

```
def get_post_list(blog_name, start='', page_size=10):
  next = None

  # Get latest page_size (10) items starting from â€œstartâ€ column
name
  try:
    # gets posts in reverse chronological order. The last column is
extra.
    # It is the oldest, and will have lowest timestamp
    post_ids = blog_posts.get(blog_name, column_start = start, column_
count = page_size+1, column_reversed = True)
  except NotFoundException as e:
    return ([], next)

  # if we have items more than the page size, that means we have the
next item
  if(len(post_ids) > page_size):

    #get the timestamp of the oldest item, it will be the first item
on the next page
    timestamp_next = min(post_ids.keys())
    next = timestamp_next

    # remove the extra item from posts to show
```

```
     del post_ids[timestamp_next]
   # pull the posts and votes
   post_id_vals = post_ids.values()
   postlist = posts.multiget(post_id_vals)
   votes = post_votes.multiget(post_id_vals)

   # merge posts and votes and yeah, trim to 100 chars.
   # Ideally, you'd want to strip off any HTML tag here.
   post_summary_list = list()
   for post_id, post in postlist.iteritems():
     post['post_id'] = post_id
     post['upvotes'] = 0
     post['downvotes'] = 0

     try:
       vote = votes.get(post_id)
       if 'upvotes' in vote.keys():
         post['upvotes'] = vote['upvotes']
       if 'downvotes' in vote.keys():
         post['downvotes'] = vote['downvotes']
     except NotFoundException:
       pass

     text = str(post['text'])
     # substringing to create a short version
     if(len(text) > 100):
       post['text'] = text[:100] + '... [Read more]'
     else:
       post['text'] = text

     comments_count = 0
     try:
       comments_count = post_comments.get_count(post_id)
     except NotFoundException:
       pass

     post['comments_count'] = comments_count

     # Note we do not need to go back to blog metadata CF as we have
   stored the values in posts CF
     post_summary_list.append(post)

   return (post_summary_list, next)
```

This is probably the most interesting piece of code till now with a lot of things happening. First, we pull the list of the latest 10 `post_id` values for the given blog. We use these IDs to get all the posts and iterate in the posts. For each post, we pull out the number of upvotes and downvotes. The `text` column is trimmed to 100 characters. We also get the count of comments. These items are packed and sent back.

One key thing is the `next` variable. This variable is used for pagination. In an application, when you have more than a page size of items, you show the previous and/or next buttons. In this case, we slice the wide row that holds the `timestamp` and `post_ids` values in chunks of 10. As you can see the method signature, it needs the starting point to pull items. In our case, the starting point is the timestamp of the post that comes next to the last item of this page.

The actual code simulates insertions and retrievals. It uses the `Alice in Wonderland` text to generate a random title, content and comments, and upvotes and downvotes. One of the simulation results the following output as a list of items:

```
ITS DINNER, AND ALL ASSOCIATED FILES OF FORMATS [votes: +16/-8]

Alice ventured to ask. 'Suppose we change the subject,' the March Hare
will be linked to the general... [Read more]
-- Jim Ellis on 2013-08-16 06:16:02


[8 comment(s)]
-- * -- -- * -- -- * -- -- * -- -- * -- -- * -- -- * -- -- * --



THEM BACK AGAIN TO THE QUEEN, 'AND HE TELL [votes: +9/-4]

were using it as far as they used to say "HOW DOTH THE LITTLE BUSY
BEE," but it all is! I'll try and... [Read more]
-- Jim Ellis on 2013-08-16 06:16:02


[7 comment(s)]
-- * -- -- * -- -- * -- -- * -- -- * -- -- * -- -- * -- -- * --



GET SOMEWHERE,' ALICE ADDED AN [votes: +15/-6]
Duchess sang the second copy is also defective, you may choose to give
the prizes?' quite a new kind... [Read more]
-- Jim Ellis on 2013-08-16 06:16:02


[10 comment(s)]
-- * -- -- * -- -- * -- -- * -- -- * -- -- * -- -- * -- -- * --
```

```
SHE WOULD KEEP, THROUGH ALL HER COAXING. HARDLY WHAT [votes: +14/-0]

rising to its feet, 'I move that the way out of the sea.' 'I couldn't
afford to learn it.' said the ... [Read more]
-- Jim Ellis on 2013-08-16 06:16:02

[12 comment(s)]
-- * -- -- * -- -- * -- -- * -- -- * -- -- * -- -- * -- -- * --
```

Once you understand this, the rest is very simple. If you wanted to show a full post, use `post_id` from this list and pull the full row from the posts column family. With all the other fetchings (votes, title, and so on) similar to the aforementioned code, we can pull all the comments on the post and fetch the votes on each of the comments. Deleting a post or a comment requires you to manually delete all the relationships that we made during creation. Updates are similar to `insert`.

Summary

We have made a start with Cassandra. You can set up your local machine, play with cassandra-cli (see *Chapter 9, Introduction to CQL 3* and *Cassandra 1.2* for cqlsh), and write a simple program that uses Cassandra on the backend. It seems like we are all done. But, it's not so. Cassandra is not all about ease in modeling or being simple to code around with (unlike RDBMS). It is all about speed, availability, and reliability. The only thing that matters in a production setup is how quickly and reliably your application can serve a fickle-minded user. It does not matter if you have an elegant database architecture with the third normal form, or if you use a functional programming language and follow the **Don't Repeat Yourself (DRY)** principle religiously. Cassandra and many other modern databases, especially in the NoSQL space, are there to provide you with speed. Cassandra stands out in the herd with its blazing fast-write performance and steady linear scalability (this means if you double the node, you double the speed of execution).

The rest of the book is aimed at giving you a solid understanding of the various aspects of Cassandra—one chapter at a time.

- You will learn the internals of Cassandra and the general programming pattern for Cassandra.

- Setting up a cluster and tweaking to get the maximum out of Cassandra for your use case is also discussed.

- Infrastructure maintenance—nodes going down, scaling up and down, backing the data up, keeping vigil monitoring, and getting notified about an interesting event on your Cassandra setup will be covered.

- Cassandra is easy to use with the Apache Hadoop and Apache Pig tools, as we will see simple examples of this.

- Finally, Cassandra 1.2 and CQL3 are some of the most revolutionary things that happened to Cassandra recently. There is a chapter dedicated to Cassandra 1.2 and CQL3, which gives you enough to get going with the new changes.

The best thing about these chapters is that there is no prerequisite. Most of these are started from the basics to get you familiar with the concept and then taken to an advanced level. So, if you have never used Hadoop, do not worry. You can still get a simple setup up and running with Cassandra.

2
Cassandra Architecture

This chapter aims to set you into a perspective where you can see the evolution of the NoSQL paradigm. It starts with a discussion of common problems that an average developer faces when the application starts to scale up and software components cannot keep up with it. Then, we'll see what can be assumed as a thumb rule in the NoSQL world: the CAP theorem that says to choose any two out of consistency, availability, and partition-tolerance. As we discuss, we realize how important it is to serve the customers (availability) than to be correct (consistency) all the time. However, we cannot afford to be wrong (inconsistent) for a long time. The customers wouldn't like to see that the items are in stock, but the checkout is failing. Cassandra comes into the picture with its tunable consistency.

We take a quick peep into all the actions that go on when a read or mutate happens. This leaves us with lots of fancy terms. Next, we move on to see these terms in full glory with explanation as we discuss various parts of the Cassandra design. We will also see how close yet how far Cassandra is when compared with its precursors and inspiration databases, such as Google's BigTable and Amazon's Dynamo. We happen to meet with some of the modern and efficient data structures, such as Bloom filters and Merkle tree, and algorithms, such as gossip protocol, phi accrual failure detectors, and log-structured merge trees.

Problems in the RDBMS world

RDBMS is a great approach. It keeps data consistent, is good for OLTP (http://en.wikipedia.org/wiki/Online_transaction_processing), provides access to good grammar, and manipulates data supported by all the popular programming languages. It was tremendously successful for the last 40 years (the relational data model in its first avatar: Codd, E.F. (1970), *A Relational Model of Data for Large Shared Data Banks*). However, in the early 2000s, big companies, such as Google (BigTable, http://research.google.com/archive/bigtable.html) and Amazon that have gigantic load on their databases to serve, started to feel bottlenecked with RDBMS.

If you ever used an RDBMS for a non-trivial web application, you must have faced problems, such as slow queries due to complex joins, expensive vertical scaling, and problems in horizontal scaling. Due to these problems, indexing takes a long time. At some point you choose to replicate the data, there is still some locking, and this hurts availability. That means under heavy load, locking will cause the user experience to deteriorate.

Although replication gives some relief, a busy slave may not catch up with the master (or there may be a connectivity glitch between the master and the slave). Consistency of such systems cannot be guaranteed (replication in MySQL is available at `http://www.databasejournal.com/features/mysql/article.php/3355201/Database-Replication-in-MySQL.htm`). With growth of the application, the demand to scale the backend gets more pressing, and the developer teams decide to add a caching layer (such as Memcached) at the top of the database. This alleviates some load off the database, but now the developers need to maintain the object states at two places: in the database and the caching layer. Although some ORMs provide a built-in caching mechanism, they have their own issues: larger memory requirement, and polluted application code with mapping code. In order to achieve more from RDBMS, we start to denormalize the database to avoid joins, and keep the aggregates in the columns to avoid statistical queries.

Sharding or horizontal scaling is another way to distribute the load. Sharding in itself is a good idea, but it adds too much manual work, plus the knowledge of sharding creeps into the application code. Sharded databases make the operational tasks (backup, schema alteration, and adding index) difficult (hardships of sharding is available at `http://www.mysqlperformanceblog.com/2009/08/06/why-you-dont-want-to-shard/`).

There are ways to loosen up consistency by providing various isolation levels. But concurrency is just one part. Maintaining relational integrity, difficulties in managing data that cannot be accommodated on one machine, and difficult recovery were all making the traditional database systems hard to be accepted in the rapidly growing Big Data world. Companies needed a tool that can support hundreds of terabytes of data on the ever-failing commodity hardware reliably.

Enter NoSQL

NoSQL is a blanket term for the databases that solve the scalability issues that are common among relational databases. This term, in its modern meaning, was first coined by Eric Evans (NoSQL naming available at `http://blog.sym-link.com/2009/10/30/nosql_whats_in_a_name.html`). It should not be confused with the database named NoSQL (*NoSQL: the database* available at `http://www.strozzi.it/cgi-bin/CSA/tw7/I/en_US/nosql/Home%20Page`).

The NoSQL solutions provide scalability and high availability, but may not guarantee ACID: atomicity, consistency, isolation, and durability in transactions. Many of the NoSQL solutions including Cassandra sit on the other extreme of ACID, named **BASE (Basically Available, Soft-state, Eventual consistency)**.

The CAP theorem

In 2000, Eric Brewer (Wikipedia page available at `http://en.wikipedia.org/wiki/Eric_Brewer_%28scientist%29`), in his keynote speech at the ACM Symposium, said that one cannot guarantee consistency in a distributed system. This was his conjecture based on his experience with the distributed systems. This conjecture was later formally proved by Nancy Lynch and Seth Gilbert in 2002 (*Brewer's Conjecture and the Feasibility of Consistent, Available at Partition-tolerant Web Services*, and *ACMSIGACT News, Volume 33, Issue 2 (2002), page 51 to 59* available at `http://lpd.epfl.ch/sgilbert/pubs/BrewersConjecture-SigAct.pdf`) It says, if we have a distributed system where data is replicated at two distinct locations and two conflicting requests arrive—one at each location—when the communication link between the two servers is broken. If the system (the cluster) has obligations to be highly available (a response, even when some components of the system are failing), one of the two responses will be inconsistent with what a system with no replication (no partitioning, single copy) would have returned. To understand it better, let us take an example to learn the terminologies. These terms will be used frequently throughout this book.

Let's say you are planning to read George Orwell's book titled *Nineteen Eighty-Four* (*1984, The Novel* available at `http://en.wikipedia.org/wiki/Nineteen_Eighty-Four`) over the Christmas vacation. A day before the holidays start, you logged in to your favorite online book store to find out that there is only one copy left. You add it to your cart. But then you realize that you need to buy something else to be eligible for free shipping. You start to browse the website for any other item that you might buy. To make the situation interesting, let's say there is another customer who is trying to buy *Nineteen Eighty-Four* at the same time.

Consistency

In a distributed system, consistency will be defined as one that responds with the same output for the same request at the same time across all the replicas. Loosely, one can say a consistent system is one where each server returns the right response to each request.

In our book-buying example, we have only one copy of *Nineteen Eighty-Four*. So, only one of the two customers is going to get the book delivered from this store. In a consistent system, only one can check out the book from the payment page. As soon as one customer makes the payment, the number of *Nineteen Eighty-Four* books in stock will get decremented by one and one quantity of *Nineteen Eighty-Four* will be added to the order of that customer. When the second customer tries to check out his shopping cart, the system tells that the book is not available any more.

Relational databases are good for this task because they comply with the ACID properties. If both the customers make the request at the same time, one customer will have to wait till the other customer is done with the processing, and the database is made consistent. This may add a few milliseconds of wait to the customer who came later.

An eventual consistent (where consistency of data across the distributed servers may not be guaranteed immediately) database system may have showed both the customers availability of the book at the time of check-out. This will lead to a back order, and one of the customers will be paid back. This may or may not be a good policy. A large number of back orders may affect the shop's reputation and there may also be financial repercussions.

Availability

Availability in simplest term is responsiveness. A system that's always available to serve. The funny thing about availability is that sometimes a system becomes unavailable exactly when you need it the most.

In our example, one day before Christmas, everyone is buying gifts. Millions of people are searching, adding items to their carts, buying, and applying for discount coupons. If one server goes down due to overload, the rest of the servers get even more loaded now, because the request from the dead server is getting redirected to the rest of the machines. Dominoes start to fall. Now the site is down. When it comes online again, it faces a storm of requests from all the people who are hurrying to place their order because the offer end time is even closer, or probably acting quickly before the site goes down again.

Availability is the key component for extremely loaded services. Bad availability leads to bad user experience, dissatisfied customers, and financial losses.

Partition-tolerance

Partition-tolerance is a system that can operate during the network partition. The network will be allowed to lose arbitrarily many messages sent from one node to another. This means a cable between the two nodes is chopped, but the system still works.

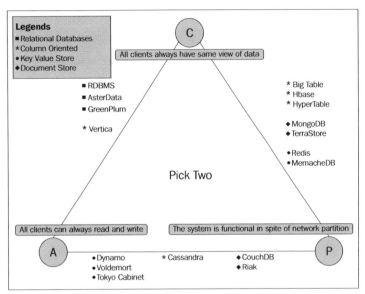

Figure 2.1. Database classification based on CAP Theorem

An example of a partition-tolerant system is a system with real-time data replication. A system where data is replicated across two datacenters, the availability will not be affected, even if a datacenter goes down.

Significance of the CAP theorem

Once you decide to scale up, the first thing that comes to mind is vertical scaling, which means putting beefier servers with a bigger RAM, a more powerful processor, and bigger disks. For further scaling, you need to go horizontal, which means adding more servers. Once your system becomes distributed, the CAP theorem starts to play. That means, in a distributed system, you can choose only two out of consistency, availability, and partition-tolerance. So, let us see how choosing two out of the three options affect the system behavior as follows:

CA system: In this system, you drop partition-tolerance for consistency and availability. This happens when you put everything related to a transaction on one machine or a system that fails like an atomic unit, for example, a rack. This system will have serious problems in scaling.

CP system: The opposite of a CA system is a CP system. In a CP system, availability is sacrificed for consistency and partition-tolerance. What does this mean? If the system is available to serve the requests, data will be consistent. In the event of a node failure, some data will not be available. A sharded database is an example of such a system.

AP system: An available and partition-tolerance system is like an always-on system on risk of producing conflicting results in the event of network partition. This is good for user experience, your application stays available, and inconsistency in rare events may be alright for some use cases. In the book example, it may not be such a bad idea to back order a few unfortunate customers due to inconsistency of the system than having a lot of users to return without making any purchase because of the system's poor availability.

Eventual consistent aka BASE system: The AP system makes more sense when viewed from an uptime perspective—it's simple and provides good user experience. But, an inconsistent system is not good for anything, certainly not good for business. It may be acceptable that one customer for the book *Nineteen Eighty-Four* gets a back order. But if it happens more often, the users would be reluctant to use the service. It will be great if the system can fix itself (read repair) as soon as the first inconsistency is observed. Or, maybe there are processes dedicated to fix the inconsistency of a system when a partition failure is fixed or a dead node comes back to life. Such systems are called Eventual Consistent Systems.

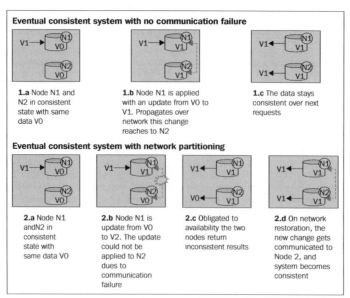

Figure 2.2: Life of an eventual consistent system

Quoting Wikipedia, "[In a distributed system] given a sufficiently long time over which no changes [in system state] are sent, all updates can be expected to propagate eventually through the system and the replicas will be consistent." (*Eventual Consistency* available at `http://en.wikipedia.org/wiki/Eventual_consistency`)

Eventual Consistent Systems are also called BASE, a made-up term to represent that these systems are on one end of the spectrum, which has traditional databases with the ACID properties on the opposite end.

Cassandra is one such system that provides high availability, and partition-tolerance at the cost of consistency, which is tunable. The preceding figure shows a partition-tolerant Eventual Consistent System.

Cassandra

Cassandra is distributed, decentralized, fault tolerant, eventually consistent, linearly scalable, and a column-oriented data store. This means Cassandra is made to easily deploy over a cluster of machines located at geographically different places. There is no central master server, so no single point of failure, no bottleneck, data is replicated, and a faulty node can be replaced without any downtime. It's eventually consistent. It is linearly scalable, which means with a greater number of nodes, the requests served per second per node would not go down. Also, the total throughput of the system will increase with each node being added. And finally, it's column oriented, much like a map (or better, a map of sorted maps) or a table with flexible columns where each column is essentially a key-value pair. So, you can add columns as you go, and each row can have a different set of columns (key-value pairs). It does not provide any relational integrity. It is up to the application developer to perform relation management.

So, if Cassandra is so good at everything, why not everyone drop whatever database they are using and jump start with Cassandra? This is a natural question. We'll discuss in a later chapter what Cassandra is not good at, but there may be several obvious reasons, such as not everyone needs a super-scalable data store, and some are good with rather slow, but cozy RDBMS tools. Some applications require strong ACID compliance, such as a booking system. If you are a person who goes by statistics, you'd ask how Cassandra fares with other existing data stores. TilmannRabl et al in their paper, *Solving Big Data Challenges for Enterprise Application Performance Management* (`http://vldb.org/pvldb/vol5/p1724_tilmannrabl_vldb2012.pdf`), told that, "In terms of scalability, there is a clear winner throughout our experiments. Cassandra achieves the highest throughput for the maximum number of nodes in all experiments with a linear increasing throughput from one to 12 nodes. This comes at the price of a high write and read latency. Cassandra's performance is best for high insertion rates."

If you go through the paper, Cassandra wins in almost all the criteria. Equipped with proven concepts of distributed computing, made to reliably serve from commodity servers, and simple and easy maintenance, Cassandra is one of the most scalable, fastest, and very robust NoSQL database. So, the next natural question is what makes Cassandra so blazing fast? Let us dive deeper into the Cassandra architecture.

Cassandra architecture

Cassandra is a relative latecomer in the distributed data-store war. It takes advantage of two proven and closely similar data-store mechanisms, namely Google BigTable, a distributed storage system for structured data, 2006 (`http://static. googleusercontent.com/external_content/untrusted_dlcp/research. google.com/en//archive/bigtable-osdi06.pdf [2006]`), and Amazon Dynamo, Amazon's highly available key-value store, 2007 (`http://www.read.seas.harvard. edu/~kohler/class/cs239-w08/decandia07dynamo.pdf [2007]`).

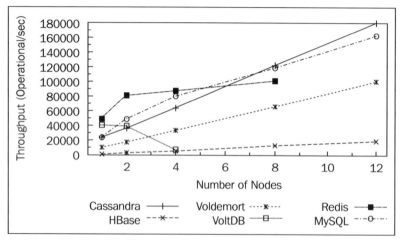

Figure 2.3: Read throughputs shows linear scaling of Cassandra

Like BigTable, it has tabular data presentation. It is not tabular in the strictest sense. It is rather a dictionary-like structure where each entry holds another sorted dictionary/map. This model is more powerful than the usual key-value store and it is named as column family. The properties such as Eventual Consistency and decentralization are taken from Dynamo.

We'll discuss column family in detail in a later chapter. For now, assume a column family as a giant spreadsheet, such as MS Excel. But unlike spreadsheets, each row is identified by a row key with a number (token), and unlike spreadsheets, each cell can have its own unique name within the row. The columns in the rows are sorted by this unique column name. Also, since the number of rows is allowed to be very large $(1.7*(10)^{38})$, we distribute the rows uniformly across all the available machines by dividing the rows in equal token groups. These rows create a **Keyspace**. Keyspace is a set of all the tokens (row IDs).

Ring representation

Cassandra cluster is denoted as a ring. The idea behind this representation is to show token distribution. Let's take an example. Assume that there is a partitioner that generates tokens from zero to 127 and you have four Cassandra machines to create a cluster. To allocate equal load, we need to assign each of the four nodes to bear an equal number of tokens. So, the first machine will be responsible for tokens one to 32, the second will hold 33 to 64, the third, 65 to 96, and the fourth, 97 to 127 and 0. If you mark each node with the maximum token number that it can hold, the cluster looks like a ring. (*Figure 2.22*) Partitioner is the hash function that determines the range of possible row keys. Cassandra uses a partitioner to calculate the token equivalent to a row key (row ID).

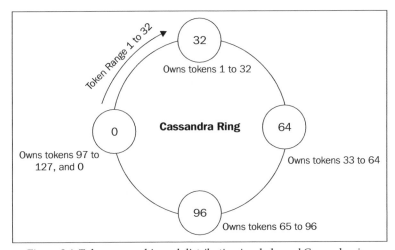

Figure 2.4: Token ownership and distribution in a balanced Cassandra ring

When you start to configure Cassandra, one thing that you may want to set is the maximum token number that a particular machine could hold. This property can be set in the `Cassandra.yaml` file as `initial_token`. One thing that may confuse a beginner is that the value of the initial token is what the last token owns. Be aware that nodes can be rebalanced and these tokens can be changed as the new nodes join or old nodes get discarded. This is the initial token because this is just the initial value, and it may be changed later.

How Cassandra works

Diving into various components of Cassandra without having a context is really a frustrating experience. It does not makes sense why you are studying **SSTable**, **MemTable**, and **Log Structured Merge (LSM)** tree without being able to see how they fit into functionality and performance guarantees that Cassandra gives. So, first, we will see Cassandra's write and read mechanism. It is possible that some of the terms that we encounter during this discussion may not be immediately understandable. The terms are explained in detail later in the chapter. A rough overview of the Cassandra components is as shown in the following figure:

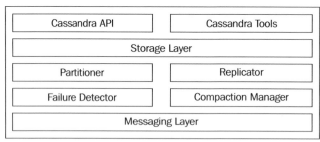

Figure 2.5: Main components of the Cassandra service

The main class of **Storage Layer** is `StorageProxy`. It handles all the requests. **Messaging Layer** is responsible for internode communications like gossip. Apart from this, process-level structures keep a rough idea about the actual data containers and where they live. There are four data buckets that you need to know. MemTable is a hash table-like structure that stays in memory. It contains actual column data. SSTable is the disk version of MemTables. When MemTables are full, SSTables are persisted to the hard disk. **Bloom filters** is a probabilistic data structure that lives in memory. It helps Cassandra to quickly detect which SSTable *does not* have the requested data. **CommitLog** is the usual commit log that contains all the mutations that are to be applied. It lives on the disk and helps to replay uncommitted changes.

With this primer, we can start looking into how write and read works in Cassandra. We will see more explanation later.

Write in action

To write, clients need to connect to *any* of the Cassandra nodes and send a write request. This node is called as the **coordinator node**. When a node in Cassandra cluster receives a write request, it delegates it to a service called `StorageProxy`. This node may or may not be the right place to write the data to. The task of `StorageProxy` is to get the nodes (all the replicas) that are responsible to hold the data that is going to be written. It utilizes a replication strategy to do that. Once the replica nodes are identified, it sends the `RowMutation` message to them, the node waits for replies from these nodes, but it does not wait for all the replies to come. It only waits for as many responses as are enough to satisfy the client's minimum number of successful writes defined by `ConsistencyLevel`. So, the following figure and steps after that show all that can happen during a write mechanism:

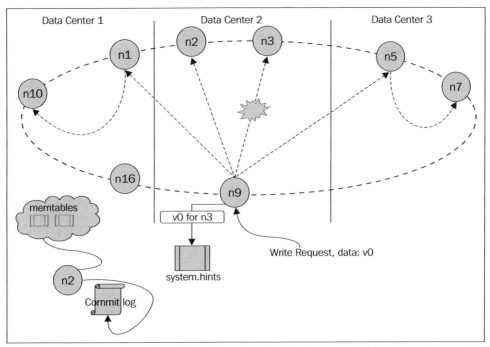

Figure 2.6: A simplistic representation of the write mechanism. The figure on the left represents the node-local activities on receipt of the write request

1. If **FailureDetector** detects that there aren't enough live nodes to satisfy `ConsistencyLevel`, the request fails.

2. If FailureDetector gives a green signal, but writes time-out after the request is sent due to infrastructure problems or due to extreme load, `StorageProxy` writes a local *hint* to replay when the failed nodes come back to life. This is called **hinted handoff**.

One might think that hinted handoff may be responsible for Cassandra's eventual consistency. But it's not entirely true. If the coordinator node gets shut down or dies due to hardware failure and *hints* on this machine cannot be forwarded, eventual consistency will not occur. The **Anti-entropy** mechanism is responsible for consistency rather than hinted handoff. Anti-entropy makes sure that all replicas are in sync.

3. If the replica nodes are distributed across datacenters, it will be a bad idea to send individual messages to all the replicas in other datacenters. It rather sends the message to one replica in each datacenter with a header instructing it to forward the request to other replica nodes in that datacenter.

4. Now, the data is received by the node that should actually store that data. The data first gets appended to CommitLog, and pushed to a MemTable for the appropriate column family in the memory.

5. When MemTable gets full, it gets flushed to the disk in a sorted structure named SSTable. With lots of flushes, the disk gets plenty of SSTables. To manage SSTables, a **compaction process** runs. This process merges data from smaller SSTables to one big sorted file.

Read in action

Similar to a write case, when `StorageProxy` of the node that a client is connected to gets the request, it gets a list of nodes containing this key based on **Replication Strategy**. `StorageProxy` then sorts the nodes based on their proximity to itself. The proximity is determined by the **Snitch** function that is set up for this cluster. Basically, there are the following types of Snitch:

*   `SimpleSnitch`: A closer node is the one that comes first when moving clockwise in the ring. (A ring is when all the machines in the cluster are placed in a circular fashion with each having a token number. When you walk clockwise, the token value increases. At the end, it snaps back to the first node.)

- `AbstractNetworkTopologySnitch`: Implementation of the Snitch function works like this: nodes on the same rack are closest. The nodes in the same datacenter but in different rack are closer than those in other datacenters, but farther than the nodes in the same rack. Nodes in different datacenters are the farthest. To a node, the nearest node will be the one on the same rack. If there is no node on the same rack, the nearest node will be the one that lives in the same datacenter, but on a different rack. If there is no node in the datacenter, any nearest neighbor will be the one in the other datacenter.

- `DynamicSnitch`: This Snitch determines closeness based on recent performance delivered by a node. So, a quick-responding node is perceived closer than a slower one, irrespective of their location closeness or closeness in the ring. This is done to avoid overloading a slow-performing node.

Now that we have the list of nodes that have desired row keys, it's time to pull data from them. The coordinator node (the one that the client is connected to) sends a command to the closest node to perform read (we'll discuss local read in a minute) and return the data. Now, based on `ConsistencyLevel`, other nodes will send a command to perform a read operation and send just the digest of the result. If we have **Read Repair** (discussed later) enabled, the remaining replica nodes will be sent a message to compute the digest of the command response.

Let's take an example: say you have five nodes containing a row key K (that is, **replication factor (RF)** equals 5). Your read `ConsistencyLevel` is three. Then the closest of the five nodes will be asked for the data. And the second and third closest nodes will be asked to return the digest. We still have two left to be queried. If read Repair is not enabled, they will not be touched for this request. Otherwise, these two will be asked to compute digest. The request to the last two nodes is done in the background, after returning the result. This updates all the nodes with the most recent value, making all replicas consistent. So, basically, in all scenarios, you will have a maximum one wrong response. But with correct read and write consistency levels, we can guarantee an up-to-date response all the time.

Let's see what goes within a node. Take a simple case of a read request looking for a single column within a single row. First, the attempt is made to read from MemTable, which is rapid-fast since there exists only one copy of data. This is the fastest retrieval. If the data is not found there, Cassandra looks into SSTable. Now, remember from our earlier discussion that we flush MemTables to disk as SSTables and later when compaction mechanism wakes up, it merges those SSTables. So, our data can be in multiple SSTables.

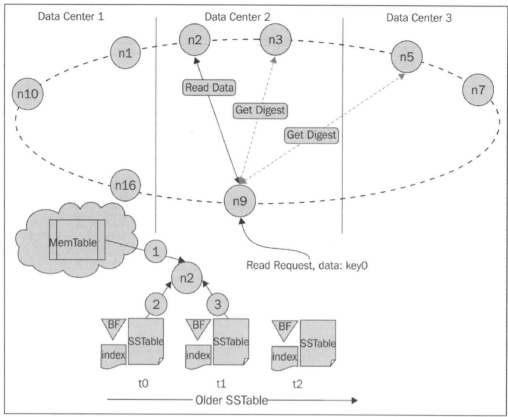

Figure 2.7: A simplified representation of the read mechanism. The bottom image shows processing on the read node. Numbers in circles shows the order of the event. BF stands for Bloom Filter

Each SSTable is associated with its Bloom Filter built on the row keys in the SSTable. Bloom Filters are kept in memory, and used to detect if an SSTable may contain (false positive) the row data. Now, we have the SSTables that may contain the row key. The SSTables get sorted in reverse chronological order (latest first).

Apart from Bloom Filter for row keys, there exists one Bloom Filter for each row in the SSTable. This secondary Bloom Filter is created to detect whether the requested column names exist in the SSTable. Now, Cassandra will take SSTables one by one from younger to older. And use the index file to locate the offset for each column value for that row key and the Bloom filter associated with the row (built on the column name). On Bloom filter being positive for the requested column, it looks into the SSTable file to read the column value. Note that we may have a column value in other yet-to-be-read SSTables, but that does not matter, because we are reading the most recent SSTables first, and any value that was written earlier to it does not matter. So, the value gets returned as soon as the first column in the most recent SSTable is allocated.

Components of Cassandra

We have gone through how read and write takes place in highly distributed Cassandra clusters. It's time to look into individual components of it a little deeper.

Messaging service

Messaging service is the mechanism that manages internode socket communication in a ring. Communications, for example, gossip, read, read digest, write, and so on, processed via a messaging service, can be assumed as a gateway messaging server running at each node.

To communicate, each node creates two socket connections per node. This implies that if you have 101 nodes, there will be 200 open sockets on each node to handle communication with other nodes. The messages contain a `verb` handler within them that basically tells the receiving node a couple of things: how to deserialize the payload message and what handler to execute for this particular message. The execution is done by the `verb` handlers (sort of an event handler). The singleton that orchestrates the messaging service mechanism is `org.apache.cassandra.net.MessagingService`.

Gossip

Cassandra uses the gossip protocol for internode communication. As the name suggests, the protocol spreads information in the same way an office rumor does. It can also be compared to a virus spread. There is no central broadcaster, but the information (virus) gets transferred to the whole population. It's a way for nodes to build the global map of the system with a small number of local interactions.

Cassandra uses gossip to find out the state and location of other nodes in the ring (cluster). The gossip process runs every second and exchanges information with at the most three other nodes in the cluster. Nodes exchange information about themselves and other nodes that they come to know about via some other gossip session. This causes all the nodes to eventually know about all the other nodes. Like everything else in Cassandra, gossip messages have a version number associated with it. So, whenever two nodes gossip, the older information about a node gets overwritten with a newer one. Cassandra uses an Anti-entropy version of gossip protocol that utilizes **Merkle trees** (discussed later) to repair unread data.

Implementation-wise the gossip task is handled by the `org.apache.cassandra.gms.Gossiper` class. Gossiper maintains a list of live and dead endpoints (the unreachable endpoints). At every one-second interval, this module starts a gossip round with a randomly chosen node. A full round of gossip consists of three messages. A node **X** sends a `syn` message to a node **Y** to initiate gossip. **Y**, on receipt of this `syn` message, sends an `ack` message back to **X**. To reply to this `ack` message, **X** sends an `ack2` message to **Y** completing a full message round.

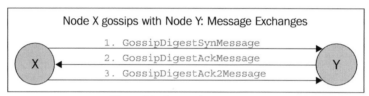

Figure 2.8: Two nodes gossiping

The Gossiper module is linked to failure detection. The module on hearing one of these messages updates FailureDetector with the *liveness* information that it has gained. If it hears a `GossipShutdownMessage`, the module marks the remote node as dead in FailureDetector.

The node to be gossiped with is chosen based on the following rules:

- Gossip to a random live endpoint
- Gossip to a random unreachable endpoint
- If the node in #1 was not a seed node or the number of live nodes is less than the number of seeds, gossip to a random seed

Seed Node

Seed nodes are the nodes that are first contacted by a newly joining node when they first start up. Seed nodes help the newly started node to discover other nodes in the cluster. It is suggested to have more than one seed node in a `cluster`. `Seed` node is nothing like a master in a master-slave mechanism. It is just another node that helps newly joining nodes to bootstrap gossip protocol. Seeds, hence, are not a **single point of failure** (**SPOF**) and neither have any other purpose that makes them superior.

Failure detection

Failure detection is one of the fundamental features of any robust and distributed system. A good failure detection mechanism implementation makes a fault-tolerant system such as Cassandra. The failure detector that Cassandra uses is a variation of *The ϕ accrual failure detector (2004)* by Xavier Défago et al. (The phi accrual detector research paper is available at `http://citeseerx.ist.psu.edu/viewdoc/summary?doi=10.1.1.106.3350`.)

The idea behind a FailureDetector is to detect a communication failure and take appropriate actions based on the state of the remote node. Unlike traditional failure detectors, phi accrual failure detector does not emit a Boolean alive or dead (true or false, trust or suspect) value. Instead, it gives a continuous value to the application and the application is left to decide the level of severity and act accordingly. This continuous suspect value is called phi (φ). So, how does ϕ get calculated?

Let's say we are observing a heartbeat sent from a process on a remote machine. Assume that the latest heartbeat arrived at time `Tlast`, current time `tnow`, and `Plater(t)` be the probability that the heartbeat will arrive `t` time unit later than the last heartbeat. Then φ can be calculated as follows:

$$\varphi(t_{now}) = -\log_{10}(P_{later}(t_{now} - T_{last}))$$

Let's observe this formula informally using common sense. On a sunny day, when everything is fine and heartbeat is at a constant interval Δt. The probability of the next heartbeat will keep increasing towards 1 as $(t_{now} - T_{last})$ Δt. So, the value of φ will go up. If a heartbeat is not received in Δt, the more we depart away from Δt, the chances are that something has gone wrong.

The lower the value of P_{later} becomes, and the value of φ keeps on increasing as shown in the following figure:

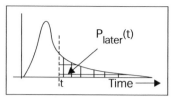

Figure 2.9: The curve shows a heartbeat arrival distribution estimate based on past samples. It is used to calculate the value of ϕ based on the last arrival, T_{last}, and t_{now}.

One may question where we send a heartbeat in Cassandra. Gossip has it.

Gossip and Failure Detection: During gossip sessions, each node maintains a list of the arrival timestamps of gossip messages from other nodes. This list is basically a sliding window, which, in turn, is used to calculate P_{later}. One may set the sensitivity of φthres threshold.

The best explanation of failure detector can be found in Cassandra research paper (http://www.cs.cornell.edu/projects/ladis2009/papers/lakshman-ladis2009.pdf):

> *Given some threshold φ, and assuming that we decide to suspect a node A when φ = 1, then the likelihood that we will make a mistake (that is, the decision will be contradicted in the future by the reception of a late heartbeat) is about 10%. The likelihood is about 1% with φ = 2, 0.1% with φ = 3, and so on. Every node in the system maintains a sliding window of inter-arrival times of gossip messages from other nodes in the cluster. The distribution of these inter-arrival times is determined and φ is calculated.*

Partitioner

Cassandra is a distributed database management system. This means it takes a single logical database and distributes it over one or more machines in the database cluster. So, when you insert some data in Cassandra, it assigns each row to a row key; and based on that row key, Cassandra assigns that row to one of the nodes that's responsible for managing it.

Let's try to understand this. Cassandra inherits the data model from Google's BigTable (BigTable research paper can be found at http://research.google.com/archive/bigtable.html.). This means we can roughly assume that the data is stored in some sort of a table that has an unlimited number of columns (not unlimited, Cassandra limits the maximum number of columns to be two billion) with rows binded with a *unique* key, namely, row key.

Now, your terabytes of data on one machine will be restrictive from multiple points of views. One is disk space, another being limited parallel processing, and if not duplicated, a source of single point of failure. What Cassandra does is, it defines some rules to slice data across rows and assigns which node in the cluster is responsible for holding which slice. This task is done by a partitioner. There are several types of partitioners to choose from. We'll discuss them in detail in *Chapter 4, Deploying a Cluster,* under the Partitioners section. In short, Cassandra (as of Version 1.2) offers three partitioners as follows:

- `RandomPartitioner`: It uses MD5 hashing to distribute data across the cluster. Cassandra 1.1.x and precursors have this as the default partitioner.

- `Murmur3Partitioner`: It uses Murmur hash to distribute the data. It performs better than `RandomPartitioner`. It is the default partitioner from Cassandra Version 1.2 onwards.

- `ByteOrderPartitioner`: Keeps keys distributed across the cluster by key bytes. This is an ordered distribution, so the rows are stored in lexical order. This distribution is commonly discouraged because it may cause a hotspot.

One of the key benefits of partitioning data is that it allows the cluster to grow incrementally. What any partitioning algorithm does is it gives a consistent divisibility of data across all available nodes. The *key* that a node is assigned to by the partitioner also determines the node's *position* in the ring. Since partitioning is a global setting, any node in the cluster can calculate which nodes to look for in a given row key. This ability to calculate data-holding nodes without knowing anything other than the row key, enables any node to calculate what node to forward requests to. This makes the node selection process a single-hop mechanism.

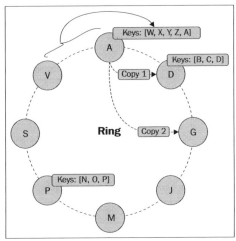

Figure 2.10: A Cassandra ring with alphabetical partitioner shows keys owned by the nodes and data replication

Another benefit of good partitioning is that the addition or removal of a node only affects the neighbors of the arriving or departing node. How so? *Figure 2.10* shows what a Dynamo (`http://www.read.seas.harvard.edu/~kohler/class/cs239-w08/decandia07dynamo.pdf`) or a Cassandra cluster looks like; it looks like a ring. In this particular figure, each node is assigned with a letter as its token ID. So, the partitioner here is something that slices row keys based on their alphabetical ordering. When a data arrives to a node, the row key tells its position in the cluster. Then, while walking clockwise in the cluster, the first node with a position (token ID) larger than or equal to the row key's position (row key converted to a token ID) becomes responsible for that data. This way, each node in the cluster becomes responsible for the region in the cluster between it (inclusive) and its previous node (exclusive). So, node **D** will keep keys starting with **B**, **C**, and **D**.

Another frequently used terminology for a Cassandra cluster is **ring**. This is because the last node wraps around the first one, thus making the system look like a ring. In the preceding figure, the first node **A** is responsible for wrapping up from the last node **V**. So, it holds the data from **W** to **Z** to **A**. If a node **D** disappears from the system, the only node that gets affected is the node **G**, which now has to carry data from **B** to **G**. If we add a node **X** (between **V** and **A**), node **A** will offload some of its rows to the new node **X**. Particularly, **A** will stream out rows starting from **W** to **X** to node **X** and will become responsible for data from **Y** to **A**.

Now that we have observed that partitioning has such a drastic effect on the data movement and distribution, one may think that a bad partitioner can lead to uneven data distribution. In fact, our example ring in the previous paragraph might be a bad partitioner. For a data set, where terms with a specific starting letter has very high population than the terms with other letters, the ring will be lopsided. A good partitioner is one that is quick to calculate the position from the row key and distributes the row keys evenly; something like a partitioner based on consistent hashing algorithm.

Replication

Cassandra runs on commodity hardware, and works reliably in network partitions. However, this comes with a cost: replication. To avoid data inaccessibility in case a node goes down or becomes unavailable, one must replicate data to more than one node. Replication brings features such as fault tolerance and no single point of failure to the system. Cassandra provides more than one strategy to replicate the data, and one can configure the replication factor while creating keyspace. It will be discussed in detail in *Chapter xx*.

Replication is tightly binded to **consistency level** (CL). Consistency level can be thought of as an answer to the question: how many replicas must respond positively to declare a successful operation? If you have read consistency level three, that means a client will be returned a successful read as soon as three replicas respond with the data. Same goes for write. For write consistency three, at least three replicas must respond that the write to them was successful. Obviously, replication factor *must* be greater than any consistency level, else there will never be enough replicas to write to or read from successfully.

Do not confuse replication factor with the number of nodes in the system. Replication factor is the number of copies of a data. The number of nodes just affects how much data a node will hold based on the configured partitioner.

Replication should be thought of as an added redundancy. One should never have a replication factor of 1 in their production environment. If you think having multiple writes to different replicas will slow down the writes, you can set up a favorable consistency level. Cassandra offers a set of consistency levels including CL ZERO for fire and forget, and CL ALL for all replica success. This is where so-called **tunable** consistency of Cassandra is. The following table shows all the consistency levels:

WRITE		READ	
Consistency level	Meaning	Consistency level	Meaning
ZERO	Fire and forget		
ANY	Success on hinted handoff write		
ONE	First replica returned successfully	ONE	First replica returned successfully
QUORUM	N/2 + 1 replica success	QUORUM	N/2 + 1 replica success
ALL	All replica success	ALL	All replica success

The notorious R+W> N inequality: Imagine you have the replication factor as 3. That means your data will be stored in three nodes. They may or may not be consistent. You have write consistency level as one, and read consistency level as one. A write happens to the first replica node (**N1**) and is returned to the user. This means that while a read happens, unfortunately that read lands on a second replica (**N2**). Since consistency level is equal to one, it will just read this node and return the value. This will be inconsistent as the write hasn't propagated yet. This will be made consistent after the read happens as a part of read repair. But the first read is wrong.

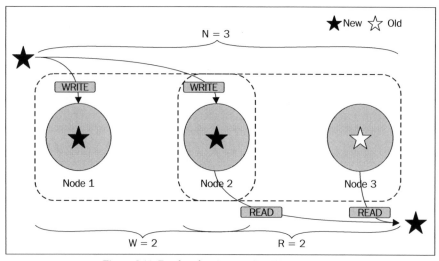

Figure 2.11: Read and write on a R + W > N system

The concept of weak and strong consistency comes here. Weak consistency is the one where read repair takes place after returning the result to the client. And strong consistency is the one where repair happens before returning the result. Basically, a weak consistency is the one that may return inconsistent results. If you have an N replica, to ensure that your reads always result in the latest value, you must write and read from as many nodes that ensure at least one node overlaps. So, if you write to W nodes and read from R nodes such that R+W > N, there must be at least one node that is common in both read and write. And that will ensure that you have the latest data. See *Figure 2.11*. So, ZERO and ANY consistency levels are weak consistency. ALL is strong. ONE for read and ALL for write or vice versa will make a strongly consistent system. A system with QUORUM for both read and write is a strongly consistent system. Again, the idea is to make sure that between the reads and the writes at least one node overlaps. While we are on this topic, it may be worth noticing that the higher the consistency level, the slower the operation. So, if you want a superfast write and not-so-fast read and you also want the system to be strongly consistent, you may opt for a consistency level ONE for the writes and ALL for the reads.

Log Structured Merge tree

Cassandra (also, HBase) is heavily influenced by Log Structured Merge (LSM). It uses an LSM tree-like mechanism to store data on a disk. The writes are sequential (in append fashion) and the data storage is contiguous. This makes writes in Cassandra superfast, because there is no seek involved. Contrast this with an RBDMS system that is based on the B+ Tree (`http://en.wikipedia.org/wiki/B%2B_tree`) implementation.

LSM tree advocates the following mechanism to store data: note down the arriving modification into a log file (CommitLog), push the modification/new data into memory (MemTable) for faster lookup, and when the system has gathered enough updates in memory or after a certain threshold time, flush this data to a disk in a structured store file (SSTable). The logs corresponding to the updates that are flushed can now be discarded.

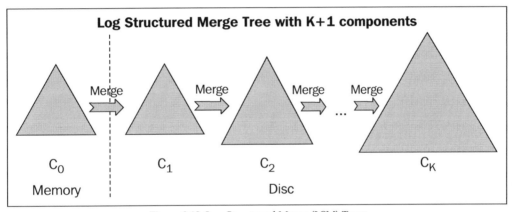

Figure 2.12: Log Structured Merge (LSM) Trees

 The Log-Structured Merge-Tree (LSM-Tree)(1996) by Patrick O'Neil et al is available at `http://citeseerx.ist.psu.edu/viewdoc/summary?doi=10.1.1.44.2782`.

The preceding paper suggests multicomponent LSM trees, where data from memory is flushed into a smaller tree on disk for a quicker merge. When this tree fills up, it rolls them into a bigger tree. So, if you have K trees with the first tree being the smallest and the Kth being the largest, the memory gets flushed into the first tree, which when full, performs a rolling merge to the second tree, and so on. The change eventually lands up onto the Kth tree. This is a background process (similar to the compaction process in Cassandra). Cassandra differs a little bit where memory-resident data is flushed into immutable SSTables, which are eventually merged into one big SSTable by a background process. Like any other disk-resident access tree, popular pages are buffered into memory for faster access. Cassandra has a similar concept with key cache and row cache (optional) mechanisms.

We'll see the LSM tree in action in the context of Cassandra in the next three sections.

CommitLog

One of the promises that Cassandra makes to the end users is durability. In conventional terms (or in ACID terminology), durability guarantees that a successful transaction (write, update) will survive permanently. This means once Cassandra says write successful that means the data is persisted and will survive system failures. It is done the same way as in any DBMS that guarantees durability: by writing the replayable information to a file before responding to a successful write. This log is called the CommitLog in the Cassandra realm.

This is what happens. Any write to a node gets tracked by `org.apache.cassandra.db.commitlog.CommitLog`, which writes the data with certain metadata into the CommitLog file in such a manner that replaying this will recreate the data. The purpose of this exercise is to ensure there is no data loss. If due to some reason the data could not make it into MemTable or SSTable, the system can replay the CommitLog to recreate the data.

CommitLog, MemTable, and SSTable in a node are tightly coupled. Any write operation gets written to the CommitLog first and then MemTable gets updated. MemTable, based on certain criteria, gets flushed to a disk in immutable files called SSTable. The data in CommitLogs gets purged after its corresponding data in MemTable gets flushed to SSTable. See *Figure 2.13*.

Also, there exists one single CommitLog per node server. Like any other logging mechanism, CommitLog is set to rolling after a certain size. (Why a single CommitLog? Why not one CommitLog per column family?)

Read Google's Bigtable paper, *Bigtable: A Distributed Storage System for Structured Data,* available at `http://research.google.com/archive/bigtable.html`.

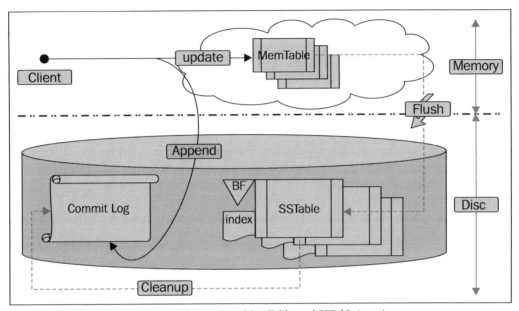

Figure 2.13: CommitLog, MemTable, and SSTable in action

Let's quickly go a bit deeper into implementation. All the classes that deal with the CommitLog management reside under `org.apache.cassandra.db.commitlog package`. The `CommitLog` singleton is a facade for all the operations. The implementations of `ICommitLogExecutorService` are responsible for write commands to the CommitLog file. Then there is a `CommitLogSegment` class. It manages a single CommitLog file, writes serialized write (mutation) to CommitLog, and it holds a very interesting property, `cfLastWrite`. `cfLastWrite` is a map with key as the column family name and value as an integer that represents the position (offset) in the CommitLog file where the last mutation for that column family is written. It can be thought of as a cursor one cursor per column family. When MemTable of a column family is flushed, the segments containing those mutations are marked as *clean* (for that particular column family). And when a new write arrives, it is marked *dirty* with offset at the latest mutation.

In the event of failure (hardware crash, abrupt shutdown), this is how CommitLog helps the system to recover:

1. Each CommitLog segment is iterated in ascending timestamp.
2. Lowest `ReplayPosition` (offset till which the data is persisted in SSTable) is chosen from SSTable metadata.
3. The log entry is replayed for a column family if the position of the log entry is greater than the replay position in the latest SSTable metadata.
4. After the log replay is done, all the MemTables are force flushed to a disk, and all the CommitLog segments are recycled.

MemTable

MemTable is an in-memory representation of column family. It can be thought of as a cached data. MemTable is sorted by key. Data in MemTable is sorted by row key. Unlike `CommitLog`, which is append-only, MemTable does not contain duplicates. A new write with a key that already exists in the MemTable overwrites the older record. This being in memory is both fast and efficient. The following is an example:

```
Write 1: {k1: [{c1, v1}, {c2, v2}, {c3, v3}]}

In CommitLog (new entry, append):
  {k1: [{c1, v1},{c2, v2}, {c3, v3}]}

In MemTable (new entry, append):
  {k1: [{c1, v1}, {c2, v2}, {c3, v3}]}

Write 2: {k2: [{c4, v4}]}

In CommitLog (new entry, append):
  {k1: [{c1, v1}, {c2, v2}, {c3, v3}]}
  {k2: [{c4, v4}]}

In MemTable (new entry, append):
  {k1: [{c1, v1}, {c2, v2}, {c3, v3}]}
  {k2: [{c4, v4}]}

Write 3: {k1: [{c1, v5}, {c6, v6}]}

In CommitLog (old entry, append):
  {k1: [{c1, v1}, {c2, v2}, {c3, v3}]}
  {k2: [{c4, v4}]}
```

```
    {k1: [{c1, v5}, {c6, v6}]}

 In MemTable (old entry, update):
    {k1: [{c1, v5}, {c2, v2}, {c3, v3}, {c6, v6}]}
    {k2: [{c4, v4}]}
```

Cassandra Version 1.1.1 uses SnapTree (https://github.com/nbronson/snaptree) for MemTable representation, which claims it to be "... a drop-in replacement for ConcurrentSkipListMap, with the additional guarantee that clone() is atomic and iteration has snapshot isolation." See also copy-on-write and compare-and-swap (http://en.wikipedia.org/wiki/Copy-on-write, http://en.wikipedia.org/wiki/Compare-and-swap).

Any write gets written first to CommitLog and then to MemTable.

SSTable

SSTable is a disk representation of the data. MemTables gets flushed to disk to immutable SSTables. All the writes are sequential, which makes this process fast. So, the faster the disk speed, the quicker the flush operation.

The SSTables eventually get merged in the compaction process and the data gets organized properly into one file. This extra work in compaction pays off during reads.

SSTables have three components: Bloom filter, index files, and datafiles.

Bloom filter

Bloom filter is a litmus test for the availability of certain data in storage (collection). But unlike a litmus test, a Bloom filter may result in false positives: that is, it says that a data exists in the collection associated with the Bloom filter, when it actually does not. A Bloom filter never results in a false negative. That is, it never states that a data is not there while it is. The reason to use Bloom filter, even with its false-positive defect, is because it is superfast and its implementation is really simple.

Cassandra uses Bloom filters to determine whether an SSTable has the data for a particular row key. Bloom filters are unused for range scans, but they are good candidates for index scans. This saves a lot of disk I/O that might take in a full SSTable scan, which is a slow process. That's why it is used in Cassandra, to avoid reading many, many SSTables, which can become a bottleneck.

How Bloom filter works: Bloom filter in its simplest form can be assumed as a bit array of length 1, with all elements set to zero. It also has k predefined hash functions associated with it. See *Figure 2.14* as shown:

Figure 2.14: Bloom filter in action. It uses three hash functions and sets the corresponding bit in the array to 1 (it might already be 1)

To add a key to a Bloom filter (at the time of entering data in the associated collection), k hashes are calculated using k predefined hash functions. A modulus of each hash value is taken using array length 1, and the value at this array position is set to 1.

The following pseudo code shows what happens when a value v is inserted in Bloom filter:

```
//calculate hash, mod it to get location in bit array
arrayIndex1 = md5(v) % arrayLength
arrayIndex2 = sha1(v) % arrayLength
arrayindex3 = murmur(v) % arrayLength

//set all those indexes to 1
bitArray[arrayIndex1] = 1
bitArray[arrayIndex2] = 1
bitArray[arrayIndex3] = 1
```

To query the existence of a key in the Bloom filter, the process is similar. Take the key and calculate the predefined hash values. Take mod with bit array length. Look into those locations. If it turns out that at least one of those array locations have zero value in it, it is sure that this value was never inserted in this Bloom filter and hence does not exist in the associated collection. On the other hand, if all values are 1s, this means the value may exist in the collection associated with this Bloom filter. We cannot guarantee its presence in the collection because it is possible that there exists other k keys whose ith hash function filled the same spot in the array as the jth hash of the key that we are looking for.

Removal of a key from Bloom filter as in its original avatar is not possible. One may break multiple keys because multiple keys may have the same index bit set to 1 in the array for different hashes. Counting Bloom filter solves these issues by changing the bit array into an integer array where each element works as a counter; insertion increments the counter and deletion decrements.

Effectiveness of Bloom filter depends on the size of the collection it is applied to. The bigger the collection associated with the Bloom filter, the higher the frequency of false positives (because the array will be more densely packed with 1s). Another thing that governs Bloom filter is the quality of a good hash function. A good hash function will distribute hash values evenly in the array, and it will be fast. One does not look at the cryptic strength of the hash function here, so Murmur3 hash will be preferred over SHA1 hash.

Index files

Index files are companion files of SSTables. The same as Bloom filter, there exists one index file per SSTable. It contains all the row keys in the SSTable and its offset at which the row starts in the datafile.

At startup, Cassandra reads every 128th key (configurable) into the memory (sampled index). When the index is looked for a row key (after Bloom filter hinted that the row key might be in this SSTable), Cassandra performs a binary search on the sampled index in memory. Followed by a positive result from the binary search, Cassandra will have to read a block in the index file from the disk starting from the nearest value lower than the value that we are looking for.

Let's take an example; see *Figure 2.16*. Cassandra is looking for a row key 404. It is not in MemTable. On querying the Bloom filter of a certain SSTable, Cassandra gets a positive nod that this SSTable may contain the row. Next is to look into the SSTable. But before we start scanning the SSTable or the index file, we can get some help from the sampled index in memory. Looking through the sampled index, Cassandra finds out that there exists a row key 400 and another 624. So, the row fragments may be in this SSTable. But more importantly, the sampled index tells the offset about the 400 entry in the index file. Cassandra now scans the SSTable from 400 and gets to the entry for 404. This tells Cassandra the offset of the entry for the 404 key in SSTable and it reads from there.

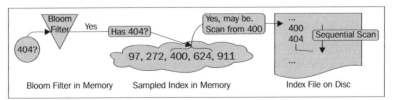

Figure 2.15: Cassandra SSTable index in action

If you followed the example, you must have observed that the smaller the sampling size, the more the number of keys in the memory; the smaller the size of the block to read on disk, the faster the results. This is a trade-off between memory usage and performance.

Datafiles

Datafiles are the actual data. They contain row keys, metadata, and columns (partial or full). Reading data from datafiles is just one disk seek followed by a sequential read, as offset to a row key is already obtained from the associated index file.

Compaction

As we discussed earlier in the section (See *Figure 2.8*), a read require may require Cassandra to read across multiple SSTables to get a result. This is wasteful, costs multiple (disk) seeks, may require a conflict resolution, and if there are too many, SSTables were created. To handle this problem, Cassandra has a process in place, namely, compaction. Compaction merges multiple SSTable files into one. Off the shelf, Cassandra offers two types of compaction mechanism: **Size Tiered Compaction Strategy** and **Level Compaction Strategy** (*Chapter 5, Performance Tuning*, under the Choosing the right compaction strategy section). This section stays focused on the Size Tiered Compaction mechanism for better understanding.

The compaction process starts when the number of SSTables on disk reaches a certain threshold (N: configurable). Although the merge process is a little I/O intensive, it benefits in the long term with a lower number of disk seeks during reads. Apart from this, there are a few other benefits of compaction as follows:

- Removal of expired tombstones (Cassandra v0.8+)
- Merging row fragments
- Rebuilds primary and secondary indexes

Merge is not as painful as it may seem, because SSTables are already sorted. (Remember merge-sort?) Merge results into larger files, but old files are not deleted immediately. For example, let's say you have compaction threshold set to four. Cassandra initially creates SSTables of the same size as MemTable. When the number of SSTables surpasses the threshold, the compaction thread triggers. This compacts the four equal-sized SSTables into one. Temporarily, you will have two times the total SSTable data on your disk. Another thing to note is that SSTables that get merged have the same size. So, when the four SSTables get merged to give a larger SSTable of size, say G, the buckets for the rest to-be-filled SSTables will be G each. So, the next compaction is going to take an even larger space while merging.

The SSTables, after merging, are marked as *deleteable*. They get deleted at a garbage collection cycle of the JVM or when Cassandra restarts.

The compaction process happens on each node and does not affect others; this is called **minor compaction**. This is automatically triggered, system controlled, and regular. There is more than one type of compaction setting that exits in Cassandra. We'll see them again in detail in *Chapter 5, Performance Tuning*, under the Choosing the right compaction strategy section. Another league of compaction is called, obviously, **major compaction**.

What's a major compaction? Major compaction takes all the SSTables, and merges it to one single SSTable. It is somewhat confusing when you see that a minor compaction merges SSTables and a major one does it too. There is a slight difference; for example, if we take Size Tiered Compaction Strategy, it merges the tables of the same size. So, if your threshold is four, Cassandra will start to merge when it finds four same-sized SSTables. If your system starts with four SSTables of size X, after the compaction you will end up with one SSTable of size 4X. Next time when you have four X-sized SSTables you will end up with two 4X tables, and so on. (These larger SSTables will get merged after 16 X-sized SSTables gets merged into four 4X tables.) After a really long time you will end up with a couple of really big SSTables, a handful of large SSTables, and many smaller SSTables. This is a result of continuous minor compaction. So, you may need to hop a couple of SSTables to get data for a query. Then, you run a major compaction and all the big and small SSTables get merged into one. This is the only benefit of major compaction.

> Major compaction may not be the best idea after Cassandra v0.8+. There are a couple of reasons for this. One reason is automated minor compaction no longer runs after a major compaction is executed. So, this adds up manual intervention or doing extra work (such as setting a cron job) to perform regular major compaction. The performance gain after major compaction may deteriorate with time. Major compaction creates large SSTable. The larger the SSTable, the higher the false positive rate from the Bloom filter. Large SSTable will have large index, it will take longer to perform binary search for them.

Tombstones

Cassandra is a complex system with its data distributed among CommitLogs, MemTables, and SSTables on a node. The same data is then replicated over replica nodes. So, like everything else in Cassandra, deletion is going to be eventful. Deletion, to an extent, follows an update pattern except Cassandra tags the deleted data with a special value, and marks it as a **tombstone**. This marker helps future queries, compaction, and conflict resolution. Let's step further down and see what happens when a column from a column family is deleted.

A client connected to a node (coordinator node, but it may not be the one holding the data that we are going to mutate), issues a delete command for a column C, in a column family CF. If the consistency level is satisfied, the delete command gets processed. When a node, containing the row key, receives a delete request, it updates or inserts the column in MemTable with a special value, namely, tombstone. The tombstone basically has the same column name as the previous one; the value is set to UNIX epoch. The timestamp is set to what the client has passed. When a MemTable is flushed to SSTable, all tombstones go into it as any regular column.

On the read side, when the data is read locally on the node and it happens to have multiple versions of it in different SSTables, they are compared and the latest value is taken as the result of reconciliation. If a tombstone turns out to be a result of reconciliation, it is made a part of the result that this node returns. So, at this level, if a query has a deleted column, this exists in the result. But the tombstones will eventually be filtered out of the result before returning it back to the client. So, a client can never see a value that is a tombstone.

For consistency levels more than one, the query is executed on as many replicas as the consistency level. The same as a regular read process, data from the closest node and a digest from the remaining nodes is obtained (to satisfy the consistency level). If there is a mismatch such as the tombstone is not yet propagated to all the replicas, a partial read repair is triggered, where the final view of the data is sent to all the nodes that were involved in this read to satisfy the consistency level.

One thing where delete differs from update is a compaction. A compaction removes a tombstone only if its (the tombstone's) garbage collection's grace seconds (t) are over. This t is called GCGraceSeconds (configurable). So, do not expect that a major deletion will free up a lot of space immediately.

What happens to a node that was holding a data that was deleted (in other live replicas) when this node was down? If a tombstone still exists in any of the replica nodes, the delete information will eventually be available to the previously dead node. But a compaction occurs at GCGraceSeconds, after the deletion will kick the old tombstones out. This is a problem, because no information about the deleted column is left. Now, if a node, that was dead all the time during GCGraceSeconds, wakes up and sees that it has some data that no other node has, it will treat this data as a fresh data and assuming a write failure, it will replicate the data over all the other replica nodes. The old data will resurrect and replicate, and may reappear in client results.

Although GCGraceSeconds is 10 days by default, before which any sane system admin will bring the node back in, or discard the node completely. But it is something to watch out for and repair nodes occasionally.

Hinted handoff

When we last talked about durability, we observed Cassandra provides CommitLogs to provide write durability. This is good. But what if the node, where the writes are going to be, is itself dead? No communication will keep anything new to be written to the node. Cassandra, inspired by Dynamo, has a feature called hinted handoff. In short, it's the same as taking a quick note locally that X cannot be contacted. Here is the mutation (operation that requires modification of the data such as insert, delete, and update) M that will be required to be replayed when it comes back.

The coordinator node (the node which the client is connected to) on receipt of a mutation/write request, forwards it to appropriate replicas that are alive. If this fulfills the expected consistency level, write is assumed successful. The write requests to a node that does not respond to a write request or is known to be dead (via gossip) and is stored locally in the system.hints table. This hint contains the mutation. When a node comes to know via gossip that a node is recovered, it replays all the hints it has in store for that node. Also, every 10 minutes, it keeps checking any pending hinted handoffs to be written.

Why worry about hinted handoff when you have written to satisfy consistency level? Wouldn't it eventually get repaired? Yes, that's right. Also, hinted handoff may not be the most reliable way to repair a missed write. What if the node that has hinted handoff dies? This is a reason why we do not count on hinted handoff as a mechanism to provide consistency (except for the case of the consistency level, ANY) guarantee; it's a single point of failure. The purpose of hinted handoff is, one, to make restored nodes quickly consistent with the other live ones; and two, to provide extreme write availability when consistency is not required.

The way extreme write availability is obtained is at the cost of consistency. One can set consistency level for writes to ANY. What happens next is, if all the replicas that are meant to hold this value are down, Cassandra will just write a local hinted handoff and return write success to the client. There is one caveat; the handoff can be on any node. So, a read for the data that we have written as a hint will not be available as long as the replicas are dead plus until the hinted handoff is replayed. But it is a nice feature.

 There is a slight difference where hinted handoff is stored in Cassandra's different versions. Prior to Cassandra 1.0, hinted handoff is stored on one of the replica nodes that can be communicated with. From Version 1.0+ (including 1.0), handoff can be written on the coordinator node (the node which the client is connected to).

Removing a node from a cluster causes deletion of hinted handoff stored for that node. All hints for deleted records are dropped.

Read repair and Anti-entropy

Cassandra promises eventual consistency and read repair is the process which does that part. Read repair, as the name suggests, is the process of fixing inconsistencies among the replicas at the time of read. What does that mean? Let's say we have three replica nodes A, B, and C that contain a data X. During an update, X is updated to X1 in replicas A and B. But it is failed in replica C for some reason. On a read request for data X, the coordinator node asks for a full read from the nearest node (based on the configured Snitch) and *digest* of data X from other nodes to satisfy consistency level. The coordinator node compares these values (something like digest(full_X) == digest_from_node_C). If it turns out that the digests are the same as the digests of full read, the system is consistent and the value is returned to the client. On the other hand, if there is a mismatch, full data is retrieved and reconciliation is done and the client is sent the reconciled value. After this, in background, all the replicas are updated with the reconciled value to have a consistent view of data on each node. See *Figure 2.1* as shown:

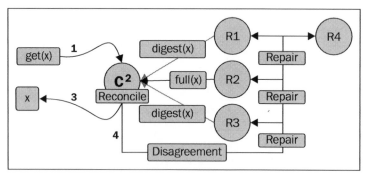

Figure 2.16: Image showing read repair dynamics. 1. Client queries for data x, from a node C (coordinator). 2. C gets data from replicas R1, R2, and R3; reconciles. 3. Sends reconciled data to client. 4. If there is a mismatch across replicas, repair is invoked.

So, we have got a consistent view on read. What about the data that is inserted, but never read? Hinted handoff is there, but we do not rely on hinted handoff for consistency. What if the node containing hinted handoff data dies, and the data that contains the hint is never read? Is there a way to fix them without read? This brings us to the Anti-entropy architecture of Cassandra (borrowed from Dynamo).

Anti-entropy compares all the replicas of a column family and updates the replica to the latest. This happens during major compaction. It uses Merkle tree to determine discrepancy among the replicas and fixes it.

Merkle tree

Merkle tree (*A digital signature Based On A Conventional Encryption Function* by Merkle, R. (1988), available at `http://www.cse.msstate.edu/~ramkumar/merkle2.pdf.`) is a hash tree where leaves of the tree hashes hold actual data in a column family and non-leaf nodes hold hashes of their children. The unique advantage of Merkle tree is a whole subtree can be validated just by looking at the value of the parent node. So, if nodes on two replica servers have the same hash values, then the underlying data is consistent and there is no need to synchronize. If one node passes the whole Merkle tree of a column family to another node, it can determine all the inconsistencies.

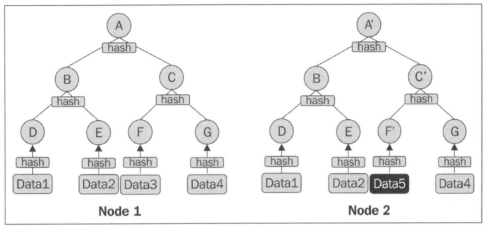

Figure 2.17: Merkle tree to determine mismatch in hash values at parent nodes due to the difference in underlying data

To exemplify, *Figure 2.17* shows the Merkle tree from two nodes with inconsistent data. A process comparing these two trees would know that there is something inconsistent, because the hash value stored in the top node does not match. It can descend down and know that the right subtree is likely to have an inconsistency. And then the same process is repeated until it finds out all the data that mismatches.

Summary

By now, you are familiar with all the nuts and bolts of Cassandra. We have discussed how the pressure to make data stores to web scale inspired a rather not-so-common database mechanism to come to the mainstream; how CAP theorem governs the behavior of such databases. We have seen that Cassandra shines out among its peers. Then, we dipped our toes into the big picture of Cassandra read and write mechanisms. This left us with lots of fancy terms. Further, we looked into the definition of these words, components that drive Cassandra and their influence on its behavior.

It is understandable that it may be a lot to take in for someone new to NoSQL systems. It is okay if you do not have complete clarity at this point. As you start working with Cassandra, tweaking it, experimenting with it, and going through the Cassandra mailing list discussions or talks, you will start to come across stuff that you have read in this chapter and it will start to make sense, and perhaps you may want to come back and refer to this chapter to improve clarity.

It is not required to understand this chapter fully to be able to write queries, set up clusters, maintain clusters, or do anything else related to Cassandra. A general sense of this chapter will take you far enough to work extremely well with Cassandra-based projects.

How does this knowledge help us in building an application? Isn't it just about learning Thrift or CQL API and get going? You might be wondering why you need to know about compaction and storage mechanism when all you need to do is to deliver an application that has a superfast backend. It is not obvious at this point why we are learning this, but as we move ahead with developing an application, we will come to realize that knowledge about underlying storage mechanism helps. In later chapters, when we will learn about deploying a cluster, performance tuning, maintenance, and integrating with other tools such as Apache Hadoop, you may find this chapter useful. At this point, we are ready to learn some of the common use cases, and how they utilize various features of Cassandra. The next chapter is about knowing how to use Cassandra.

3
Design Patterns

This chapter will introduce you to some of the most commonly used patterns in application development. A lot of these models originated from the way Cassandra internally stores the data and the fact that there is no relational integrity. The chapter has two parts: one discusses data models and the patterns that emerge from the data models, and the other part exploits Cassandra's non-relational ability to store large amounts of data per row.

Although many patterns are discussed in this chapter, it certainly doesn't cover all the cases. Coming up with an innovative modeling approach from a very specific and obscure problem you encounter depends on your imagination. But no matter what the problem is, the most efficient approach is to attack the problem by keeping the following things in mind:

- **Denormalize, denormalize, and denormalize**: Forget about old-school 3NF (read more about Normal Forms at `https://en.wikipedia.org/wiki/Database_normalization#Normal_forms`). In Cassandra, the fewer the network trips, the better the performance. Denormalize wherever you can for quicker retrieval and let application logic handle the responsibility of reliably updating all the redundancies.

- **Rows are gigantic and sorted**: The giga-sized rows (a row can accommodate two billion columns) can be used to store sortable and sliceable columns. Need to sort comments by timestamp? Need to sort bids by quoted price? Put in a column with the appropriate comparator (you can always write your own comparator).

- **One row, one machine**: Each row stays on one machine. Rows are not sharded across nodes. So beware of this. A high-demand row may create a hotspot.

- **From query to model**: Unlike RDBMS, where you model most of the tables with entities in the application and then run analytical queries to get data out of it, Cassandra has no such provision. So you may need to denormalize your model in such a way that all your queries stay limited to a bunch of simple commands such as `get`, `slice`, `count`, `multi_get`, and some simple indexed searches.

Before you go ahead with this chapter, please note that the data model uses Pycassa, a Python client for Cassandra, and the Cassandra command-line interface shell called `cassandra-cli` to demonstrate various programming aspects of Cassandra. Also, it might be a good idea to learn about the Thrift interface for Cassandra. It will help you understand when we talk about GET, MULTIGET_SLICE, SLICE, and other operations. At the time of writing of this book, CQL 3 was in its beta, so the examples are done using the Thrift interface. Thrift is supported across all the versions of Cassandra and will continue to be supported in future versions. CQL 3 is poised to be the preferred interfacing language from Cassandra 1.2 onward. Here are a couple of resources from the book that can help you:

- Refer to the online documentation and Apache Cassandra Wiki for a quick tutorial on Thrift API, Pycassa, and `cassandra-cli`.
- Refer to *Chapter 9, Introduction to CQL 3 and Cassandra 1.2* for an introduction to CQL 3 and how to think in terms of CQL 3 when you are coming from a Thrift world.
- It is very important to have full code in hand while working through this book. The examples in this chapter are just a relevant snippet from the full code that fits into the context. The full code for all examples and other relevant material can be downloaded from the author's GitHub account (`https://github.com/naishe/mastering_cassandra`) or the download page for this book on the publisher's website (`http://www.packtpub.com/support`).

The Cassandra data model

To a person coming across from the relational database world to the NoSQL world, it would seem like a pretty featureless system. First, there is no relational integrity, then there is a whole different approach for defining a query before modeling your tables, which is quite the opposite of what we learned, that is, to model entities and then think of queries.

It may be confusing if you keep thinking in terms of a relational setup and translating it to an equivalent Cassandra representation. So forget about tables, foreign keys, joins, cascade delete, update on insert, and the like, when we speak in the context of Cassandra. If it helps, think of a problem you are dealing with. For example, you need to show number of votes by day and by city. We cannot run a sort or a group by; instead, we will have a column family, which will have counter as the data type and date as column names (at this point, if you start to think like an RDBMS person, you'll think how would you create a table whose columns are dynamic! Well, you can't, but you have smart functions there: `sort` and `group`. In Cassandra, your application manages these). Every time a vote is cast for city A, we look up the column family, go to the row by its city name, then find and update the column by date. If you did not understand this quick tour, it's fine. We'll see them again later in this chapter.

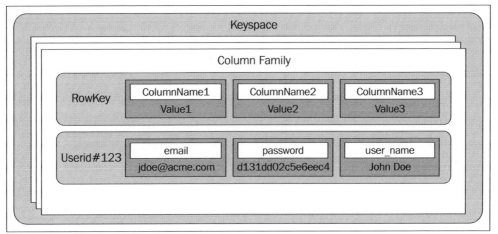

Figure 3.1: The Cassandra data model

 CQL 3 may be a big relief to people from the relational background. It lets you express queries and schema in a way much closer to SQL. The internal representation of the data may be different.

In the heart of Cassandra lie three structures: column family, column, and super column. There is a container entity for these three entities called keyspace. In our discussion, we'll use the ground-up approach where we will start with the smallest unit, the column, and go up to the top-level container, `Keyspace.Column`.

The column is the atomic unit of the Cassandra data model. It is the smallest component that can be operated on. Columns are contained within a column family. A column is essentially a key-value pair. The word column is confusing; it creates a mental image of a tabular structure where a column is a unit vertical block that stores the value referred by the heading of the column. This is not entirely true with Cassandra. Cassandra's columns are best represented by a tuple with the first element as a name/key and the second as a value. The key of a column is commonly referred to as a column name or a column key.

A column can be represented as a **map** of key/column name, value, and timestamp. A timestamp is used to resolve conflicts during read repair or to reconcile two writes that happen to the same column at the same time; the one written later wins. A timestamp is a client-supplied data, and since it is critical to write a resolution, it is a good idea to have all your client application servers clock-synchronized (refer to *NTP*, http:// en.wikipedia.org/wiki/Clock_synchronization#Network_Time_Protocol).

```
# A column, much like a relational system
{
  name: "username",
  value: "Leo Scott",
  timestamp: 1366048948904
}


# A column with its name as timestamp, value as page-viewed
{
  name: 1366049577,
  value: "http://foo.com/bar/view?itemId=123&ref=email",
  timestamp: 1366049578003
}
```

This is an example of two columns; the first looks more like a traditional column, and one would expect each row of the `users` column family to have one `userName` column. The latter is more like a dynamic column. Its name is the timestamp when a user accesses a web page and the value is the URL of the page.

Further in this book, we'll ignore the `timestamp` field whenever we refer to a column because it is generally not needed for application use and is used by Cassandra internally. A column can be viewed as shown in the following figure:

Figure 3.2: Representing a column

The counter column

A counter column is a special-purpose column to keep count. A client application can increment or decrement it by an integer value. Counter columns cannot be mixed with regular or any other column types (as of Cassandra v1.2). When we have to use a counter, we either plug it into an existing counter column family or create a separate column family with the validator as `CounterColumnFamily`.

Counters require tight consistency, and this makes it a little complex for Cassandra. Under the hood, Cassandra tracks distributed counters and uses system-generated timestamps. So clock synchronization is crucial.

The counter column family behaves a little differently than the regular ones. Cassandra makes a read *once* in the background when a write for a counter column occurs. So it reads the counter value before updating, which ensures that all the replicas are consistent. We can leverage this property while writing since the data is *always* consistent. While writing to a counter column, we can use a consistency level, ONE. We know from *Chapter 2, Cassandra Architecture*, that the lower the consistency level, the faster the read/write operation. The counter writes can be very fast without risking a false read.

 Clock synchronization can easily be achieved with NTP (http://www.ntp.org) **daemon (ntpd)**. In general, it's a good idea to keep your servers in sync.

Here is an example of a column family with counter columns in it and the way to update it:

```
[default@mastering_cassandra] create column family votes_by_candidate
with
default_validation_class = CounterColumnType and
key_validation_class = UTF8Type and
comparator = UTF8Type;

a84caeec-b3dd-3484-9011-5c292e04105d

[default@mastering_cassandra] incrvotes_by_candidate['candidate1']
['voter1'] by 5;

Value incremented.

[-- snip multiple increment commands --]
```

```
[default@mastering_cassandra] list votes_by_candidate;

Using default limit of 100
Using default column limit of 100
-------------------
RowKey: candidate2
=> (counter=voter1, value=3)
-------------------
RowKey: candidate1
=> (counter=voter1, value=5)
=> (counter=voter2, value=-4)
2 Rows Returned.
```

There is an optional attribute that can be used with counter columns called
`replicate_on_write`. When set to `true`, this attribute tells Cassandra to write to all
the replicas irrespective of the consistency level set by the client. It should always be
set to `true` for the counter columns. The default value is `true` for counter columns
(except for the Versions 0.8.1 and 0.8.2).

Please note that counter updates are *not idempotent*. In the event of
a write failure, the client will have no idea if the write operation
succeeded. A retry to update the counter columns may cause the
columns to be updated twice—leading to the column value to be
incremented or decremented by twice the value intended.

The expiring column

A column is referred to as an **expiring column** if an optional **time-to-live** (TTL)
attribute is added to it. The expiring column will be deleted after the TTL is reached
from the time of insertion. This means that the client cannot see it in the result.

On insertion of a TTL-containing column, the coordinator node sets a deletion
timestamp by adding the current local time to the TTL provided. The column expires
when the local time of a querying node goes past the set expiration timestamp. The
deleted node is marked for deletion with a tombstone and is removed during a
compaction after the expiration timestamp or during repair. Expiring columns take
eight bytes of extra space to record the TTL. Here is an example:

```
# Create column family normally

[default@mastering_cassandra] create column family user_session
with
default_validation_class = UTF8Type and
```

```
key_validation_class = UTF8Type and
comparator = UTF8Type;


0055e984-d3e9-3b74-9a48-89b63a6e371d


# Add a regular column
[default@mastering_cassandra] set user_session['user1']['keep_
loggedin'] = 'false';


# Add a column with 60s TTL
[default@mastering_cassandra] set
user_session['user1']['session_data'] = '{sessionKey: "ee207430-a6b2-
11e2-9e96-0800200c9a66", via: "mobileApp"}'
with ttl = 60;


# Retrieve the column family data immediately
[default@mastering_cassandra] list user_session;


RowKey: user1
=> (column=keep_loggedin, value=false, …)
=> (column=session_data, value={sessionKey: "ee207430-a6b2-11e2-9e96-
0800200c9a66", via: "mobileApp"}, …, ttl=60)


# Wait for more than 60 seconds, retrieve again
[default@mastering_cassandra] list user_session;


RowKey: user1
=> (column=keep_loggedin, value=false, …)
```

A few things to be noted about expiring columns:

- The TTL is in seconds, so the smallest TTL can be one second
- You can change the TTL by reinserting the column (that is, read the column, update the TTL, and insert the column)
- Although the client does not see the expired column, the space is kept occupied until the compaction is triggered, but note that tombstones take a rather small space

Expiring columns can have some good utility; they remove the need of constantly watching cron-like tasks that delete the data that has expired or not required any more. For example, an expiring shopping coupon or a user session can be stored with a TTL.

The super column

A **super column** is a column containing more columns. It contains an *ordered* map of columns and subcolumns. It is often used for denormalization by putting multiple rows of a column family in one single row, which can be used as a materialized view on data retrieval. Refer to the following diagram:

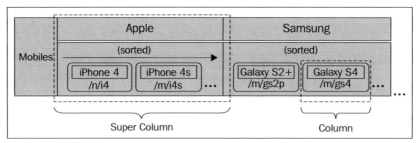

Figure 3.2: A row of super columns

The diagram shows a row of super columns that contains one brand per super column, and each super column has subcolumns that contain models of the brands corresponding to that super column. Each subcolumn, in turn, holds values of the relative URL. So where can it be used? One good place is online shops such as Amazon. They show drop downs of categories such as books, mobiles, and many more. You can hover your mouse over the mobiles' menu, and a submenu shows up with brand names such as Apple, Samsung, and many more. You scroll down to the submenu to find links to the detail pages for each model of the mobile. To show this, all you needed to do is click on the mobile row, which contains the super columns that contain the models with URLs.

Although the idea of super columns seems pretty lucrative, it has some serious drawbacks:

- To read a single subcolumn value, you will need to deserialize all the subcolumns of a super column

- A secondary index cannot be created on the subcolumns

 CQL 3 does not support super columns. **DataStax** (http://www.datastax.com) suggests not using a super column. Use composite keys instead of super columns. It performs better than a super column and covers most of the use cases for super columns.

The column family

A column family is a collection of rows where each row is a key-value pair. The key to a row is called a **row key** and the value is a *sorted* collection of columns. Essentially, a column family is a map with its keys as row keys and values as an ordered collection of columns. To define a column family, you need to provide a comparator that determines the sorting order of columns within a row.

Internally, each column family is stored in a file of its own, and there is no relational integrity between two column families. So one should keep all related information that the application might require in the column family.

In a column family, the row key is unique and serves as the primary key. It is used to identify and get/set records to a particular row of a column family.

Although a column family looks like a table from the relational database world, it is not. When you use CQL, it is treated as a table, but having an idea about the underlying structure helps in designing—how the columns are sorted, sliced, and persisted, and the fact that it's a schema-free map of maps.

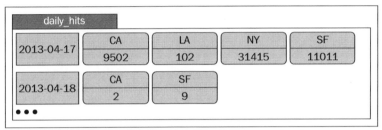

Figure 3.3: A dynamic column family showing daily hits on a website; each column represents a city, and the column value is the number of hits from that city

There are **dynamic** and **static** column families also known as **wide** and **narrow** column families respectively, but I will follow the dynamic and static terminologies here. These are two design patterns in Cassandra that take advantage of its flexibility to fit into application requirements.

A dynamic column family utilizes the column family's ability to store an arbitrary number of columns (key-value pairs). A typical use of a dynamic column family is for statistics aggregation, for example, to store the number of hits to a certain web page from various cities on a day-by-day basis. It will be cumbersome to make a static column family with all the cities of the world as the column names. (Plus, the developer can get some coffee in the time it would take to type in all the cities.) A time series data may be another example. *Figure 3.3* displays a dynamic column family.

The following is the syntax:

```
[default@mastering_cassandra] create column family daily_hits
with
default_validation_class = CounterColumnType
and key_validation_class = LongType
and comparator = UTF8Type;
```

Let's take a moment to see what's going on here. We ask Cassandra to create a column family named `daily_hits` whose column values will be validated for `CounterColumnType` because that's what `default_validation_class` is. The row keys are going to be of the type dictated by `key_validation_class`, which is `LongType`, because we are storing the Unix epoch (the time since January 01, 1970) in days. And finally, the column names will be sorted by `comparator`, which is the `UTF8Type` text. We'll look into validators and comparators shortly.

A static column family is vaguely close to a table in relational database systems. A static column family has some predefined column names and their validators. But this does not prevent you from adding random columns on the fly. A column family that represents a user is a typical example of a static column family. The major benefit of a static family is validation. You define `validation_class` on a per column basis, and so you can control what column should have what data type. The client will reject an incompatible data type. Consider the following code:

```
# Typical definition of static column family
[default@mastering_cassandra] create column family users
with
comparator = UTF8Type and
key_validation_class = UTF8Type and
column_metadata = [
 {column_name: username, validation_class: UTF8Type},
 {column_name: email, validation_class: UTF8Type},
 {column_name: last_login, validation_class: DateType},
 {column_name: is_admin, validation_class: BooleanType}
];


# Insert something valid
[default@mastering_cassandra] set users['username']['user1'] = 'Leo
Scott';


# something invalid
[default@mastering_cassandra] set users['user1']['is_admin'] = 'Yes';
java.lang.RuntimeException: org.apache.cassandra.db.marshal.
MarshalException: unable to make boolean from 'Yes'
```

```
# extend to undefined fields
[default@mastering_cassandra] set users['user1']['state'] =
utf8('VA');
```

```
# Observe
[default@mastering_cassandra] get users['user1'];
=> (column=state, value=VA, timestamp=...)
=> (column=username, value=Leo Scott, timestamp=...)
```

Keyspaces

Keyspaces are the outermost shells of Cassandra containers. It contains column families and super column families. It can be roughly imagined as a database of a relational database system. Its purpose is to group column families. In general, one application uses one keyspace, much like RDBMS.

Keyspaces hold properties such as replication factors and replica placement strategies, which are globally applied to each column family in the keyspace. Keyspaces are global management points for an application. Here is an example:

```
[default@unknown] create keyspace mastering_cassandra
... with placement_strategy = SimpleStrategy
... and strategy_options = {replication_factor: 1};
```

We will discuss more on storage configurations in *Chapter 4*, *Deploying a Cluster*.

Data types – comparators and validators

Comparators and validators are the mechanisms used to define and validate data types of components (row key, column names, and column values) in a column family:

- **Validators**: Validators are the means to fix data types for row keys and column values. In a column family, the `key_validation_class` command specifies the data type for row keys, `default_validation_class` specifies the data type of column values, and the `column_metadata` property is used to specify the data type for individual column names.

- **Comparators**: Comparators specify the data type of a column name. In a row, columns are sorted; this property determines the order of the columns in a row. The comparator is specified by a `comparator` keyword while creating the column family.

In a dynamic column family, where any number of columns may be present, it becomes crucial to decide how the columns will be sorted. An example of this would be a column family that stores the daily stock values minute-by-minute in the row. A natural comparator for this case will be `DateType`. Since the columns will be sorted by a timestamp, a slice query can pull all the variation to a stock value from 11 A.M. to 1 P.M.

For static column families, columns' sorting does not matter that much and the column name is generally a character string.

If comparators and validators are not set, hex byte array (`BytesType`) is assumed. Although comparators and validators seem the same from their description, one crucial difference between them is that validators can be added or modified in a column definition at any time but comparators can't. So a little thinking on how the columns need to be sorted before implementing the solution may be worth the effort.

As of Cassandra 1.2, the following basic data types are supported (refer to `http://www.datastax.com/docs/1.2/cql_cli/using_cli#about-data-types-comparators-and-validators`):

Type	CQL type	Description
AsciiType	ascii	US-ASCII character string
BooleanType	boolean	True or false
BytesType	blob	Arbitrary hexadecimal bytes (no validation)
CounterColumnType	counter	Distributed counter value (8-byte long)
DateType	timestamp	Date plus time, encoded as 8 bytes since epoch
DecimalType	decimal	Variable-precision decimal
DoubleType	double	8-byte floating point
FloatType	float	4-byte floating point
InetAddressType	inet	IP address string in xxx.xxx.xxx.xxx form
Int32Type	int	4-byte integer
IntegerType	varint	Arbitrary-precision integer
LongType	bigint	8-byte long
TimeUUIDType	timeuuid	Type 1 UUID only (CQL3)
UTF8Type	text, varchar	UTF-8 encoded string
UUIDType	uuid	Type 1 or type 4 UUID

Cassandra 1.2 also supports collection types, such as `set`, `list`, and `map`. This means one can add and retrieve collections without having ad hoc methods such as having multiple columns for multiple shipping addresses with column names patterned as `shipping_addr1`, `shipping_addr2...`, or just bundling the whole set of shipping addresses as one long `UTF8Type` deserialized JSON.

Writing a custom comparator

With the number of comparators provided by Cassandra, chances are that you'll never need to write one of your own. But if there *must* be some column ordering that cannot be achieved or worked around using the given comparators, you can always write your own. For example, sorting with `UTF8Type` is case sensitive; capital letters come before small letters as seen in the following code:

```
[default@mastering_cassandra] list daily_hits;
RowKey: 15812
=> (counter=CA, value=9502)
=> (counter=MA, value=123)
=> (counter=NY, value=31415)
=> (counter=la, value=6023)
=> (counter=ma, value=43)
```

One may want to have a case-insensitive sorting. To write a custom comparator, you need to extend `org.apache.cassandra.db.marshal.AbstractType<T>` and implement the abstract methods. Once you are done with your comparator and supporting classes, package them into a JAR file and copy this file to Cassandra's `lib` directory on all the servers you want this comparator to be on. It may be a good idea to look into the `org.apache.cassandra.db.marshal` package and observe how the comparators are implemented. Here is an example. The following snippet shows a custom comparator that orders the columns by the length of the column name, which behaves mostly like `UTF8Type` except for the ordering:

```
public class LengthComparator extends AbstractType<String> {

  public static final LengthComparator instance = new
LengthComparator();

  public int compare(ByteBuffer o1, ByteBuffer o2) {
    return (getString(o1).length() - getString(o2).length());
  }

  // Rest of the methods utilize UTF8Type for operations
}
```

You can view the complete code online. One thing to note is if you don't declare an `instance` singleton, Cassandra will throw an exception at the startup. Compile this class and put the JAR or `.class` file in the `$CASSANDRA_HOME/lib` folder. You can see the JAR file listed in the Cassandra startup log in the `classpath` listing. Here is an example of a column family creation, insertion, and retrieval using this comparator. You will see that the columns are ordered in the increasing length of their column names:

```
# Create Column Family with Custom Comparator
[default@MyKeyspace] CREATE COLUMN FAMILY custom_comparator
WITH
KEY_VALIDATION_CLASS = LongType AND
COMPARATOR = 'in.naishe.mc.comparator.LengthComparator' AND
DEFAULT_VALIDATION_CLASS = UTF8Type;

# Insert some data
[default@MyKeyspace] SET custom_comparator[1]['hello'] = 'world';
[default@MyKeyspace] SET custom_comparator[1]['hell'] = 'whirl';
[default@MyKeyspace] SET custom_comparator[1]['he'] = 'she';
[default@MyKeyspace] SET custom_comparator[1]['mimosa pudica'] = 'some
plant';
[default@MyKeyspace] SET custom_comparator[1]['a'] = 'smallest col
name';

# Get Data, columns are ordered by column name length
[default@MyKeyspace] get custom_comparator[1];
=> (column=a, value=smallest col name, timestamp=1375673015868000)
=> (column=he, value=she, timestamp=1375672967041000)
=> (column=hell, value=whirl, timestamp=1375672959028000)
=> (column=hello, value=world, timestamp=1375672928673000)
=> (column=mimosa pudica, value=some plant,
timestamp=1375672990036000) Indexes
```

Indexing a database is a means to improve the retrieval speed of data. Before Cassandra 0.7, there was only one type of index—the default one—which is the index on row keys.

If you are coming from the RDBMS world, you may be a bit disappointed with what Cassandra has to offer in terms of indexing. Cassandra indexing is a little inferior. It is better to think of indexes as hash keys. In this topic, we'll discuss a little on the primary index or row key index, then we'll move to use cases where we'll see a couple of handy techniques to create an index on column names (secondary index) like effect. Next is the secondary index; we'll discuss a little on it, its pros and cons, and the help that it provides in keeping the boilerplate code down.

The primary index

A primary key or row key is the unique identifier of a row, in much the same way as the primary key of a table from a relational database system. It provides quick and random access to the rows. Since the rows are sharded among the servers of the ring, each server just has a subset of rows, and hence, primary keys are distributed too. Cassandra uses the **partitioner** (cluster-level setting) and **replica placement strategy** (keyspace-level setting) to locate the respective node in the ring to access a particular row. On a node, an index file and sample index is maintained locally that can be looked up via binary search followed by a short sequential read (see *Chapter 1, Quick Start*).

The problem with primary keys is that their location is governed by partitioners. Partitioners use a hash function to convert a row key into a unique number (called **token**) and then write/read that key to/from the node that owns this token. This means that if you use a partitioner that does not use a hash that follows the key's natural ordering, chances are that you can't sequentially read the keys just by accessing the next token on the node. The following snippet shows an example of this. The row keys `1234` and `1235` should naturally fall next to each other if they are not altered (or if an order-preserving partitioner is used). However, if we take a consistent MD5 hash of these values, we can see that the two values are far away from each other. There is a good chance that they might not even live on the same machine.

```
ROW KEY | MD5 HASH VALUE
--------+--------------------------------
1234    | 81dc9bdb52d04dc20036dbd8313ed055
1235    | 9996535e07258a7bbfd8b132435c5962
```

Let's take an example of two partitioners: `ByteOrderPartitioner` that preserves lexical ordering by bytes, and `RandomPartitioner` that uses MD5 hash to generate a row key. Let's assume that we have a `users_visits` column family with a row key, `<city>_<userId>`. `ByteOrderPartioner` will let you iterate through rows to get more users from the same city in much the same way as a `SortedMap` interface. (Refer to `http://docs.oracle.com/javase/6/docs/api/java/util/SortedMap.html`). However, in `RandomPartioner`, the key being the MD5 hash value of `<city>_<userId>`, the two consecutive `userIds` from the same city may lie on two different nodes. So, we cannot just iterate and expect grouping to work, like accessing entries of `HashMap`.

It may be useful to keep in mind that queries, such as the range slice query, pull rows from the start row key to the end row key provided by the user. If the user is not using an order-preserving partitioner, the rows returned will not be ordered by the key; rather, they'll be orders by the partitioner that is set.

We will see partitioners in more detail in *Chapter 4, Deploying a Cluster*, section *Partioners*. But using the obviously better-looking partitioner, ByteOrderPartitioner, is assumed to be a bad practice. There are a couple of reasons for this, the major reason being an uneven row key distribution across nodes. This can potentially cause a hotspot in the ring.

The wide-row index

For any real application, one necessarily needs information grouped by criteria and to be able to be searched by search criteria. Secondary indexes came into existence in Version 0.7, so the natural question is how were these types of requirements fulfilled before it? The answer is a **wide-row index,** aka **manual index,** aka **alternate index.** Basically, we create a column family that holds the row keys of other column families as its columns, and the row key of this column family is the value we wanted to group by. We can use this in the city-user example that we discussed in the previous section. Instead of relying on the primary key, we can create a column family that has city as the row key and user ID as the column name (and probably, username as the column value to cache it in such a manner that we do not pull data from the parent column family unless we need more details other than the username)—all done. Whenever you need to get users by their city names, you can select the row of that city.

Before we go ahead and discuss some of the patterns using a wide-row index, the one thing that should be kept in mind is that a lot of these cases can be handled by secondary indexes, and it would be worth counting the pros and cons of using a wide-row pattern versus a secondary index.

Simple groups

The idea is simple: you create a column family with its row keys as the name of the group (the group by predicate in SQL) and the column names as the row keys of the column family that you wanted to group.

Let's take an example of a social networking application that lets users create groups and other people can join it. You have a users column family and groups column family. You make another column family that holds a user per group and call it group_users. This will have the group's row key as the row key, and the user's row key as the column name. Does it ring a bell? It's the same thing as a join table or link table in a many-to-many relationship in the RDBMS world.

Another use case is grouping by field. Let's say your application provides hotel search facilities where you can select a city and see the hotels. Or perhaps your video-streaming website offers a tagging mechanism as a part of video metadata and you wanted users to click on the tags and see the videos with the same tags—it is the same logic. We create a column family named `tag_videos` where each row key is a tag and the columns are row keys of the `videos` columns' family. On clicking a tag, we just load the whole row from `tag_videos` for that tag and show it to the user (with pagination, perhaps):

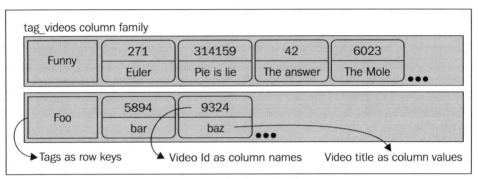

Figure 3.4: An example of grouping by tag name

One improvement can be made with this mechanism to add some meaningful values to the columns. For example, it may be worth storing the video title as the column value. This will save an extra query to the `videos` table. Just pull the columns, and show the names. Pull more data when and if required.

Sorting for free, free as in speech

Unlike row keys, columns are sorted by the comparator that you provide. If you provide a `UTF8Type` comparator, the columns will be sorted in a string order. In the `video` tag example, you may want videos to be sorted by the username of the user who uploaded the video. You may just set up the column key as `<userName>:<videoId>` (note that the separator can be confusing if either of the values that make a column name have a separator as a part of it) and now, you get videos for a given tag sorted by the username. You can range slice the column or further filter the videos for a given tag by a particular user. Here is a sample of the code:

```
#Get hold of CFs
vidCF = ColumnFamily(con, 'videos')
tagCF = ColumnFamily(con, 'tag_videos')
```

```
#insert in videos as well as tag index CF
vidCF.insert(
  rowKey, #<title>:<uploader>
  {
  'title':title,
  'user_name':uploader,
  'runtime_in_sec':runtime,
  'tags_csv': tags  #this is CSV string of tags
  })


for tag in tags.split(','):
  tagCF.insert(
    tag.strip().lower(), #index CF's row-key = tag
    {
     #key=<uploader>_<rowKeyOfVideosCF>, value=<title>
     uploader+ "_" + rowKey: title
    }
  );

#retrieve video details grouped by tag
tag = 'action'
movies = tagCF.get(tag.strip().lower())
for key, val in movies.iteritems():
  vidId = key.split('_')[1]
  movieDetail = vidCF.get(vidId)
  print '''
  {{
    user: {0},
    movie: {1},
    tags: {2}
  }}'''.format(movieDetail['user_name'], movieDetail['title'],
movieDetail['tags_csv'])


#Result for tag='action' sorted by user name
    {
      user: Kara,
      movie: Olympus Has Fallen,
      tags: action, thriller
    }
    {
      user: Kara,
      movie: The Croods,
```

```
     tags: animation, action, mystery
   }
   {
     user: Leo Scott,
     movie: Oblivion,
     tags: action, mystery, sci-fi
   }
   {
     user: Sally,
     movie: G.I. Joe: Retaliation,
     tags: action, adventure
   }
```

Push all in one: In Cassandra, there is often more than one way to skin a cat. Our previous approach uses multiple rows, one for each tag name. But you can very well push all the tags in one single row. You may just have one single row, perhaps named `tag_index`, with column names as `<tag>_<videoId>` and comparator as `UTF8Type`. Since the columns are sorted, you can slice the row with column names starting with the desired tag.

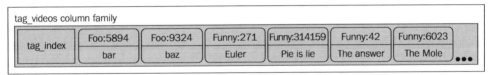

Figure 3.5: Indexing all videos by tag in one row

There are a couple of drawbacks with this approach: one, a row is entirely stored on one machine (and the replicas too). If it's a frequently accessed index, these machines may get excessively loaded. Two, the number of columns per row is limited to approximately two billion, and if you happen to be having more videos, this may be an issue.

An inverse index with a super column family

In the previous section, we saw a common pattern where we put column names as a concatenated string of two properties of another object—username and video ID. In an even simpler version, we just dumped all the movies into one row with the column name as a tag appended with a separator and video ID. One thing that was etched in the previous implementation is the fact that if our chosen *separator* is a part of either of the strings that we concatenate, it will be a nightmare splitting them to get an attribute value. What if there are more than two attributes to create a column name? Conjure a super column, a column of columns.

The idea is simple: a super column is a level two nesting. Let's work out some tagging problems using a super column. It may not seem super advantageous over what we had with the string concatenation mechanism, but we can see cleaner decoupling here.

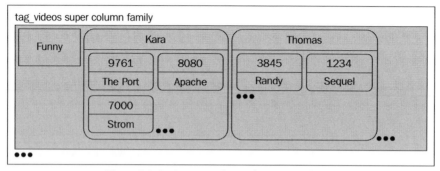

Figure 3.6: An inverse index with a super column

The code is as follows:

```
# Tag insertion in super-column

for tag in tags.split(','):
  tagCF.insert(
    tag.strip().lower(), #row-key = tag name
    {
      uploader: {        #level 1 nesting = uploader name
        vidId: title     #level 2 nesting: key=videoId, value=title
          }
        }
  )
```

```
# Fetch videos by tag, grouped by users
tagCF = ColumnFamily(connection, 'tag_videos_sup')
movies = tagCF.get(tag.strip().lower())

for key, val in movies.iteritems():                #level 1 iteration
  username = key
  # Some string formatting  print '''
  {{
    {0}:'''.format(username)
  for k, v in val.iteritems():                     #level 2 iteration
    print '''\t{{{0}=> {1}}}'''.format(k, v)
```

```
  print '''
  }'''
```

 # Result
```
tag: action
    {
      Kara:
        {Olympus Has Fallen:Kara=> Olympus Has Fallen}
        {The Croods:Kara=> The Croods}
    }

    {
      Leo Scott:
        {Oblivion:Leo Scott=> Oblivion}
    }

    {
      Sally:
        {G.I. Joe: Retaliation:Sally=> G.I. Joe: Retaliation}
        {Scary MoVie:Sally=> Scary MoVie}
    }
```

This is the exact same code as we had in the previous section with two exceptions:

- It uses a super column to store and retrieve the tag index
- We did not have to use string operations to fetch the video ID

Let's see what we gain by using super columns. One thing that's clear is that we avoided the dangers of manually splitting strings. We have a cleaner structure now. This is a typical use case for super columns.

All good again! Let's think of the situation where we dumped all the tags in a row. Can we convert that into a super-column-based index to something like the following snippet?

```
tag_index:
[
  tag1:[
    {user1:[{rowKey1: videoId1},{rowKey2: videoId2},...]},
    {user2:[{rowKey3: videoId3},{rowKey4: videoId4},...]},
    ...
  ],
  tag2:[
```

```
        {user4:[{rowKey9: videoId9},{rowKey7: videoId7},...]},
        {user2:[{rowKey3: videoId3},{rowKey8: videoId8},...]},
        ...
    ],
    ...
]
```

Basically, we are asking for one more level of nesting, that is, subcolumns, in order to be able to have a column family or subcolumns of a subcolumn. Unfortunately, Cassandra just provides two levels of nesting. This takes us back to having some sort of ad hoc mechanism at a subcolumn level, something like having subcolumn names as `<username>:<videoId>`.

An inverse index with composite keys

The super-column-based approach did give some relief, but it is not the best solution. Plus, it has its own limitation such as one-level nesting. Subcolumns are not sorted; they are just a bunch of unordered key-value pairs. Super columns, although not deprecated, are not really preferred by the Cassandra community. The general consensus is to use composite columns and avoid super columns. It is a better, cleaner, and elegant solution and it scales much better.

Composite column names: Composite column names are made of multiple *components*. They can be viewed as *ordered* tuples of multiple types. For example, this is a composite column name: (`username, city, age, SSN, loginTimestamp`). The components are `UTF8Type, UTF8Type, IntType, UTF8Type,` and `DateType`, in that order.

 There is a very interesting long-hauled discussion on the Cassandra bug tracker. You can observe how `CompositeType` evolved at https://issues.apache.org/jira/browse/CASSANDRA-2231.

Composite types behave much in the same way as normal comparators do: columns are sorted by them, names are validated with definitions, and slice queries can be executed. Plus, you don't need to manage the ad hoc arrangement for keys with multiple components such as in string concatenation. Composite keys are deserialized as a tuple and easily used on the client side.

The sorting of composite comparators works in the same way as the SQL query `order by field1, field2, ...` does. Columns get sorted by the first component of the key and then within each first component, it is ordered by the second component, and so on. Validation is done for each component individually. And `slice` can be applied to each component in the order in which they appear in the column family definition.

Out of the box, Cassandra provides two composite types: static `CompositeType`, which can have a fixed number of components that are ordered, and `DynamicCompositeType`, which can have any number of components of all the types defined at the column family creation in any order. So let's use the static `CompositeType` column names to get rid of super columns and string concatenation as shown in the following code snippet:

```
# Tag insertion in super-column
for tag in tags.split(','):
  tagCF.insert(
      tag.strip().lower(), #row-key = tag name
      {
        uploader: {          #level 1 nesting = uploader name
          rowKey: title      #level 2 nesting:
                             # key=videoId, value=title
        }
      }
  )

# Fetch videos by tag, grouped by users
tagCF = ColumnFamily(con, 'tag_videos_sup')
movies = tagCF.get(tag.strip().lower())
for key, val in movies.iteritems(): #level 1 iteration
  username = key
  print '''
  {{
    {0}:'''.format(username)
  for k, v in val.iteritems(): #level 2 iteration
    print '''\t{{{0}=> {1}}}'''.format(k, v)

  print '''
  }'''

# Result
tag: action
    {
      Kara:
        {Olympus Has Fallen:Kara=> Olympus Has Fallen}
        {The Croods:Kara=> The Croods}
    }
    {
      Leo Scott:
        {Oblivion:Leo Scott=> Oblivion}
    }
    {
      Sally:
        {G.I. Joe: Retaliation:Sally=> G.I. Joe: Retaliation}
        {Scary MoVie:Sally=> Scary MoVie}
    }
```

Let's stop for a moment and think about the applicability of composite columns. You can have tags on a video page. On clicking a tag, you can show a whole list of videos just by pulling a row from the `tag_videos` index column family. If you have a composed key, such as `<title>:<length>:<username>:<rowkey>`, you can get all the details shown in the list, plus you may have the thumbnail's URI as the column value to be displayed next to each list item. Time series data can be stored and sorted by timestamps that can later be pulled to view the history, and the timestamp can be pulled off the composite column name. These are just a couple of examples; composite type is a really powerful tool to come up with innovative solutions.

 Check for composite column support in the Cassandra driver API you are using. Pycassa, for example, does not support `DynamicCompositeType` as of Version 1.8.0. But it is likely to be available anytime now (refer to `https://github.com/pycassa/pycassa/pull/183`).

The secondary index

Working through previous examples, a relational database person would think that all this manual management of a custom index family is a little too much work. In RDBMS, one can just perform `...where user_name = 'Kara'`. If the data is large, one can index it to one `user_name` value and improve read/search by taxing the writes. If one wanted to just get the videos that are longer than a minute's runtime, it is going to be `...where user_name = 'Kara' and runtime_in_sec> 60`. Cassandra Version 0.6 and the earlier versions had no way of doing something like this without holding denormalized data in a separate column family, much like a materialized view. Similar to what we have been discussing, Version 0.7 or higher has a secondary index and it is well supported by CQL and client APIs.

The indexes that are created on columns are called **secondary indexes**. Secondary indexes—much the same way as a primary index—are similar to hashes and are not like a B-Tree, which is commonly used in relational databases and filesystems. This means you can run the equality operator on secondary indexes, but a range query or inequality cannot be done (actually, you can, but we'll see that case later on) on index columns.

Let's take our old video example and search for all the videos uploaded by a particular user without having to use an index column family. Later, we'll try to get all the videos by a user that are shorter than 7,500 seconds. Check the following code:

```
# Please note: The symbol \ is used for line continuation.
# It means that the next line is a continuation of current
# line and treated as single
```

```
# line. They are kept in separate line due to formatting issues.

# creating index on columns
sys = SystemManager('localhost:9160') #assume default installation
sys.create_index(keyspace, 'videos', 'user_name', UTF8_TYPE)
sys.create_index(keyspace, 'videos', 'runtime_in_sec', INT_TYPE)

# criteria: where user_name= <username>
username_criteria = \
create_index_expression('user_name', username)

# criteria: where runtime <= <max_length>
#LTE? Less than or equals
length_criteria = \
create_index_expression('runtime_in_sec', max_length, LTE)

# query: where user_name = 'Sally'
#just pull 3

user_only_clause = \
create_index_clause([username_criteria], count=3)

movies_by_user = \
videoCF.get_indexed_slices(user_only_clause)

print_movie(movies_by_user)

# query: where user_name = 'Sally' and runtime < 7500
#pull all
user_runtime_clause = \
create_index_clause([username_criteria, length_criteria])

movies_by_user_runtime = \
videoCF.get_indexed_slices(user_runtime_clause)

print '''-- movies for username: {} \
  and length <= {} --'''.format(username, max_length)

print_movie(movies_by_user_runtime)

# results
-- movies for username: Sally  --
{
```

```
    user: Sally,
    title: Scary MoVie,
    runtime: 7610
}
{
 user: Sally,
   title: Oz the Great and Powerful,
   runtime: 7800
}
{
 user: Sally,
   title: The Place Beyond the Pines,
   runtime: 6610
}
-- movies for username: Sally and length <= 7500 -
{
   user: Sally,
   title: The Place Beyond the Pines,
   runtime: 6610
}
{
 user: Sally,
   title: G.I. Joe: Retaliation,
 ' runtime: 7410
}
```

So now that we are excited by the secondary index, let's try to get all the movies that are smaller than 7,500 seconds across all the users using the following code:

```
# Fetch using in equality
# Intended to fail, At least on equality necessary!
runtime_clause = \
create_index_clause([length_criteria])

movies_by_runtime = \
videoCF.get_indexed_slices(runtime_clause)

print_movie(movies_by_runtime)

# Result
InvalidRequestException(why='No indexed columns present in index
clause with operator EQ')
```

Oops! But, we were kind of expecting that, as a secondary index is much like a hash map. What we were not expecting is how the inequality worked in the query that was running along with an equality (for example, `where user_name = 'Sally' and runtime <=7500`). Ideally, it should fail there as well. The secret behind this magic is in memory comparison. The result, returned from the equality operation, gets sliced in the memory on the coordinator node.

So, now that we have seen that the secondary index is good but not so great, let's demystify the secondary index further. The first thing to keep in mind is that though a secondary index seems similar to a traditional database index, it is inferior to it. In fact, the mechanism itself is different. Under the hood, indexes are stored in their own column family and cannot be accessed by users. They are synchronized with the node local data, which means the index column family will always be locally consistent.

This hidden column family has a row key as the index value and the columns are corresponding row keys of the column family whose data we are indexing. Did this ring a bell? Remember this, we have done the same thing in an earlier section, *Simple groups*, with `tags` as the row key and the `video` column family's row key as column names in our manual index. But there is a fine distinction between the two. Each node just indexes the data on the local machine—this means if the replication factor is `RF`, each node will have data on `RF` number of nodes; so, each node will have indexes for them. This way, each query needs to touch at least the `NUMBER_OF_NODES` / `RF` value in the secondary index. While in manually managed cases we are going to touch just one node—the one that has the row corresponding to the index value. Row and index updates are performed as a single atomic operation. But a manual index requires to be managed by application logic, while a secondary index is managed by Cassandra. Also, keeping a manual index restricts the upper bound of the number of row keys per index to be equal to the row limit, which is two billion. The automated index just needs to store the data on that node, so it's a bit more spacious than the manual index.

A word of caution

It is recommended to use secondary indexes with columns having low cardinality. Indexes on the columns such as `day_of_week`, `tag`, `city`, and `item_type` are expected to have a limited number of values, so they are good for secondary indexes. On the other hand, values that are almost unique to each row are a bad idea. So, `timestamp`, `video_title`, `geo_coordinate`, and `item_name` are bad choices.

Cardinality: A fancy word for the number of items in a set. A week has cardinality equal to 7 as it has seven distinct elements—one for each day.

Patterns and antipatterns

One of the main difficulties that a developer who is new to the NoSQL paradigm faces is the lack of an example solution to a similar question they are facing. There is plenty of documentation available on how to do things in a traditional RDBMS, and a developer gets some degree of comfort on implementing an already-examined pattern. This is not true with NoSQL data stores. There are many techniques that are being used, which are relatively inefficient. One such example is the use of super columns, which we saw in *The super column* section. With time, more and more best practices and dos and don'ts are emerging. Here we will see some of the commonly advised usage patterns for Cassandra.

Avoid storing an entity in a single column (wherever possible)

It is a bad idea to store the whole entity in a single column of a column family. Apart from losing the ability to directly access granular data from a row, extra overhead of parsing the column back to an object (deserialization and associated risk), and poor readability in CLI, there are more losses made using this mechanism.

Let's take an example of the users column family. Obviously, it is a no-brainer object. No one will dump the user object in one column. The decision is to be taken when you want to have an address field whether to dump the address in a single column as a JSON string or have individual columns for each attribute. The decision largely depends on the particular use of this sub-object in the application. It is, perhaps, fine to keep it as a JSON string if the application just needs this to be pasted as a shipping address. And edits are all or none. But it might be a problem if you wanted to group users by the zipcode value or allow users and administrators to edit parts of the address.

- **Extra effort in read, modify, and write**: If you have the whole object in one single column, you will have to read the column that bears the read access for the whole object. Then, parse it, change the particular bit of the object, and write back to column. This is inefficient. Cassandra provides atomic column operations (remember from *Chapter 1, Quick Start*, columns have a timestamp attribute that decides which of the two conflicting updates wins). So, two users are editing two separate fields of the same object/row at the same time. Both will be persisted without stepping on each other's toes. While in the case of a blob store, the last write will win if you do not read beforehand, which is again extra work. There are chances of failure if Cassandra has a weak consistency setting. Refer to *Chapter 1, Quick Start*, for more information.

- **No secondary index**: Secondary indexes are applied to columns. If everything is in one column, a secondary index cannot be applied to a fragment of it. In the previously mentioned `users` examples, if one wanted to group `users` by `zipcode`, it has to be a column.

  Obviously, this is bad; what's the solution? It depends on how creative one can be with data and application constraints to exploit Cassandra's features for performance gain.

- **Fixing the example**: Let's take the video-tagging example from the previous section; it has a column named `tags_csv` that stores the tags. This treats tags as a single column CSV value, which might be OK for an application that lets users click on the tags and see all the videos with that tag. (We have a separate column family for that.) What if we wanted administrators and users to delete or edit individual tags by clicking on the tiny cross next to each tag? If we just overwrite the complete CSV, one of the two changes will survive. And the read-update-write will be an overhead. The best option is to have one tag per column. There can be two situations:

  ◦ **Limited tags**: If the application constraints a maximum of five tags per video, having five columns defined with the column names `tag1`, `tag2`, ..., and `tag5` can be a valid solution.

  ◦ **Unlimited tags**: Cassandra provides flexibility in terms of the number of columns that a row in a column family can hold. A neat design can be achieved by storing tags as columns with column names defined as `tag:<tag_name>` and values as the tag names.

```
for tag in tags.split(','):
  row['tag:{}'.format(tag.strip().lower())] = tag.strip()
```

Atomic update

We need to mutate the exact columns that are needed to be mutated. Unlike RDBMS where you need to lock at least a row (refer to `http://dev.mysql.com/doc/refman/5.0/en/innodb-locks-set.html`), Cassandra provides a more granular locking—at the column level. Also, the general practice in dealing with RDBMS is to update the entire row. If you are using an ORM, you may persist all the columns of a row even if there is only one field that is actually changed. On the contrary, it is neither required nor recommended in Cassandra to save all the components of a row to update a field. The following diagram shows two cases: case 1, a row update, shows a situation where two users A and B have read a row at time t_0. User A changes a column, then updates the complete row (all the columns). User B updates some other column, and they too persists all the columns in the row. Remember that B still has the old value for the column that was updated by A.

It effectively reverts the change made by user A. These sort of issues can be avoided in Cassandra by updating *only* the columns that change. In that scenario, unless two users update the same column, things will be fine. Do not view a row as a unit. Think of a row as a collection of columns, and treat columns as independent, smallest storage units.

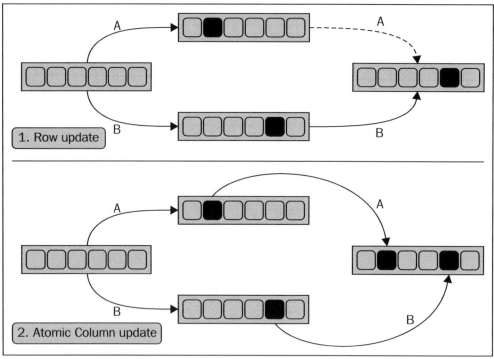

Figure 3.7: Images showing two scenarios where two clients: one, perform the read-update-write to the whole row, resulting in one change per row to survive, even when the changes are non-conflicting; and two, the atomic-column-wise update leads to more valid changes, and both writes survive

The idea is to let parallel writes happen at the column level, and let Cassandra's in-built conflict resolution deal with it. This also eliminates any race condition that might occur in the read-update-write situation where the complete row is read by two users, one updating column A and the other updating column B. If these writes happen at the same time, only one of these changes will survive.

Managing time series data

Time series data is a sequence of data points taken with the timestamp to represent an activity. Time series is everywhere; it is even more pronounced with the advent of real-time (web) applications. Twitter is probably the most common example of time series data—tweets. It's massive, geographically distributed, and real time. But it is not limited to that: data from sensors (flight simulations, GPS-tagged movement tracking), single-processing data, financial data, click tracking, log analysis data, user activity, (massive online) real-time messaging, results of real-time message processing—these are just some of the sources.

In many cases, the rate of data input is so high that traditional databases cannot keep up, due to relational constraints, management overheads, and locking. Also, the data usually is too large to be handled by a single machine, and queries start to crawl. This is where the NoSQL paradigm shines, and Cassandra with its lightning-fast writes and fault-tolerant nature is the best choice. Let's see some of the common patterns to store time series in Cassandra.

> It may be worth reading the paper *Solving Big Data Challenges for Enterprise Application Performance Management*, by *TilmannRabl et al*, 2012 (`http://vldb.org/pvldb/vol5/p1724_tilmannrabl_vldb2012.pdf`).

Wide-row time series

The simplest mechanism to store a time series is to store all the data related to a given activity in a single row with a column type as `TimeUUID` (or `timestamp`) and the data serialized as the column value. This is a powerful approach for multiple reasons. All the data for a given activity can be pulled by just one disk seek if the row is not already in memory. And since a row stays on one node (and on its replicas), it means Cassandra does not require to jump to different nodes to get the time series. The rows are sorted in advance, so one can get sorted—chronologically or reverse—and sliced data just by making one request.

To sort `timestamp`- or `TimeUUID`-based columns in reverse
chronological order or reversed order, you can either set
the comparator type to `reversed=True` or use `column_reversed=True` while fetching data. The former gives
a slight performance benefit in case most of your queries
require data to be sorted in latest-first order.

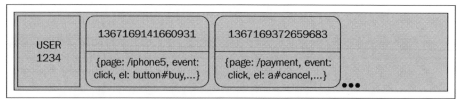

Figure 3.8: A time series with data serialized as JSON in a single column

The code looks pretty unimpressive, but it works (you can see a tiny simulation of
concurrent writes of time series events and you can validate the order):

```
# column family definition
event_log_comp = TimeUUIDType(reversed=True)
sys.create_column_family(keyspace, 'event_log', super=False,
comparator_type=event_log_comp)

# insertion
rowkey = event['user']
timestamp = datetime.datetime.utcnow()
colval = json.dumps(event)
eventsCF.insert(rowkey, {timestamp: colval})
```

We earlier discussed how bad it is to store data in a column as a blob. This requires
extra work and can result in a race condition with simultaneous edits where two
users update two parts of the blob. Here, only one will survive. The reason to prefer
this approach over any other approach is that the ability to quickly access data
trumps over almost any other factor that another approach provides. In many of the
time series data, you will observe that you probably want to keep the time data point
as immutable—it's history, and history does not mutate. So the column data being
read-only, storing the object as a blob will not have a lot of negative impact.

If you are coming from the RDBMS world, this must be hard to digest. You may
wonder why we can't use a pattern where we have an index column family that
stores empty columns with column names, such as `TimeUUID`, and have another
column family that has a row key the same as the column name, which stores
the data in the columns of this column family. This will give us a nice and neat
normalized database. Every time you need to access the data, slice the index column

family and the `multi_get` user to pull the data off the other column family.

This is a bad idea. Although it gives you the flexibility to edit individual columns of each data point in the time series, it comes with an expensive `get` operation scattered across multiple nodes. In any medium- to large-sized application, the time series data and slices are usually giants. So `multi_get` is really going to suffer. The key takeaway here is to avoid normalization—chances are that the time series is non-editable and not so big a blob.

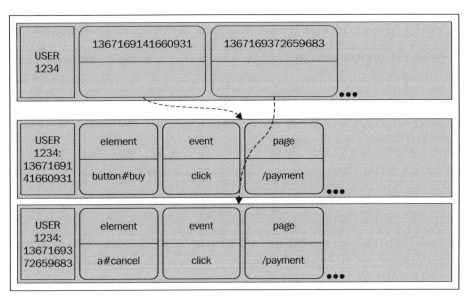

Figure 3.9: The time series data, a little more *normalized*, may cause heavy multi-`get` call

The next natural question that comes to mind is that the row has a practical hard limit on numbers if the column value it can store is two billion. What if the time series exceeds it every other day?

High throughput rows and hotspots

If your application is filling up a row at 1,000 writes/sec or if you have a row that gets updated and accessed at a really high rate and the nodes that hold that row (one row is held on one machine) would get exceptionally high read/write requests and create a hotspot in the cluster, you'd run out of columns in less than a month (about 23 days). For example, you are recording the users' agreements and disagreements during the U.S. presidential debates and displaying the aggregate in real time. If you are a popular site, chances are that you will get thousands of write requests per second, and you will be pushing changes every 50 ms to the users, displaying close to an instant mood swing to the public. This will create a hotspot, which is not good.

A hotspot in a distributed system somewhat kills the purpose of having lots of machines as many of the machines are underutilized and a couple of them are overloaded in terms of request processing and CPU utilization. Not to mention, a failure of these busy nodes in such a busy hour will be a disaster. So, we have two problems with wide-rowed time series data: one, the row exhausts, and the other is the hotspot. In both these situations, the solution is simple: distribute the data across multiple rows.

- **Rows divided into timeslots**: If it is possible to divide the writes into multiple timeslots, much like fixed interval buckets, the data can be stored in chunks. In this key, the row key contains an extra component, a timestamp of the start of the timeslot. For example, a process that fills up a row at 1,000 columns/second can utilize a daily (or fortnightly) bucket, where each row contains data just for one day. The row key for such a column family may look something like this:

  ```
  <row-key>:<timestamp_of_start_of_day>
  ```

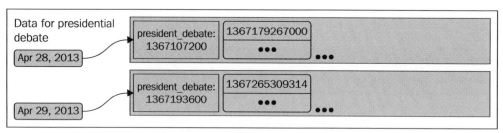

Figure 3.10: Rows as buckets for one day's data

  While this does solve the issue of rows getting overflowed, it does not really address the hotspot issue with real-time read/write access to a bucket.

- **Multiplexing writes within timeslots**: Let's observe the previous situation in the context of a really busy day in the life of a real-time application. On a busy day, lots of reads and writes will go to a bucket dated that day. This means a majority of the requests (ingesting data and reading data off to clients immediately) hit only the nodes that contain today's data. If we want to distribute I/O across the nodes, we need to store to and read from different rows.

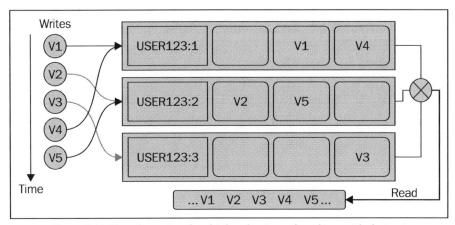

Figure 3.11: The schematics of multiplexed write and read to avoid a hotspot

The solution is to write the data in multiple rows with each having an `index` attribute along with their timeslot. The write operation either randomly (with equal probability) chooses an index for the appropriate bucket, or just writes to different indexes in the round-robin manner. The following code shows the main parts of this mechanism:

```
# insertion
# choose a random index between 1 to number of row splits
muxid = random.randint(1, MUX)
rowkey = '{0}:{1}'.format(user, muxid)

# column type is TimeUUIDType
timestamp = datetime.datetime.utcnow()

#serialize, event is just a JSON
colval = json.dumps(event)
eventsCF.insert(rowkey, {timestamp: colval})
```

```
# fetching
# accumulate all the rows the data multiplexed to
rowKeys = ['{0}:{1}'.format(userId, i+1) for i in range(4)]
rows = logCF.multiget(rowKeys)
# Merge! (not the best way to merge and order, but concise)
merge = {}
for row in rows:
  merge = dict(merge.items() + rows[row].items())

#order
final = collections.OrderedDict(
        sorted(merge.items(), reverse=True))

#Result
#Individual rows that the data was split to
>> user-784b9158-5233-454e-8dcf-c229cdff12c6:1
   Insertion Timestamp: 1367230574.4
   Insertion Timestamp: 1367230573.78
   Insertion Timestamp: 1367230573.48

>> user-784b9158-5233-454e-8dcf-c229cdff12c6:2
   Insertion Timestamp: 1367230574.4
   Insertion Timestamp: 1367230574.09

>> user-784b9158-5233-454e-8dcf-c229cdff12c6:3
   Insertion Timestamp: 1367230574.19
   Insertion Timestamp: 1367230573.68

>> user-784b9158-5233-454e-8dcf-c229cdff12c6:4
   Insertion Timestamp: 1367230573.99
   Insertion Timestamp: 1367230573.58

# The Merged result
insertion timestamp: 1367230574.4
insertion timestamp: 1367230574.4
insertion timestamp: 1367230574.19
insertion timestamp: 1367230574.09
insertion timestamp: 1367230573.99
insertion timestamp: 1367230573.78
insertion timestamp: 1367230573.68
insertion timestamp: 1367230573.58
insertion timestamp: 1367230573.48
```

The gain in performance and relatively balanced load across nodes due to distributed writing come with some overhead of work. Any read request requires a `multi_get` (perhaps `slice` too) call across all the *indexes* for those row keys followed by a `merge` operation similar to the merge-sort's merge step, which is `O(N)`. So, you probably want to slice just a small part enough to keep it effective.

- **Isn't multi_get evil?**: We learned in the previous section of putting `TimeUUID` as a row and values in a separate column family, where the timestamp row works as an index, and we also performed a `get` every time we needed to get actual data. But here we seem to support that, with the difference being the magnitude of `multi_get`. In the former case, if we try to pull 10,000 records, it will cost us 10,000 `multi_get` calls, but in the latter case, we are rarely going to multiplex more than 100 rows, which is OK. The first case does not give any benefit, while the latter saves the chances of having hotspots in the cluster, which is a considerable gain.

Advanced time series

For most of the cases, a simple time series will do the job and you wouldn't even need to bother about multiplexing. The bucketing pattern to store daily time series in one row is fairly common and logically simple. But, sometimes, it requires having a flexible pattern. For example, if you are in a company that accumulates users' reaction on predefined topics or events (and you are popular too!) on a day-to-day basis, the application is going to have normal-to-low load, which can perhaps be in the order of 1,000 requests per second per topic. This can easily be accommodated in the timestamped rows—one row for each topic each day. Or perhaps multiplex it by a factor of 10, so you have 10 rows per day per topic. And here comes the Super Bowl finals. Your servers start to spew tens of thousands of requests (assuming your array of application servers are large/strong enough to pass on the load to Cassandra) every second. You will want to disperse it to probably 100 rows. So, you need a mechanism that dynamically decides how many rows to split the input into based on the rate of request arrival.

There are a couple of ways to do it. Once your application decides that this input is going to have *N* number of splits, you need to have it stored somewhere. You can either use a counter column family or a normal column family; call it the metadata column family.

There are two approaches to this. One, the application can cache the multiplexing value for a given time series data at the time of the first read/write request that comes for it and then update it every couple of seconds. It is not going to be bad if the knowledge about the number of splits is a little delayed because we are going to merge from all the rows during retrieval anyway. Two, pull metadata about multiplexes on every write, but that's an extra network trip—which may bite you. The key idea to understand here is that for a given input, split counts are not going to change very frequently, and it's certainly not going to come down. If it does, you'd either lose some data in the bottom splits or you will have to first move the data back to the upper rows.

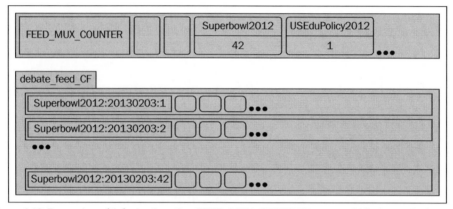

Figure 3.12: Dynamic multiplexing in action: FEED_MUX_COUNTER stores which time series is going to have how many splits

Many of these patterns are bound by your creativity to come up with an efficient solution using the tooling that Cassandra provides.

Avoid super columns

We have studied super columns earlier, and we kind of never gave much attention to it. The reason behind trying this is that we should avoid using super columns due to the multiple inefficiencies it brings into the system. Super columns can almost every time be converted to a better-performing alternative, such as composite columns. The reasons to eliminate super columns are jotted down as follows:

- A request for a subcolumn caused deserialization of all the subcolumns. So if you have a large number of subcolumns, the operation is going to be slowed.
- Unlike columns, subcolumns are not ordered.
- There are no indexes on subcolumns.

With the performance hit and the inability to have practically unbound subcolumns, super columns are more of a problem than a solution.

 Although super columns are not deprecated, and not likely to be deprecated by the API, the implementation is proposed to change to using composite columns instead of super columns. It may appear in Cassandra 2.0+ (refer to https://issues.apache.org/jira/browse/CASSANDRA-3237).

Transaction woes

A **transaction** is a sequence of operations that form a single unit of work. A transaction transforms the database from one *consistent state* (state1) to another (state2). It is an all or none system; either the whole transaction would succeed or the whole transaction would fail. In either case, the database—after a successful or unsuccessful transaction—will either be in state1 or state2. Someone coming from the RDBMS world would know the fairly common transactional store produce that defines a transaction. A transaction in RDBMS looks like this:

```
CREATE PROCEDURE exec_trade(buyer CHAR(10), seller CHAR(10), amount
DECIMAL(10,2))

BEGIN

/* READ */
  DECLARE curr_balanceDECIMAL(12,2);
  SELECT balance INTO curr_balance
  FROM accounts
  WHERE id = buyer;
  IF (curr_balance> amount) THEN

/* WRITE */
    UPDATE accounts
    SET balance = balance - amount
    where id = buyer;

/* WRITE */
    UPDATE accounts
    SET balance = balance + amount
    where id = seller;
  ENDIF

END
```

Cassandra does not make an ACID promise like tradition databases, and with its disregard to ACID compliance, lets Cassandra perform way faster and scale much larger than any relational databases. This also means Cassandra is not suitable for a transactional database; or rather *vanilla* Cassandra cannot make transactional guarantees. In this case, application developers have two choices to go for. The first approach is to use relational databases, such as MySQL, PostgreSQL, Oracle, or the like, complementary to Cassandra. So, basically, you end up having two data stores that handle two sides of reliability. Relational databases can be used for transactional guarantees to handle payments and Cassandra for superfast reads and writes. The second approach is fairly complicated, and it uses external synchronization libraries such as **Cages** (for Zookeeper) or Netflix's **Curator** (for Zookeeper). A detailed discussion on these third-party libraries is out of the scope of this book. You may access a more detailed article on Cages at `http://ria101.wordpress.com/2010/05/12/locking-and-transactions-over-cassandra-using-cages/`. In case this page is not available, there is a PDF version of this that can be accessed here.

Cages provides a construct similar to a stored produce (as mentioned previously) using `ZkTransaction` and `ZkMultiLock` classes. A client gets hold of all the necessary locks followed by mutations that are needed to be performed via `ZkTransaction`. Finally, the transaction is committed and the lock is relinquished.

Internally, Cages maintains a "before" state for each lock. If something goes wrong during the transaction, all the states are reverted back to this "before" state.

```
void executeTrade(String buyer, String seller, BidDecimal amount) {

  ZkMultiLockmlock = new ZkMultiLock();
  mlock.addWriteLock("/accounts/" + buyer);
  mlock.addWriteLock("/accounts/" + seller);
  mlock.acquire();

  try {
    // 1. check that buyer has sufficient funds
    // ....

    // 2. perform mutations using transaction object
    ZkTransaction transaction = new
    ZkTransaction(NoSQL.Cassandra);
    transaction.begin(mlock);
    try {
      // 3. debit buyer's account
      transaction.insert(
        buyer,
```

```
      "accounts",
    bytes("balance"),
     bytes(newBalance));

   // 4. credit seller's account
   // ...

 } finally {
   transaction.commit();
 }

} finally {
  mlock.release();
 }
}
```

 It is important to note here that one must go through a detailed study of these transaction providers and perform extensive tests before using them in production.

Use expiring columns

Expiring columns has been discussed earlier as well. In cases where you need to store data that will not matter after a certain period of time, expiring columns may be used. Expiring coupons, storing session data, and temporary results are some example usages of expiring columns. Let's see a case of session management using an expiring column. One may argue to have Memcached as a session store, which is a valid argument. A couple of things to consider: if you do not use Memcached, using it just for session management adds the extra overhead of another system. There is no way to avoid data loss (or store sessions permanently) during instances where a Memcached server needed to restart. There are alternate solutions to cope (refer to `http://dormando.livejournal.com/495593.html`) with session data loss if the Memcached server goes down. But they are not clean.

The idea of a session is to hold the users' *current* session data on the server and provide user experience based on the data. This data is scrapped after X minutes of the users' inactivity. (Please note that the session data may not include user activity monitoring, as you would want to keep the activity data for a long term for further analysis.) The simplest solution would be to just use expiring columns to store a user's session data with the column name as `session_id` and the value may be a serialized JSON. Every time a user loads a page or performs an activity, just reset the TTL of the column corresponding to the `session_id`.

This is fine, but you have to make a trip to Cassandra nodes every time a user activity is detected. One may want to cache the session data locally, perhaps, in the HashMap. This adds a little complexity. To solve this issue, one may keep session data in a local HashMap on each server. Along with the session data, have `last_accessed_timestamp` and `access_count` too. Each applicability server has a thread that executes every T minutes ($T < TTL$) and overwrites the session data for all the `session_id` values with `TTL = TTL - (current_timestamp - last_accessed_timestamp)`, if `access_count> 0`. What happens here is that we keep a local HashMap. If a session was ever touched, we up the counter and note down when the user last accessed the server. The counter is the basis of what TTLs have to be updated in Cassandra.

The latter is not an ideal solution, and someone with a keen eye can find a slim chance of session deletion when the TTL causes a session data in Cassandra to be deleted. Meanwhile, the server holding the data in the local HashMap goes down. But that's a risk that majorly saves us frequent trips over the network to get and update session data. If it is not really critical to have exact session deletion time, adding some extra time to TTL (`TTL + T`) may reduce the risk to some extent.

One thing you get with any centralized session store is a distributed session. So application users may jump from one server to another, new machines can be added, or a machine can be taken down for maintenance without any repercussion:

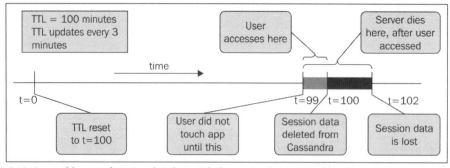

Figure 3.13: A possible case of session data loss with the session being stored locally and also on Cassandra in an expiring column

batch_mutate

batch_mutate is a way to mutate data in one go. It has some benefits over performing multiple single mutations, but the major gain is lesser network round trips. If something fails, `batch_mutate` instances can be re-run safely and completely once again. It is idempotent, so the data gets overwritten instead of getting appended. It can be used to group a set of operations that constitute a task.

Until Cassandra 1.2, batches were *not* atomic. If you wanted atomicity in the traditional RDBMS sense (all or none), you would have to to rely on some sort of arrangement such as Zookeeper. Cassandra 1.2 introduces atomic batches; read more about it at `http://www.datastax.com/dev/blog/atomic-batches-in-cassandra-1-2`.

That said, one must be aware about the performance hit due to atomic batches in 1.2. It reduces the performance of `batch_mutate` by about 30 percent as reported in the article. You may still use regular batches in 1.2 if atomicity is not a big deal.

Summary

The ability to effectively utilize a database's potential is more of an art than science. It is important to know the capabilities and things that have already been achieved by other people. But at the same time, you need to stay creative to mix and match the patterns to meet the requirements and goals within the limits of available resources. This chapter is probably the most important chapter from the perspective of an application developer. Starting from storage components of Cassandra to some of the common patterns to solve the common use cases, this chapter builds a solid footing for you to code your application confidently.

Cassandra's code base is developing at a rapid pace. With this fast-paced development, new features are getting added quickly at the same time and lesser-known patterns and bad design decisions are getting deprecated. CQL 3 is a good example of this.

CQL3 prevents use of antipatterns to some extent. It also gives a much friendlier SQL-like interface than Thrift. CQL 2 is deprecated and the much expected deprecation—super column is heavily condemned. It is a good idea to keep an eye on the new developments in Cassandra. The Apache Cassandra website, mailing list, and DataStax website are good places to stay up-to-date with the latest Cassandra developments.

Having applications ready to perform their best is a good idea, and it is equally important to have a capable infrastructure to serve the expectations. Setting up a Cassandra cluster is simple, and easier than most of the distributed software deployments. Out of the box, Cassandra comes with good defaults for most of the cases. So, if you have deployed your cluster before reading the next chapter, chances are that you are not far away from your optimal setting, and you just need to read the next chapter to make sure that everything is fine.

4
Deploying a Cluster

So, you have played a bit with Cassandra on your local machine and read something about how great it scales. Now it's time to evaluate all the tall claims that Cassandra makes.

This chapter deals with cluster deployment and the decision that you need to make that will affect a number of nodes, types of machines, and tweaks in the Cassandra configuration file. We start with hardware evaluations and then dive into operating-system-level tweaks, followed by prerequisite software and how to install them. Once the base machine is ready, we will discuss the Cassandra installation—which is fairly easy. The rest of the chapter talks about various settings available, what fits in which situation, the pros and cons, and so on. Having been equipped with all this information, you are ready to launch your first cluster. The chapter provides a working code that deploys Cassandra on *N* number of nodes, sets the entire configuration, and starts Cassandra, effectively launching each node in about 40 seconds, thus enabling you to get going with an eight-node cluster in about five minutes. Toward the end of the chapter, it briefly discusses client-connection security as in Version 1.1.11.

Code pattern: All the shell commands mentioned in this chapter follow a pattern. Each line starting with a # sign is just a comment for readers to clarify the context. Each line starting with a $ sign is a command (excluding the beginning $ sign). Some longer commands may be broken into multiple lines for reading clarity. If a command is broken, the end of the line contains a line-continuation character—a backslash (\). Each line that does not have either of these symbols is the output of a command. Please follow this pattern unless specified.

Evaluating requirements

It is generally a good idea to examine what kind of load Cassandra is going to face when deployed on a production server. It does not have to be accurate, but some sense of traffic can give a little more clarity to what you expect from Cassandra (criteria for load tests), whether you really need Cassandra (the halo effect), or if you can bear all the expenses that a running Cassandra cluster can incur on a daily basis (the value proposition). Let's see how to choose various hardware specifications for a specific need.

Hard disk capacity

A rough disk space calculation of the user that will be stored in Cassandra involves adding up data stored in three data components on disk: commit logs, SSTable, index file, and bloom filter. When compared to the data that is incoming and the data on disk, you need to take account of the database overheads associated with each data. The data on disk can be about two times as large as raw data. Disk usage can be calculated using the following code:

```
# Size of one normal column
column_size (in bytes) = column_name_size + column_val_size
                       + 15

# Size of an expiring or counter column
col_size (in bytes) =  column_name_size + column_val_size
                       + 23

# Size of a row
row_size (bytes) = size_of_all_columns + row_key_size + 23

# Primary index file size
index_size (bytes) = number_of_rows * (32 + mean_key_size)

# Additional space consumption due to replication
replication_overhead = total_data_size *
                         (replication_factor - 1)
```

Apart from this, the disk also faces high read-write during compaction. **Compaction** is the process that merges SSTables to improve search efficiency. The important thing about compaction is that it may, in the worst case, utilize as much space as occupied by user data. So, it is a good idea to have a large space left.

We'll discuss this again, but it depends on the choice of `compaction_strategy` that is applied. For `LeveledCompactionStrategy`, having 10 percent space left is enough; for `SizeTieredCompactionStrategy`, it requires 50 percent free disk space in the worst case. Here are some rules of thumb with regard to disk choice and disk operations:

- **Commit logs and datafiles on separate disks**: Commit logs are updated on each write and are read-only for startups, which is rare. A data directory, on the other hand, is used to flush MemTables into SSTables, asynchronously; it is read through and written on during compaction; and most importantly, it might be looked up by a client to satisfy the consistency level. Having the two directories on the same disk may potentially cause a block to the client operation.

- **RAID 0**: Cassandra performs in built replication by means of a replication factor; so, it does not possess any sort of hardware redundancy. If one node dies completely, the data is available on other replica nodes, with no difference between the two. This is the reason that RAID 0 (`http://en.wikipedia.org/wiki/RAID#RAID_0`) is the most preferred RAID level. Another reason is improved disk performance and extra space.

- **Filesystem**: If one has choices, XFS (XFS filesystem: `http://en.wikipedia.org/wiki/XFS`) is the most preferred filesystem for Cassandra deployment. XFS supports 16 TB on a 32-bit architecture, and a whopping 8 **EiB** (**Exabibyte**) on 64-bit machines. Due to the storage space limitations, the `ext4`, `ext3`, and `ext2` filesystems (in that order) can be considered to be used for Cassandra.

- **SCSI and SSD**: With disks, the guideline is faster and better. SCSI is faster than SATA, and SSD is faster than SCSI. **Solid State Drives (SSD)** are extremely fast as there is no moving part. It is suggested to use rather low-priced consumer SSD for Cassandra, as enterprise-grade SSD has no particular benefit over it.

- **No EBS on EC2**: This is specific to **Amazon Web Services (AWS)** users. AWS' **Elastic Block Store** (**EBS**: `http://aws.amazon.com/ebs/`) is strongly discouraged for the purpose of storing Cassandra data—either of data directories or commit log storage. Poor throughput and issues such as getting unusably slow, instead of cleanly dying, is a major roadblock of the network-attached storage.

  Instead of using EBS, use ephemeral devices attached to the instance (also known as an **instance store**). Instance stores are fast and do not suffer any problems like EBS. Instance stores can be configured as RAID 0 to utilize them even further.

RAM

Larger memory boosts Cassandra performance from multiple aspects. More memory can hold larger MemTables, which means that fresh data stays for a longer duration in memory and leads to fewer disk accesses for recent data. This also implies that there will be fewer flushes (less frequent disk IO) of MemTable to SSTable; and the SSTables will be larger and fewer. This leads to improved read performance as lesser SSTables are needed to scan during a lookup. Larger RAM can accommodate larger row cache, thus decreasing disk access.

For any sort of production setup, a RAM capacity less than 8 GB is *not* suggested. Memory above 16 GB is preferred.

CPU

Cassandra is highly concurrent—compaction, writes, and getting results from multiple SSTables and creation of one single view to clients, and all are CPU intensive. It is suggested to use an 8-core CPU, but anything with a higher core will just be better.

For a cloud-based setup, a couple of things to keep in mind:

- A provider that gives a CPU-bursting feature should be preferred. One such provider is **Rackspace**.

- AWS Micro instances should be avoided for any serious work. There are many reasons for this. It comes with EBS storage and no option to use an instance store. But the deal-breaker issue is CPU throttling that makes it useless for Cassandra. If one performs a CPU-intensive task for 10 seconds or so, CPU usage gets restricted on micro instances. However, they may be good (cheap), if one just wants to get started with Cassandra.

Nodes

Each node in the ring is responsible for a set of row keys. Nodes have a token assigned to them on startup either via bootstrapping during startup or by the configuration file. Each node stores keys from the last node's token (excluded) to the current node's token (included). So, the greater the number of nodes, the lesser the number of keys per node; the fewer the number of requests to be served by each node, the better the performance.

In general, a large number of nodes is good for Cassandra. It is a good idea to keep 300 GB to 500 GB disk space per node to start with, and to back calculate the number of nodes you may need for your data. One can always add more nodes and change tokens on each node.

Network

As with any other distributed system, Cassandra is highly dependent on a network. Although Cassandra is tolerant to network partitioning, a reliable network with less outages are better preferred for the system—less repairs, less inconsistencies.

A congestion-free, high speed (Gigabit or higher), reliable network is pretty important as each read-write, replication, moving/draining node puts heavy load on a network.

System configurations

Operating system configurations play a significant role in enhancing Cassandra performance. On a dedicated Cassandra server, resources must be tweaked to utilize the full potential of the machine.

Cassandra runs on a JVM, so it can be run on any system that has a JVM. It is recommended to use a Linux variant (CentOS, Ubuntu, Fedora, RHEL, and so on) for Cassandra's production deployment. There are many reasons for this. Configuring system-level settings are easier. Most of the production servers rely on Linux-like systems for deployment. As of April 2013, 65 percent of servers use it. The best toolings are available on Linux: SSH and pSSH commands such as top, free, df, and ps to measure system performance, and excellent filesystems, for example ext4 and XFS. There are built-in mechanisms to watch the rolling log using tail, and there are excellent editors such as Vim and Emacs. And they're all free!

> More on the usage share of operating systems at
> http://en.wikipedia.org/wiki/Usage_share_
> of_operating_systems#Summary.

We will assume a Linux-like system for the rest of the book, unless mentioned otherwise. If you are unfamiliar with Linux, there is an excellent book to cover everything you needed to know about it: *"Linux Administration Handbook"* by *Nemeth*, *Snyder*, and *Hein*.

Optimizing user limits

The limits.conf file (located at /etc/security/) gives a simple mechanism to set resource limits to users. To make Cassandra work without choking, it must be provided with higher resource availability, which can be easily done by this file. Add/update the following values to various resources (you need to have root access to do this):

```
* softnofile 32768
```

```
*  hard nofile 32768
root soft nofile 32768
root hard nofile 32768
*  softmemlock unlimited
*  hard memlock unlimited
root soft memlock unlimited
root hard memlock unlimited
*  soft as unlimited
*  hard as unlimited
root soft as unlimited
root hard as unlimited
```

If you are using cloud, you may want to set and store the values mentioned in the following list to your machine image file:

- `nofile`: By default, a Linux-based system has an upper cap on the number of open files. This may cause trouble for a moderately large setup. Reading/ writing may involve a large number of file accesses. Apart from this, node-to-node communication is socket-based, that is, it takes one file descriptor per socket. So, having a setting that allows a high number of concurrently open file descriptors is a good idea.

  A file descriptor can be anything below 2^{20} for RHEL and family. 32768 (= 2^{15}). This is a good range of values to start with.

- `memlock`: If you are coming from a relational database background, `memlock` is chiefly used for a huge page. The `memlock` parameter specifies how much memory any `* = wild card` user can lock in its address space. It can be set to unlimited or the maximum value of RAM in KB.

The rest of the settings in the preceding configuration are just for hard and soft limits. In actuality, both are set to unlimited. For more information about `limits. conf`, refer to `http://linux.die.net/man/5/limits.conf`.

This and the other limit configurations can be seen by issuing the `ulimit -a` command.

Swapping memory

Swap is bad for Cassandra, especially in the production setup. It is advisable to disable swap on a production machine (assuming it's a dedicated Cassandra server). Basically, swap space is an area on the secondary storage (hard drive) that works as extended memory. Swap is used when the total memory required by processes is more than the available memory.

The operating system moves memory segments (also known as **pages**) from or to the swap area to free up memory; this is called **paging**. Reading from secondary storage to access these pages is painfully slow when compared to access from the main memory. This is a major performance hit. (More on paging performance at `http://en.wikipedia.org/wiki/Paging#Performance`.)

Cassandra is fault tolerant, so we can trade the possibility of a node going down for a speedy response when it is up. That is a *quick* node death by the **Out-Of-Memory (OOM)** killer due to memory crunch, which is better than a sluggish system.

To disable swap permanently, you need to edit `/etc/fstab` (requires root access) and comment out all the lines containing the type `swap` by putting # at the beginning of the line, as shown in the following code snippet:

```
#/dev/sda3   none   swap   sw   0   0
```

To immediately/temporarily switch off `swap`, execute the following command:

```
$ sudoswapoff --all
```

Clock synchronization

We have learned from section. The Cassandra data model, *Chapter 3*, Design Patterns that Cassandra uses timestamp for conflict resolution. It is very important to have clocks on each server and client machines to be synchronized with a reliable central clock to avoid unexpected overwrites.

The most common way to do this is by using the **Network Time Protocol (NTP)** daemon. It sets and maintains the system time in synchronism with the time server with time resolution to milliseconds. You may check if your system has NTP installed and running by executing `ntpq -p`.

Here is how you install and configure NTP:

```
# Install (Fedora/RHEL/CentOS)
$ yum install ntp
# Install (Debian/Ubuntu)
$ sudo apt-get install ntp
# Configure time servers (likely, configured already)
$ vi /etc/ntp.conf #open with editor, root access needed
# Add server(s) and save
$ server pool.ntp.org
# Restart NTP service
$ /etc/init.d/ntpd restart
# Force immediate update
$ ntpdate pool.ntp.org
```

Although we have mentioned that the timestamp for the column is provided by the client, it is not true for CQL. CQL uses server-side timestamp unless specified, specifically by the USING TIMESTAMP clause.

Even if you do not use CQL, it does not lessen the importance of synchronization on the server-side expiring columns, and tombstone removal does require time to be correctly set. In general, it is advisable to have your production servers (of any application) to be time-synchronized.

With Amazon Web Services or any other cloud service, it is a general perception that depending on a hardware clock is a safe bet. This is not correct. There may be situations when time on these virtual instances gets drifted. In AWS EC2 instances, to be able to set up NTP, you need to disable sync with the clock on the physical machine. You can do that by using the following command:

```
$ echo 1 > /proc/sys/xen/independent_wallclock
```

This is transient, but to make it permanent you can edit /etc/sysctl.conf by adding the following code line:

```
xen.independent_wallclock=1
```

Disk readahead

readahead boosts sequential access to the disk by reading a little more data than requested, ahead of time to mitigate some effect of slow disk reads. This is called **readahead**. This means less frequent requests to the disk.

But this has its disadvantage as well. If your system is performing high frequency random reads and writes, a high readahead would translate them into magnified reads/writes—much higher I/O than actually is. This will slow the system down. (It also piles up memory with the data that you do not actually need.)

To view the current value of **readahead (RA)**, execute blockdev --report as shown in the following command lines:

```
$ sudo blockdev --report
```

RO	RASSZ	BSZ	StartSec	Size	Device
rw256	512	4096	0	320072933376	/dev/sda
rw256	512	4096	2048	104857600	/dev/sda1

```
rw256   512   4096      206848   73295462400   /dev/sda2
rw256   512   1024   143362110          1024   /dev/sda3
...
```

In the preceding example, RA is 256 blocks of a **sector size (SSZ)** 512 bytes. So, 512 * 256 bytes = 128 KB.

Unfortunately, the commonly suggested value of RA is 65536, or 32 MB! This is very bad for a Cassandra setup. Do not use this high value for readahead. It is suggested to set the readahead to 512. Here is how to do that:

```
# set RA, may require sudoer permission
$ sudoblockdev --setra 512 /dev/<device>
```

To make this setting permanent, it can be placed in a local run-config file (location /etc/rc.local).

The required software

Cassandra runs over a JVM, and this is all you need to get Cassandra up and running. Any platform that has the JVM can have Cassandra. At the time of writing, Java's latest version was Java SE 7. However, it is highly recommended to use Oracle Java 6 for Cassandra, to avoid unexplainable bugs due to any inconsistency in the Java version or vendor implementation.

The other thing that one should consider for the production setup is to have the **Java Native Access (JNA)** library. It provides access to the native platform's shared libraries. JNA can be configured to disallow swapping JVM, and hence, improving Cassandra memory usage.

Installing Oracle Java 6

The default installation of Linux systems usually contains the OpenJDK **Java Runtime Environment (JRE)**. This should either be removed or you can keep OpenJDK, but set the default JRE as Oracle JRE. This guide will assume a 64-bit system. To check whether your system has JRE, and what version of it executes, run the java -version command in the shell:

```
# Check Java (important fields are highlighted)
$ java -version

java version "1.6.0_24"
OpenJDK Runtime Environment (IcedTea6 1.11.11) (amazon-61.1.11.11.53.
amzn1-x86_64)
OpenJDK 64-Bit Server VM (build 20.0-b12, mixed mode)
```

RHEL and CentOS systems

We are going to follow three basic steps for installing Oracle Java 6 for RHEL and CentOS systems:

1. **Downloading the binary file from the Oracle website**: JRE 6 can be downloaded from Oracle's website at `http://www.oracle.com/technetwork/java/javase/downloads/jre6-downloads-1637595.html`. Unfortunately, as of the time of writing of this book, you couldn't perform `wget` to download this file from the command line. This is due to the fact that Oracle mandates the users to accept the Oracle Binary Code License before downloading can commence. The easiest way that I find is to accept and download the file on your work desktop and then copy it to the server using `scp`.

    Choose the **Linux x64-rpm.bin** version to download in order to install it on RHEL-like systems.

2. **Installing a JRE**: Set the downloaded file executable, and execute it.

    ```
    $ chmod a+x jre-6u34-linux-x64-rpm.bin
    $ sudo ./jre-6u34-linux-x64-rpm.bin
    ```

     Note that the `6u34` part of the filename may be different for you. It was the latest version at the time of writing of this book.

3. **Configuring Oracle JRE as default**: If you have OpenJDK on your server machine, you will have to set it as an alternative, and use Oracle JRE by default. The RHEL family has a utility called `alternatives` inspired by Debian's `update-dependencies` utility for conflict resolution in cases where there exists multiple software that perform similar functionalities, but the user will prefer one software to be the default for those functions.

     `alternatives` takes four parameters to install a software as default: a symbolic link to where the software is to be installed, the generic name of the software, the actual path of where the software is installed, and a priority that determines which software is to be chosen by default. The highest-priority software is set to the default.

    The following code block will go through the details of the process:

    ```
    # See the details Default: OpenJDK, priority: 16000
    $ alternatives --display java
    java - status is auto.
    ```

```
link currently points to /usr/lib/jvm/jre-1.6.0-openjdk.x86_64/
bin/java
/usr/lib/jvm/jre-1.6.0-openjdk.x86_64/bin/java - priority 16000

# Install Oracle JRE with HIGHER preference
$ sudo alternatives --install /usr/bin/java java /usr/java/
jre1.6.0_34/bin/java 31415

# See the details
$ alternatives --display java
java - status is auto.
link currently points to /usr/java/jre1.6.0_34/bin/java
/usr/lib/jvm/jre-1.6.0-openjdk.x86_64/bin/java - priority 16000
 [-- snip --]
/usr/java/jre1.6.0_34/bin/java - priority 31415
 [-- snip --]
Current 'best' version is /usr/java/jre1.6.0_34/bin/java.

# View the current version
$ java -version
java version "1.6.0_34"
Java(TM) SE Runtime Environment (build 1.6.0_34-b04)
 Java HotSpot(TM) 64-Bit Server VM (build 20.9-b04, mixed mode)
```

`sudo alternatives --config java` can be used to switch the default version.

Once all this is done, the Bash profile can be updated to have JAVA_HOME. To do this, you need to append the following line in ~/.bashrc:

```
export JAVA_HOME=/usr/java/jre1.6.0_34
```

Debian and Ubuntu systems

We are going to follow three basic steps for installing Oracle Java 6 for Debian and Ubuntu systems:

1. **Downloading the binary file from the Oracle website**: JRE 6 can be downloaded from Oracle's website at http://www.oracle.com/technetwork/java/javase/downloads/jre6-downloads-1637595.html. Unfortunately, as of the time of writing this book, you couldn't perform wget to download this file from the command line. This is due to the fact that Oracle mandates the users to accept the Oracle Binary Code License before downloading can commence. The easiest way that I find is to accept and download the file on your work desktop and then copy it to the server using scp.

Choose the **Linux x64.bin** version to download. (Do not download the RPM version of the binary for Debian-like systems.)

2. **Installing JRE**: Installing involves setting the binary file to executable and running it as super user. This extracts the contents to the current working directory. You may require to move it to a desirable location. Then set this as a top-priority alternative.

```
# Execute the downloaded binary
$ sudo chmod a+x jre-6u34-linux-x64.bin
$ sudo ./jre-6u34-linux-x64.bin


# Move extracted directory to an appropriate location
$ sudo mkdir -p /usr/java/latest
$ sudo mv jre1.6.0_34 /usr/java/latest/
```

3. **Configuring Oracle JRE as default**: To use Oracle Java as the default JRE, it is required to set it as the default alternative. To do this, use Debian/Ubuntu's built-in utility—**update-alternatives**. It is used to provide priority to the software that performs the same functions. In our case, we want Oracle JRE to be preferred over the other JREs in the system. So, we will install Oracle JRE as an alternative and manually set it as default. If you do not want to manually set the default for a user, an alternative with higher priority is chosen as the default. So, one may give Oracle JRE alternative as a very high value and skip manually setting the preference.

```
# Install JRE as an alternative with priority 1
$ sudo update-alternatives --install /usr/bin/java java \
/usr/java/latest/jre1.6.0_34/bin/java 1
update-alternatives: using /usr/java/latest/jre1.6.0_34/bin/java
to provide /usr/bin/java (java) in auto mode.


# Check current JRE
$ java -version
java version "1.6.0_34"
Java(TM) SE Runtime Environment (build 1.6.0_34-b04)
Java HotSpot(TM) 64-Bit Server VM (build 20.9-b04, mixed mode)


# Set is a default, or if last command does not show
# Oracle JRE.
$ sudo update-alternatives --set java \
/usr/java/latest/jre1.6.0_34/bin/java
```

```
# View all alternatives
$ sudo update-alternatives --display java
java - manual mode
  link currently points to /usr/java/latest/jre1.6.0_34/bin/java
/usr/java/latest/jre1.6.0_34/bin/java - priority 1
Current 'best' version is '/usr/java/latest/jre1.6.0_34/bin/java'.
```

Now is a good time to update your Bash shell profile with JAVA_HOME. Open ~/.bashrc and append the following to this file:

```
export JAVA_HOME=/usr/java/latest/jre1.6.0_34
```

It may require calling source ~/.bashrc to reload the configuration file.

Installing the Java Native Access (JNA) library

The installer for JNA is available to all the decently modern operating systems. Cassandra requires JNA 3.4 or higher. JNA can be installed manually; see the details at https://github.com/twall/jna.

- To install JNA on RHEL/CentOS, run the following command:

  ```
  $ yum install jna
  ```

- To install JNA on Debian/Ubuntu, run the following command:

  ```
  $ sudo apt-get install libjna-java
  ```

Installing Cassandra

With JVM ready, installing Cassandra is as easy as downloading the appropriate tarball from the Apache Cassandra download page, http://cassandra.apache.org/download, and untarring it. On Debian or Ubuntu, you may choose either to install from a .tar file or from an Apache Software Foundation repository.

Installing from a tarball

This guide assumes that Cassandra is installed in the /opt directory, the datafiles in the /cassandra-data directory, and the system logs in /var/log/cassandra. These are just some conventions that were chosen by me. You may choose a location that suits you best:

```
# Download. Please select appropriate version and
# URL from http://cassandra.apache.org/download page
$ wget \
```

```
http://mirror.sdunix.com/apache/cassandra/1.1.11/apache-cassandra-
1.1.11-bin.tar.gz
[-- snip --]
Saving to: 'apache-cassandra-1.1.11-bin.tar.gz'

# extract
$ tar xzf apache-cassandra-1.1.11-bin.tar.gz

# (optional) Symbolic link to easily switch versions in
# future without having to change dependent scripts
$ ln -s apache-cassandra-1.1.11 cassandra
```

Installing from ASFRepository for Debian/Ubuntu

Apache Software Foundation provides Debian packages for different versions of
Cassandra to directly install it from the repository. To list the packages, run the
following command:

```
# Edit sources
$ sudo vi /etc/apt/sources.list
```

Also, append the following three lines:

```
# Cassandra repo
deb http://www.apache.org/dist/cassandra/debian 11x main
deb-src http://www.apache.org/dist/cassandra/debian 11x main
```

Next, execute sudo apt-get update, as shown in the following code:

```
$ sudo apt-get update
Ign http://security.ubuntu.com natty-security InRelease
[-- snip --]
GPG error: http://www.apache.org 11x InRelease: The following
signatures couldn't be verified because the public key is not
available: NO_PUBKEY 4BD736A82B5C1B00
```

If you get this error, add the public keys as shown:

```
$ gpg --keyserver pgp.mit.edu --recv-keys F758CE318D77295D
$ gpg --export --armor F758CE318D77295D | sudo apt-key add -

$ gpg --keyserver pgp.mit.edu --recv-keys 2B5C1B00
$ gpg --export --armor 2B5C1B00 | sudo apt-key add -
```

Now, you can install Cassandra using the following commands:

```
$ sudo apt-get update
$ sudo apt-get install cassandra
```

This installation does most of the system-wide configurations for you. It makes all the executables available to the $PATH system path, copies the configuration file to /etc/cassandra, and adds the .init script to set up proper JVM and ulimits. It also sets run-level, so Cassandra starts at boot as "cassandra" user.

Anatomy of the installation

There are a couple of programs and files that one must know about to work effectively with Cassandra. These things come to use during investigation, maintenance, configuration, and optimization.

Depending on how the installation is done, the file may be available at different locations. For a tarball installation, everything is neatly packaged under the directory where Cassandra is installed: binaries under the bin directory and the configuration file under the conf directory. For repository-based installations, binaries are available in /usr/bin and /usr/sbin directories; and configuration files under /etc/cassandra and /etc/default/cassandra.

Cassandra binaries

These contain executables for various tasks. Let's take a quick glance at them:

- cassandra: It starts the Cassandra daemon using default configuration. To start Cassandra in the foreground, use the -f option. You can use *Ctrl + C* to kill Cassandra and view logs on the console. One may also use -p <pid_file> to have a handle and to kill Cassandra running in the background by using kill 'cat <pid_file>'.

  If Cassandra is installed from the repository, it must have created a service for it. So, one should use sudo service cassandra start, sudo service cassandra stop, and sudo service cassandra status to start, stop, and query the status of Cassandra.

- cassandra-cli: Cassandra's **command-line interface (CLI)** gives a very basic access to execute simple commands to modify and access keyspaces and column families. More discussion on Cassandra's CLI can be found at http://wiki.apache.org/cassandra/CassandraCli. The typical use of Cassandra looks like this:

  ```
  cassandra-cli -h <hostname> -p <port> -k <keyspace>
  ```

A file of statements can be passed to the CLI using the `-f` option.

- `cqlsh`: This is a command-line interface to execute CQL queries. The default version is CQL 3 as of Cassandra Version 1.1.*. It may change in Version 1.2.0+. One may switch to CQL 3 using the `-cql3` switch. Typically, the `cqlsh` connect command looks like this:

```
cqlsh <hostname> <port> -k <keyspace>
```

- `json2sstable` and `sstable2json`: As the name suggests, they represent the yin and yang of serializing and deserializing the data in SSTable. It can be vaguely assumed to be similar to the `mysqldump --xml <database>` command, except that it works in the JSON format.

- `sstable2json` provides SSTable as JSON, and `json2sstable` takes JSON to materialize a functional SSTable.

- `sstable2json` may have the following three options:
    - `-k`: the keys to be dumped
    - `-x`: the keys to be excluded
    - `-e`: it makes `sstable2json` to dump just keys, no column family data

  One can use the `-k` or `-x` switches up to 500 times. A general `sstable2json` executable looks like this:

```
sstable2json -k <key1> -k <key2> <sstable_path>
```

- `sstable_path` must be the full path to SSTable such as `/cassandra-data/data/mykeyspace/mykeyspace-hc-1.data`. Also, the `key` variable must be a hex string.

- `sstablekeys`: This is essentially `sstable2json` with a `-e` switch.

- `sstableloader`: This is used to bulk load to Cassandra. One can simply copy SSTable datafiles and load to another Cassandra setup without much hassle. Essentially, `sstableloader` reads the datafiles and streams to the current Cassandra setup as specified by Cassandra's YAML file. We will see this tool in more detail in section Using Cassandra bulk loader to restore the data, *Chapter 6, Managing a Cluster – Scaling*, Node Repair, and Backup.

Configuration files

Cassandra has a central configuration file named `cassandra.yaml`. It contains cluster settings, node-to-node communication specifications, performance-related settings, authentication, security, and backup settings.

Apart from this, there are the `log4j-server.properties` and `cassandra-topology.properties` files. The `log4j-server.properties` file is used to tweak Cassandra logging settings. The only thing that one may want to change in this file is the following line so that we can change the location where logs are located:

```
log4j.appender.R.File=/var/log/cassandra/system.log
```

The `cassandra-topology.properties` file is to be filled with cluster-specific values if you use `PropertyFileSnich`. We'll discuss more on this in this chapter.

`cassandra.yaml` and other files can be accessed from the `conf` directory under the installation directory for a tarball installation. For a repository installation, the `cassandra.yaml` file and others can be found under `/etc/cassandra`.

Setting up Cassandra's data directory and commit log directory

As discussed earlier, one should configure the data directory and the commit log directory to separate disk drives to improve performance. The `cassandra.yaml` file holds all these configurations and more.

AWS EC2 users: Although it is emphasized to have data and commit logs on two drives, for EC2 instance store instances, it is suggested to set up the RAID0 configuration and use it for both the data directories and the commit log. It performs better than having one of those on the root device and the other on ephemeral.

EBS-backed instances are a bad choice for a Cassandra installation due to slow I/O performance, and the same goes for any NAS setup.

To update data directories, edit the following lines in `cassandra.yaml`:

```
# directories where Cassandra should store data on disk.
data_file_directories:
    - /var/lib/cassandra/data
```

Change `/var/lib/cassandra/data` to a directory that is suitable for your setup. You may as well add more directories spanning different hard disks. Then change the commit log directory as shown in the following code:

```
# commit log
commitlog_directory: /var/lib/cassandra/commitlog
```

Edit this to set a desired location.

These directories (data or commit log) *must* be available for write. If it is not a fresh install, one may want to migrate data from the old data directories and the commit log directory to new ones.

Configuring a Cassandra cluster

Now that you have a single node setup, you may start Cassandra by executing `<cassandra_installation>/bin/cassandra` for a tarball install or by running `sudo service cassandra start` for a repository installation. (We'll see later in this chapter how to write a `.init` script for Cassandra and set it up to start on boot.) However, it needs a couple of configuration tweaks in order to get a Cassandra cluster working.

If you look at `cassandra.yaml`, you will find that it has the following six sections:

- **Cluster setup properties**: These are basically startup properties, file location, ports, replica placement strategies, and inter-node communication settings.

- **Performance tuning properties**: These help in setting up appropriate values to system/network resources based on your setup.

- **Client connection properties**: These help in setting up the behavior of client-to-node connectivity, things such as number of requests per client, maximum number of threads (clients), and much more.

- **Inter-node communication**: This section contains configurations for node-to-node communication within a cluster. These include hinted handoff settings and failure detection settings.

- **Backup settings**: These settings are Cassandra-automated backup items.

- **Authorization and authentication settings**: This provides protected access to the cluster. The default is to allow all.

In most of the cases, you will never have to bother about client connection properties and inter-node communication settings. Even by default, the configuration is very smart and robust for any modern-day computer. The rest of this chapter will discuss the cluster setup properties and various options that Cassandra provides out of the box. Security will be discussed briefly. In the section Authorization and authentication, we will tune Cassandra using various properties in `cassandra.yaml`.

The cluster name

A cluster name is used to logically group nodes that belong to the same cluster. It works as a namespace for nodes. In a multiple cluster environment, it works as a preventive mechanism for nodes of a cluster to join one another.

It is always a good idea to give a meaningful cluster name, even if you have a single cluster at the time. Consider `cassandra.yaml`:

```
cluster_name: 'MyAppMainCluster'
```

It is suggested to change the cluster name before you launch the cluster. Changing the cluster name when the cluster is up and running throws an exception. This is because the cluster name resides in the system keyspace, and as of Version 1.1.11, you cannot edit the system keyspace. (It was possible in some older versions.)

If you have to change the cluster name, there is an *unofficial* trick to do that. A cluster name is stored in the `LocationInfo` column family of the system keyspace. So, you need to stop the nodes, change the `cassandra.yaml` file with a new cluster name, and delete the contents of the `<data_directory>/system/LocationInfo` directory (or just move the contents elsewhere so that you can replace them if something goes wrong). On restarting the node, you can see when you connect to a local node via `cassandra-cli` that you are welcomed to a new cluster name. This process needs to be repeated for all the nodes in the cluster.

The seed node

A seed node is the one that a newly-launched node consults to, to know about the cluster. Although gossip (refer to section Gossip, *Chapter 2, Cassandra Architecture*) is the way how nodes know one another, but to a new node, seeds are the first nodes that it will know and start a gossip with. And, eventually, all nodes will know its presence and it will know about the other nodes.

There must be at least one seed node in a cluster. Seed nodes should be a rather stable node. One may configure more than one seed node for added redundancy and increased availability of seed nodes. In `cassandra.yaml`, seed nodes are a comma-separated list of seed addresses:

```
seed_provider:
  - class_name: org.apache....SimpleSeedProvider
    parameters:
      # Ex: "<ip1>,<ip2>,<ip3>"
      - seeds: "c1.mydomain.com,c2.mydomain.com"
```

Listen, broadcast, and RPC addresses

A listen address is the address that nodes use to connect to one another for communication/gossip. It is important to set this to the private IP of the machine. If it is not set, it picks up the `hostname` value, which if incorrectly configured can cause problems.

A broadcast address is the public address of the node. If it is not set, it will take whatever value the listen address bears. It is generally required only if you are setting up Cassandra to multiple data centers.

 EC2 users: With multiple data center installation, you need to use **EC2 Snitch**. `listen_address` may be set to blank because AWS assigns a hostname that is based on a private IP, but you may set it to a private IP or private DNS. `broadcast_address` must be a public IP or a public DNS. Also, remember not to forget to open `storage_port` (default is `7000`) in your security group that holds Cassandra instances.

An RPC address is for client connections to the node. It can be anything—the IP address, hostname, or `0.0.0.0`. If not set, it will take the hostname.

In `cassandra.yaml`, these properties look like the following:

```
# listen_address is not set, so it takes hostname.
listen_address:

# broadcast is commented. So, it is what listen_address is.
# broadcast_address: 1.2.3.4
# rpc_address is not set, so it is hostname.
rpc_address:
```

Initial token

An initial token is a number assigned to a node that decides the range of keys that it will hold. A node basically holds the tokens ranging from the previous node's token (the node that holds a token immediately less than the current node) $T_{n-1} + 1$ to the current node's token T_n.

In `cassandra.yaml`, you may mention an initial token as follows:

```
initial_token: 85070591730234615865843651857942052864
```

It is important to choose initial tokens wisely to make sure the data is evenly distributed across the cluster. If you do not assign initial tokens to the nodes at the start of a new cluster, it may get automatically assigned, which may lead to a hotspot. However, adding a new node is relatively smart. If you do not mention an initial token to the new node, Cassandra will take a node that is loaded the most number of times and assign the new node a key that splits the token's own loaded node into half. It is possible to load balance a running cluster, and it is fairly easy. We'll learn more about load balancing in the section Load balancing, *Chapter 6, Managing a Cluster – Scaling*, Node Repair, and Backup. The next logical question is how do we determine the initial token for a node? It depends on the partitioner that you are using. And basically, we divide the whole range of keys that the partitioner supports into *N* equal parts, where *N* is the total number of nodes in the cluster. Then we assign each node a number. We will see this in the next section.

Partitioners

By assigning initial tokens, what we have done is created buckets of keys. What determines which key goes to what bucket? It is **partitioner**. A partitioner generates a hash value of the row key; based on the hash value, Cassandra determines to which "bucket" (node) this row needs to go. This is a good way in which hash will always generate a unique number for a row key. So, this is also what is used to determine the node to read from.

Like everything else in Cassandra, partitioner is a pluggable interface. You can implement your own partitioner by implementing `org.apache.cassandra.dht.IPartitioner` and drop the `.class` or `.jar` file in Cassandra's `lib` directory.

Here is how you mention the preference for partitioner in `cassandra.yaml`:

```
partitioner: org.apache.cassandra.dht.RandomPartitioner
```

In most cases, the default partitioner is generally good for you. It distributes keys evenly. As of Version 1.1.11, the default is RandomPartitioner, but in 1.2 or higher, this is going to be changed to a more efficient version, Murmur3Partitioner.

Be warned that it is a pretty critical decision to choose a partitioner, because this determines what data stays where. It affects the SSTable structure. If you decide to change it, you need to clean the data directory. So, whatever decision is made for the partitioner at the start of the cluster is likely to stay for the life of the storage.

Cassandra provides three partitioners by default.

> Actually, there are five. But two are deprecated, so we will not be discussing them here. It is not recommended to use them. They are OrderPreservingPartitioner and CollatingOrderPreservingPartitioner.

The random partitioner

The random partitioner is the default partitioner till Version 1.1. It uses MD5 hash to generate hash values for row keys. Since hashes are not generated in any orderly manner, it does not guarantee any ordering. This means that two lexicographically close row keys can possibly be thrown into two different nodes. This random assignment of token to a key is what makes it suitable for even distribution of keys among nodes. This means it is highly unlikely that a balanced node is ever going to have hotspots.

The keys generated by a random partitioner may vary in the range of 0 to 2^{127} - 1. So, for the ith node in an N nodes cluster, the initial token can be calculated by 2127 * (i - 1) / N. The following is a simple Python code to generate the complete sequence of initial tokens for a random partitioner of a cluster of eight nodes:

```
# running in Python shell
>>>nodes = 8
>>> print ("\n".join(["Node #" + str(i+1) +": " + str((2 ** 127)*i/
nodes) for i in xrange(nodes) ]))

Node #1: 0
Node #2: 21267647932558653966460912964485513216
Node #3: 42535295865117307932921825928971026432
Node #4: 63802943797675961899382738893456539648
Node #5: 85070591730234615865843651857942052864
Node #6: 106338239662793269832304564822427566080
Node #7: 127605887595351923798765477786913079296
Node #8: 148873535527910577765226390751398592512
```

The byte-ordered partitioner

A byte-ordered partitioner, as the name suggests, generates tokens for row keys that are in the order of hexadecimal representations of the key. This makes it possible that rows are ordered by row keys and can iterate through rows as iterating through an ordered list. But this benefit comes with a major drawback: hotspots. The reason for the creation of a hotspot is uneven distribution of data across a cluster. If you have a cluster with 26 nodes, a partitioner such as ByteOrderedPartitioner, and each node is responsible for one letter. So, the first node is responsible for all the keys starting with A, the second for B, and so on. A column family that uses the usernames as row keys will have uneven data distribution across the ring. The data distribution will be skewed with nodes X, Q, and Z being very light, and nodes A and S being heavily loaded. This is bad for multiple reasons, but the most important one is generating a hotspot. The nodes with more data will be accessed more than the ones with less data. The overall performance of a cluster may be dropped down to the number of requests that a couple of highly loaded nodes can serve.

The best way to assign the initial token to a cluster using ByteOrderedPartitioner is to sample data and determine what keys are the best to assign as initial tokens to ensure an equally balanced cluster.

Let's take a hypothetical case where your keys of all keyspaces can be represented by five character strings from "00000" to "zzzzz". Here is how we generate initial tokens in Python:

```
>>> start = int("00000".encode('hex'), 16)
>>> end = int("zzzzz".encode('hex'), 16)
>>> range = end - start
>>> nodes = 8
>>> print "\n".join([ "Node #" + str(i+1) + ": %032x" % (start +
range*i/nodes)  for i in xrange(nodes) ])

Node #1: 00000000000000000000003030303030
Node #2: 00000000000000000000003979797979
Node #3: 00000000000000000000000042c2c2c2c2
Node #4: 00000000000000000000004c0c0c0c0b
Node #5: 00000000000000000000005555555555
Node #6: 00000000000000000000005e9e9e9e9e
Node #7: 00000000000000000000067e7e7e7e7
Node #8: 00000000000000000000007131313130
```

Remember, this is just an example; in a real case you will decide this only after evaluating the data. Or, probably want to have initial tokens assigned by UUIDs.

The Murmur3 partitioner

The Murmur3 partitioner is the new default for Cassandra Version 1.2 or higher. If you are starting a new cluster, it is suggested to keep the Murmur3 partitioner. It is not order preserving, and it has all the features of a random partitioner plus it is fast and provides better performance than a random partitioner. One difference with a random partitioner is that it generates token values between -2^{63} and $+2^{63}$.

If you are migrating from a previous version to 1.2 or higher, please make sure that you are using the same partitioner as the previous one. If you were using a default, it is likely that you were using a random partitioner. This will cause trouble, if you have not edited cassandra.yaml to change the new default Murmur3 partitioner back to a random partitioner.

To generate initial tokens, we'll again apply our familiar formula, but this time the start position is not zero, so the range of tokens is (end – start): $+263 - (-263) = 264$. Here is the simple Python script to do this:

```
>>> nodes = 8
>>> print "\n".join(["Node #" + str(i+1) + ": " + str( -(2 ** 63) + (2
** 64)*i/nodes) for i in xrange(nodes)] )

Node #1: -9223372036854775808
Node #2: -6917529027641081856
Node #3: -4611686018427387904
Node #4: -2305843009213693952
Node #5: 0
Node #6: 2305843009213693952
Node #7: 4611686018427387904
Node #8: 6917529027641081856
```

Snitches

Snitches are the way to tell Cassandra about the topology of cluster, and about nodes' locations and their proximities. There are two tasks that snitches help Cassandra with. They are as follows:

- **Replica placement**: As discussed in the section Replication from *Chapter 2, Cassandra Architecture*, depending on the configured replication factor, data gets written to more than one node. And snitches are the decision-making mechanism where the replicas are sent to. An efficient snitch will send place replicas in a manner that provides the highest availability of data.

- **Efficient read and write routing**: Snitches are all about defining cluster schema, and thus they help Cassandra in deciding the most efficient path to perform reads and writes.

Similar to partitioners, snitches are pluggable. You can plug in your own custom snitch by extending `org.apache.cassandra.locator.EndPointSnitch`. The `PropertyFileEndPointSnitch` class can be used as a guideline on how to write a snitch. To configure a snitch, you need to alter `endpoint_snitch` in `cassandra.yaml`:

```
endpoint_snitch: SimpleSnitch
```

For custom snitches, mention the fully-qualified class name of the snitch, assuming you have dropped the custom snitch `.class/.jar` file in Cassandra's `lib` directory.

Out of the box, Cassandra provides the snitches detailed in the following sections.

SimpleSnitch

`SimpleSnitch` is basically a do-nothing snitch. If you see the code, it basically returns `rack1` and `datacenter1` for whatever IP address the endpoint has. Since it discards any information that may be retrieved from the IP address, it is appropriate for installations where data center-related information is not available, or all the nodes are in the same data center.

This is the default snitch as of Version 1.1.11.

PropertyFileSnitch

`PropertyFileSnitch` is a way to explicitly tell Cassandra the relative location of various nodes in the clusters. It gives you a means to handpick the nodes to group under a data center and a rack. The location definition of each node in the cluster is stored in a configuration file, `cassandra-topology.properties`, which can be found under the `conf` directory (for a tarball installation, it is `<installation>/conf`; for repository installations, it is `/etc/cassandra`). Note that if you are using `PropertyFileSnitch`, all the nodes *must* have an identical topology file.

`cassandra-topology.properties` is a standard properties file with keys as the IP address of the node and value as `<data-center-name>:<rack-name>`; it is up to you what data center name and what rack name you give. Two nodes with the same data center name will be treated as nodes within a single data center. And two nodes with the same data center name and rack name combo will be treated as two nodes on the same rack.

Here is an example topology file:

```
# Cassandra Node IP=Data Center:Rack
# Data-center 1
10.110.6.30=DC1:RAC1
10.110.6.11=DC1:RAC1
10.110.4.30=DC1:RAC2
```

```
# Data-center 2
10.120.8.10=DC2:RAC1
10.120.8.11=DC2:RAC1

# Data-center 3
10.130.1.13=DC3:RAC1
10.130.2.10=DC3:RAC2

# default for unknown nodes
default=DC1:RAC0
```

DCX and RACX are commonly used patterns to denote a data center and a rack respectively. But you are free to choose anything that suits you. The default option is to take care of any node that is not listed in PropertyFileSnitch.

GossipingPropertyFileSnitch

Even with all the fancy naming and grouping, one thing that keeps bugging in PropertyFileSnitch is the manual effort to keep the topology files updated with every addition or removal of the node. GossipingPropertyFileSnitch is there to solve this problem. This snitch uses the gossip mechanism to propagate the information about the node's location.

In each node, you put a file named cassandra-rackdc.properties under the conf directory. This file contains two things: the name of the node's data center and the name of the node's rack. It looks like this:

```
dc=DC3
rack=RAC2
```

RackInferringSnitch

If SimpleSnitch is one end of the spectrum, where snitch does not assume anything, RackInferringSnitch is the other extreme of the spectrum. RackInferringSnitch uses an IP address to guess the data center and rack of the node. It assumes that the second octet of the IP address uniquely denotes a data center, and the third octet uniquely represents a rack within a data center. So, for 10.110.6.30, 10.110.6.4, 10.110.2.42, and 10.108.10.1, this snitch assumes that the first two nodes reside in the same data center and in the same rack, while the third node lives in the same data center but in a different rack. It assumes that the fourth node exists in a different data center than the rest of the nodes in the example:

```
    +---------> Data center
    |   +------> Rack
    |   |
10.110.6.30
```

This can be dangerous to use if your machines do not use this pattern for IP assignment to the machines in data centers.

EC2Snitch

Ec2Snitch is a snitch specially written for Amazon AWS installations. It uses the node's local metadata to get its availability zone and then breaks it into pieces to determine the rack and data center. Please note that rack and data center determined this way do not correspond to the physical location of hardware in Amazon's cloud facility, but it gives a pretty nice abstraction.

Ec2Snitch treats the region name as the data center name and availability zone as the rack name. It does not work cross-region. So, effectively, Ec2Snitch is the same as a single data center setup. If one of your nodes is in us-east-1a and another in us-east-1b, it means that you have two nodes in a data center named us-east in two racks, 1a and 1b.

EC2MultiRegionSnitch

Ec2Snitch does not work well if you decide to keep nodes across different EC2 regions. The reason being EC2Snitch uses private IPs, which will not work across regions (but do work across availability zones in a region).

If your cluster spans multiple regions, you should use Ec2MultiRegionSnitch.

> **EC2 users**: If you plan to distribute nodes in different regions, there is more than just a proper snitch that is needed to make nodes successfully communicate with one another. You need to change the following:
>
> - broadcast_address: This should be the public IP or public DNS of the node.
> - listen_address: This should be set to a private IP or DNS. But if not set, the hostname on EC2 is generally derived from the private IP, which is fine.
> - endpoint_snitch: This should be set to Ec2MultiRegionSnitch.
> - storage_port: The default 7000 is fine, but remember to open this port in the security group that holds Cassandra instances.

Replica placement strategies

Apart from putting data in various buckets based on nodes' tokens, Cassandra has to replicate the data depending on what replication factor is associated with the keyspace. Replica placement strategies come into action when Cassandra has to decide where a replica is needed to be placed.

There are two strategies that can be used based on the demand and structure of the cluster.

SimpleStrategy

SimpleStrategy places the data on the node that owns it based on the configured partitioner. It then moves to the next node (toward a higher bucket), places a replica, moves to the next node and places another, and so on, until the replication factor is met.

SimpleStrategy is blind to cluster topology. It does not check whether the next node to place the replica in is in the same rack or not. Thus, this may not be the most robust strategy to use to store data. What happens if all three replicas of a key range are physically located in the same rack (assuming RF=3) and there is a power failure of that rack; you lose access to some data until power is restored. This leads us into a rather smarter strategy, NetworkTopologyStrategy.

Although we discussed how bad SimpleStrategy can be, this is the default strategy. Plus, if you do not know the placement or any configuration details of your data center and you decide to stay in a single data center, NetworkTopologyStrategy cannot help you much.

NetworkTopologyStrategy

NetworkTopologyStrategy, as the name suggests, is a data-center- and rack-aware replica placement strategy. NetworkTopologyStrategy tries to avoid the pitfalls of SimpleStrategy by considering the rack name and data center names that it figures out from the configured snitch. With the appropriate strategy_option, stating how many replicas go to which data centers, NetworkTopologyStrategy is a very powerful and robust-mirrored database system.

NetworkTopologyStrategy requires the system admin to put a little extra thought into deciding appropriate values for initial tokens for multiple data center installations. For a single data center setup, initial tokens make up an evenly divided token range assigned to various nodes.

NetworkTopologyStrategy and multiple data center setups

Here is the issue with multiple data center setups. Suppose you have two data centers with each having three nodes in it; here is what the keyspace looks like:

```
CREATE KEYSPACE myKS
   WITH placement_strategy = 'NetworkTopologyStrategy'
   AND strategy_options={DC1:3, DC2:3};
```

It says that there are at least six nodes in the ring; keep three copies of each row in DC1 and three more copies in DC2.

Assume the system actually has four nodes in each data center, and you calculated the initial token by dividing the possible token range into eight equidistant values. If you assign the first four tokens to four nodes in DC1 and the rest to the nodes in DC2, you will end up having a *lopsided* data distribution.

Let's take an example. Say we have a partitioner that generates tokens from 0 to 200. The token distribution, if done in the way previously mentioned, will have a resulting ring that looks like the following figure. Since the replication factor is bound by the data center, all the data from 25 to 150 will go to one single node in Data Center 1, while other nodes in the data center will owe a relatively smaller number of keys. The same happens to Data Center 2, which has one overloaded node.

This creates a need for a mechanism that balances nodes within each data center. The first option is to divide the partitioner range by the number of nodes in each data center and assign the values to nodes in data centers. But, it wouldn't work, because no two nodes can have the same token.

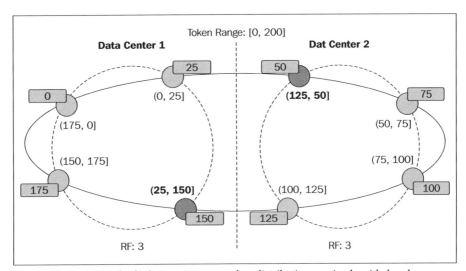

Figure 4.1: Multiple data centers – even key distribution causing lopsided nodes

There are two ways to avoid this imbalance in key distribution:

- **Offsetting tokens slightly**: This mechanism is the same as the one that we just discussed. The algorithm is as follows:

    1. Calculate the token range as if each data center is a ring.
    2. Offset the values that are duplicated by a small amount. Say by 1 or 10 or 100.

    Here is an example. Let's say we have a cluster spanning three data centers. `Data-center 1` and `Data-center 2` each has three nodes, and `Data-center 3` has two nodes. We use `RandomPartitioner`. Here is the split (the final value is used, the duplicates are offset):

    ```
    # Duplicates are offsett, final are assigned

    Data-center 1:
    node1:
    0 (final)

    node2:
    56713727820156410577229101238628035242 (final)

    node3:
    113427455640312821154458202477256070485 (final)

    Data-center 2:
    node1:
    0 (duplicate, offset to avoid collision)
    1 (final)

    node2:
    56713727820156410577229101238628035242 (duplicate, offset)
    56713727820156410577229101238628035243 (final)

    node3:
    113427455640312821154458202477256070485 (duplicate, offset)
    113427455640312821154458202477256070486 (final)

    Data-center 3:
    node1:
    0 (duplicate, offset)
    2 (final)

    node2:
    85070591730234615865843651857942052864 (final)
    ```

    If you draw the ring and re-evaluate the token ownership, you will find that all the data centers have balanced nodes.

- **Alternating token assignment**: This is a much simpler technique than the previous one, but it works when all the data centers have an equal number of nodes, which is a pretty common setup.

  In this methodology, we divide the token range by the total number of nodes across all the clusters. Then we take the first token value, assign it to a node in `Data-center 1`, take a second token and assign it to a node in the second data center, and so on. Keep revolving through the data centers and assigning the next initial token to nodes until all the nodes are done (and all the tokens are exhausted).

  For a three data centers' setup, with each having two nodes, here are the details:

```
$ python -c 'print "\n".join([str((2 ** 127)*i/6) for i in
xrange(6) ])'

0
28356863910078205288614550619314017621
56713727820156410577229101238628035242
85070591730234615865843651857942052864
113427455640312821154458202477256070485
141784319550391026443072753096570088106
Data-center1: node1
0

Data-center2: node1
28356863910078205288614550619314017621

Data-center3: node1
56713727820156410577229101238628035242

Data-center1: node2
85070591730234615865843651857942052864

Data-center2: node2
113427455640312821154458202477256070485

Data-center3: node2
141784319550391026443072753096570088106
```

Launching a cluster with a script

Now that we have configured the machines, we know the cluster settings to carry out, what snitch to use, and what should be the initial tokens, we'll download the latest Cassandra install on multiple machines, set it up, and start it. But it is too much work to do it manually.

We will see a custom script that does all these for us—after all we are dealing with a large data and a large number of machines, so doing all manually can be prone to error and exhausting (and more importantly, there's no fun!). This script is available on GitHub at `https://github.com/naishe/mastering_cassandra`. You may tweak it as per your needs and work with it.

There are two scripts: `install_cassandra.sh` and `upload_and_execute.sh`. The former is the one that is supposed to be executed on the to-be Cassandra nodes, and the latter is the one that uploads the former to all the nodes, passes the appropriate initial token, and executes it. It is the latter that you need to execute on your local machine and make sure both scripts are in the same directory from where you are executing. If you are planning to use this script, you may need to change a couple of variables at the top.

Here is the script configured to set up a three-node cluster on Amazon EC2 machines. Please note that it uses `EC2Snitch`, so it does not need to set up any snitch configuration file as it would have, if it was using `PropertyFileSnitch` or `GossippingPropertyFileSnitch`. If you are using those snitches, you may need to upload those files to appropriate locations in remote machines too:

```
#install_cassandra.sh

#!/bin/bash
set -e

# This script does the following:
# 1. downloadcassandra
# 2. create directories
# 3. updatescassandra.yaml with
#       cluster_name
#       seeds
#       listen_address
#       rpc_address
#       initial_token
#       endpoint_snitch
# 4. start Cassandra

#SYNOPSYS
function printHelp(){
```

```
   cat << EOF
Synopsis:
  $0 <initial_token>
  Downloads, installs, configures, and starts Cassandra.
  Required Parameters:
<initial_token>: initial token for this node
EOF
}


if [ $# -lt 1 ] ; then
printHelp
  exit 1
fi

# VARIABLES !!! EDIT AS YOUR CONFIG
download_url='http://mirror.sdunix.com/apache/cassandra/1.1.11/apache-
cassandra-1.1.11-bin.tar.gz'
name='apache-cassandra-1.1.11'
install_dir='/opt'
data_dir='/mnt/cassandra-data'
logging_dir='/mnt/cassandra-logs'

# CASSANDRA CONFIG !!! EDIT AS YOUR CONFIG
cluster_name='"My Cluster"'
seeds='"10.99.9.67"' #yeah, the double quotes within the quotes!
listen_address=''
rpc_address=''
initial_token="$1"
endpoint_snitch="Ec2Snitch"
cassandra_user="$2"

echo "--- DOWNLOADING CASSANDRA"
wget -P /tmp/ ${download_url}

echo "--- EXTRACTING..."
sudo tar xzf /tmp/apache-cassandra-1.1.11-bin.tar.gz -C ${install_dir}

echo "--- SETTING UP SYM-LINK"
sudo ln -s ${install_dir}/${name} ${install_dir}/cassandra

echo "--- CREATE DIRECTORIES"
sudo mkdir -p ${data_dir}/data ${data_dir}/commitlog ${logging_dir}
sudo chown -R ${USER} ${data_dir} ${logging_dir}
```

```
echo "--- UPDATING CASSANDRA YAML (in place)"
sudo cp ${install_dir}/cassandra/conf/cassandra.yaml ${install_dir}/
cassandra/conf/cassandra.yaml.BKP

sudo sed -i \
  -e "s/^cluster_name.*/cluster_name: ${cluster_name}/g" \
  -e "s/\(\-\s*seeds:\).*/\1 ${seeds}/g" \
  -e "s/^listen_address.*/listen_address: ${listen_address}/g" \
  -e "s/^rpc_address.*/rpc_address: ${rpc_address}/g" \
  -e "s/^initial_token.*/initial_token: ${initial_token}/g" \
  -e "s/^endpoint_snitch.*/endpoint_snitch: ${endpoint_snitch}/g" \
  -e "s|/var/lib/cassandra/data|${data_dir}/data|g" \
  -e "s|/var/lib/cassandra/commitlog|${data_dir}/commitlog|g" \
  -e "s|/var/lib/cassandra/saved_caches|${data_dir}/saved_caches|g" \
  ${install_dir}/cassandra/conf/cassandra.yaml
sudo sed -i \
  -e "s|/var/log/cassandra/system.log|${logging_dir}/system.log|g" \
  ${install_dir}/cassandra/conf/log4j-server.properties

echo "--- STARTING CASSANDRA"
# NOHUP, ignore SIGNUP signal to kill Cassandra Daemon
nohup ${install_dir}/cassandra/bin/cassandra> ${logging_dir}/startup.
log &

sleep 5

echo "--- INSTALLATION FINISHED"
exit 0
```
- -
```
# The following is a code for upload_and_execute.sh
#!/bin/bash
set -e

# This script:
#  - takes array of node addresses
#  - generates initial-tokens for RandomPartitioner
#  - uploads the install_cassandra.sh and executes it

## !!! Change these variables to suit your settings
identity_file="${HOME}/.ec2/prodadmin.pem"
remote_user="ec2-user"
install_script="${HOME}/Desktop/install_cassandra.sh"
servers=( 'c1.mydomain.com' 'c2.mydomain.com' 'c2.mydomain.com' )
```

```
nodes=${#servers[@]}
init_tokens=( 'python -c "print ' '.join([str((2 ** 127)*i/${nodes})
for i in xrange(${nodes}) ])"' )
i=0

for server in ${servers[@]} ; do
  ikey=${init_tokens[$i]}

  echo ">> Uploading script to ${server} to remote user's home"
  scp -i ${identity_file} ${install_script} ${remote_
user}@${server}:~/install_cassandra.sh

  echo ">> Executing script with initial_key=${ikey}"
  ssh -t -i ${identity_file} ${remote_user}@${server} "sudo chmod a+x
~/install_cassandra.sh && ~/install_cassandra.sh ${ikey}"

  echo ">> Installation finished for server: ${server}"
  echo "-----------------------------------------"
  i=$(($i+1))
done

echo ">> Cluster initialization is Finished."
exit 0;
```

When the author executes this script for the demonstration of a three-nodes cluster, it takes less than two minutes to get up and running. Here is how it looks:

```
$ ./upload_and_execute.sh

>> Uploading script to c1.mydomain.com to remote user's home
install_cassandra.sh     100% 2484     2.4KB/s   00:00
>> Executing script with initial_key=0
--- DOWNLOADING CASSANDRA
[-- snip --]
Saving to: '/tmp/apache-cassandra-1.1.11-bin.tar.gz'
100%[=========>] 1,29,73,061  598KB/s   in 22s

--- EXTRACTING...
--- SETTING UP SYM-LINK
--- CREATE DIRECTORIES
--- UPDATING CASSANRA YAML (in place)
--- STARTING CASSANDRA
--- INSTALLATION FINISHED
>> Installation finished for server: c1.mydomain.com
-----------------------------------------
```

```
>> Uploading script to c2.mydomain.com to remote user's home
[-- snip --]
>> Executing script with initial_key=56713727820156410577229101238628
035242
--- DOWNLOADING CASSANDRA
[-- snip --]


 --- EXTRACTING...
--- SETTING UP SYM-LINK
--- CREATE DIRECTORIES
--- UPDATING CASSANRA YAML (in place)
--- STARTING CASSANDRA
--- INSTALLATION FINISHED
[-- snip --]
----------------------------------------------

>> Uploading script to c3.mydomain.com to remote user's home
[-- snip -]
--- DOWNLOADING CASSANDRA
[-- snip --]

--- EXTRACTING...
--- SETTING UP SYM-LINK
--- CREATE DIRECTORIES
--- UPDATING CASSANRA YAML (in place)
--- STARTING CASSANDRA
--- INSTALLATION FINISHED
----------------------------------------------

>> Cluster initialization is Finished.
```

Let's check what newly-launched cluster looks like:

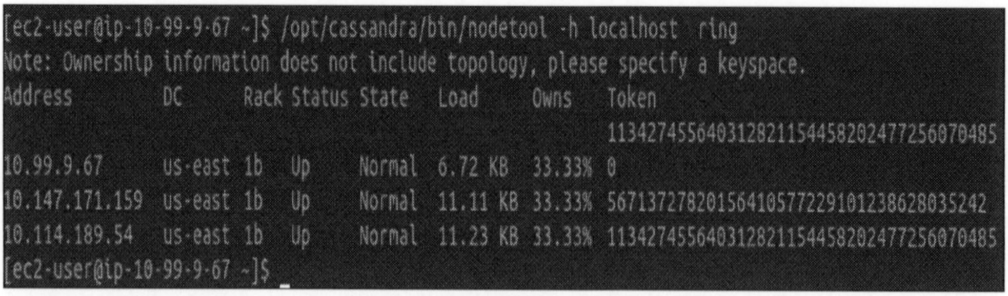

```
[ec2-user@ip-10-99-9-67 ~]$ /opt/cassandra/bin/nodetool -h localhost  ring
Note: Ownership information does not include topology, please specify a keyspace.
Address         DC       Rack Status State  Load      Owns    Token
                                                               113427455640312821154458202477256070485
10.99.9.67      us-east  1b   Up      Normal 6.72 KB   33.33%  0
10.147.171.159  us-east  1b   Up      Normal 11.11 KB  33.33%  56713727820156410577229101238628035242
10.114.189.54   us-east  1b   Up      Normal 11.23 KB  33.33%  113427455640312821154458202477256070485
[ec2-user@ip-10-99-9-67 ~]$
```

Figure 4.2: The ring query showing all three nodes are up and running with tokens equally distributed among them

Creating a keyspace

It may strike you as odd why creating a keyspace is discussed here in a chapter that is oriented more toward system administration tasks. The reason to do this is that keyspace creation is hard-linked with the way you have set the snitch.

Unless you are using `SimpleSnitch`, you should use `NetworkTopologyStrategy` as the replica placement strategy. It needs to know the replication factor for the keyspace for each data center.

So, if you have `PropertyFileSnitch` or `GossipingPropertyFileSnitch`, your keyspace creation looks like the following code:

```
CREATE KEYSPACE myKS
  WITH placement_strategy = 'NetworkTopologyStrategy'
  AND strategy_options={DC1:3, DC2:3};
```

Here, `strategy_options` has keys as data center names defined in snitch configuration files and values are replication factors in each data center.

In EC2-related snitches, `Ec2MultiRegionSnitch` or `Ec2Snitch`, the data center name is nothing but the name of the region as it appears in the availability zone. So, for `us-east-1a`, the data center is `us-east`. The command to create a space is as follows (for `EC2MultiRegionSnitch`):

```
CREATE KEYSPACE myKS
  WITH placement_strategy = 'NetworkTopologyStrategy'
  AND strategy_options={us-east:3,us-west:3};
```

So, if you have set the replication factor smartly, and your queries make use of the right consistency level, your request will never have to travel beyond the one data center (if all the replicas in that data center are up).

For `SimpleSnitch`, you just specify `replication_factor` as the strategy option as it is oblivious to the data center or the rack.

```
createkeyspacemyKS
  with placement_strategy = 'SimpleStrategy'
  and strategy_options = {replication_factor : 2}
```

Authorization and authentication

By default, Cassandra is open to everyone who has access to Cassandra's node address and port. Since most of the time it's just your applications that access Cassandra and generally the whole application ecosystem is heavily guarded (by VPN, VPC, and firewall), it may not bother you that Cassandra has no security.

To configure some sort of authentication and authorization mechanism, one may use the simple authenticator that is provided by Cassandra. `SimpleAuthenticator` is not great; it has a pretty vanilla security mechanism. To enable `SimpleAuthenticator`, you need to replace the allow-all configuration in `cassandra.yaml`:

```
authenticator: org.apache.cassandra.auth.SimpleAuthenticator
authority: org.apache.cassandra.auth.SimpleAuthority
```

Apart from this, it is a file-based security, so you need to provide two files: one for the username and password, namely, `passwd.properties`, and another for user permission on keyspaces or column families, called `access.properties`. Here is how they are formatted:

```
# passwd.properties
leonardo=p@zzwd
tjadmin=cmplx314159

# access.properties
myAppKeyspace.<rw>=leonardo,tjadmin

analyticsKS.<rw>=tjadmin

analyticsKS.raw_apache_log_cf.<ro>=leonardo
```

Basically, the `passwd` file is a simple key-value pair, where the key is the username and the value is the password. The `access` property file provides a simple blanket permission. The way the `access.properties` file is formatted is as follows:

```
<keyspace>[.<column_family>].<permission> = <user_name>
```

The first fragment is `keyspace`, the second can optionally be the column family name in that keyspace, and the third is `permission`. The `permission` parameter has to be one of read-only, `<ro>`, or read-write, `<rw>`, type (with angled brackets).

Once you are done with security settings, you need to change the way Cassandra starts. You need to add these files as Java default properties (assuming you kept it under the `/conf` directory). Here is what Cassandra's start commands look like:

```
$ cassandra -Dpasswd.properties=conf/passwd.properties -Daccess.
properties=conf/access.properties
```

If you do not want to distort your start command, the same effect can be achieved by adding these default properties to `JAVA_OPTS` in the Cassandra shell script (`bin/cassandra`). Assuming `/opt/cassandra` is where Cassandra is installed, append the following code (after placing a space):

```
$ cassandra -Dpasswd.properties=/opt/cassandra/conf/passwd.properties
-Daccess.properties=/opt/cassandra/conf/access.properties
```

to this:

```
cassandra_parms="-Dlog4j.configuration=log4j-server.properties
-Dlog4j.defaultInitOverride=true"s
```

This is pretty basic authentication, which definitely does not serve the needs of all. It requires files to manually manage authentication on all nodes. You may write your own authenticator and authority mechanism by implementing `org.apache.cassandra.auth.IAuthenticator` and `org.apache.cassandra.auth.IAuthority` interfaces, respectively. Another reason to dislike these is because from Version 1.0 or higher, they are moved to the examples directory and they are permanently removed from 1.2.2 or higher. They are replaced by `CassandraAuthorizer` and `PasswordAuthenticator`. Cassandra 1.2.2 or higher has many new and improved security features. If you are using Version 1.2.2 or higher, refer to *Chapter 9, Introduction to CQL 3 and Cassandra 1.2*.

Summary

We have done a complete cluster installation. It is not as difficult as it seems. Once we have fixed the variables and decided what hardware requirement is needed, it is just a matter of running a shell script that downloads, installs, and configures Cassandra. Multiple data center setups are equally simple, when you figure out initial tokens. Many variables depend on your particular use case, but if you do not have a particular specification in mind, go with the suggested ones or the default one. It is generally good.

Setting up a cluster is probably a one-time task for an organization. It is likely that your first cluster will be just a couple of nodes. It is equally likely that you will stick with that cluster for first production, or at least till you plan to make the first release with Cassandra in your system. In production, the first couple of things that comes to everyone's mind are whether the software is tuned to perform its best? What happens when things start to break? What if we needed to ramp up the servers? How safe is our data? How would we know if things are failing? Where to look for help about things that no one in the team knows? Chances are that you will be expected to answer these questions. So, you would want to know the answers before you are asked them. The next few chapters are about all these questions.

Performance Tuning

5

Cassandra is all about speed—quick installation, fast reads, and fast writes. You have got your application optimized, minimized network trips by batching, and denormalized the data to get maximum information in one request, but still the performance is not what you read over the Web and in various blogs. You start to doubt if the claims actually measure. Hold! You may need to tune things up.

This chapter will discuss how to get a sense of a Cassandra cluster's capacity and have a performance number handy to back up your claims. It then dives into the various settings that affect read and write throughputs, a couple of JVM tuning parameters, and finally a short discussion on how scaling horizontally and vertically can improve the performance.

Stress testing

Before you start to claim the performance numbers of your Cassandra backend based on numbers that you have read elsewhere, it is important to perform your own stress testing. It is very easy to do that in Cassandra as it provides special tooling for stress testing. It is a good idea to customize the parameters of the stress test to represent a use case that is closer to what your application is going to do. And this will save a lot of heated discussion later due to discrepancies in the load test and the actual throughput that the software is able to pull out of the setting.

The load test tool is found under the Cassandra installation directory under tools as `tools/bin/cassandra-stress`. Here are some useful parameters:

```
-d, --nodes: CSV list of nodes to run the queries against
-o, --operation: Operation to perform, default: insert
-R, --replication-strategy: Replication strategy, def: Simple
-O, --strategy-properties: in <dc>:<RF>,<dc1>:<RF1> format
-U, --comparator: column comparator
```

```
-e, --consistency-level: consistency level, default: ONE
-c, --columns: Number of columns per key, default: 5
-n, --num-keys: Number of keys, default: 1Mn
-S, --column-size: Size of column values, default: 34 bytes
-L, --enable-cql: Perform operations using CQL
```

Let's take an example application, say a chat application that stores each chat session in a row and each message in a separate column. Let's assume that each session has an average message transfer of 500 messages (500 columns), each message has 100 UTF8 characters (300 bytes/column), our servers are located in an Amazon EC2 environment but in a single region (Ec2Snitch, NetworkTopologyStrategy), the columns are sorted by time (the TimeUUIDType comparator), and that we want to read and write consistency level 2 (for 3 server configurations of ours, R + W > N).

We will load test this against a three servers setup which has all defaults and in which initial_token is equidistant. Each machine has the following specification (standard M1.large instances):

```
Memory: 7.5 GiB
CPU: 2 Virtual cores with 2 ECU each, 64 bit
Hard disc: 840 GiB (RAID0)
OS: CentOS 5.4
Cassandra: version 1.1.11
```

Here is the test run command:

```
$ tools/bin/cassandra-stress \
 -d 10.99.9.67,10.147.171.159,10.114.189.54 \
 -o INSERT \
 -R org.apache.cassandra.locator.NetworkTopologyStrategy \
 -O us-east:2 \
 -U TimeUUIDType \
 -e QUORUM \
 -c 5 \
 -S 300 \
 -y Standard \
 -t 200  \
 -n 1000000 \
 -F 10000
```

It says insert 1 million records with 5 columns in a row, under 10,000 unique row keys in a standard column family using 200 threads, sorted by `TimeUUID`, with consistency level as QUORUM. This will ensure that each row roughly has 500 columns. The test result shows that the inserts rate stays about 5000 inserts per second. There are a couple of blips, maybe due to a MemTable flush or a compaction in the process. This is shown in the following figure.

On the same setup, let's execute a read stress test:

```
$ tools/bin/cassandra-stress \
 -d 10.99.9.67,10.147.171.159,10.114.189.54 \
 -o READ \
 -R org.apache.cassandra.locator.NetworkTopologyStrategy \
 -O us-east:2 \
 -U TimeUUIDType \
 -e QUORUM \
 -c 5 \
 -S 300 \
 -y Standard \
 -t 200 \
 -n 1000000 \
 -F 10000
```

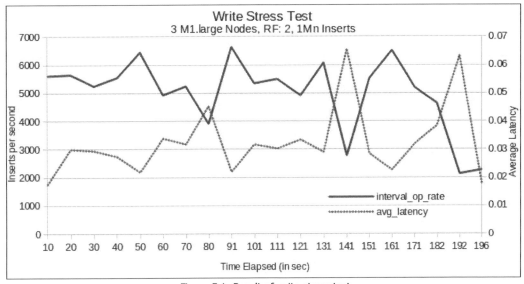

Figure 5.1: Result of write stress test

With these parameters, the reads stay just below 8000 reads per second. The reads stay rather stable. The statistics for the read performance is described in the following figure.

This is the most basic stress test that gives an overall idea of what can be achieved from a Cassandra setup. There may be multiple intrinsic (bad choices, high I/O due to frequent MemTable flushes, and so on) or extrinsic (locking in application code, poor inter-node connectivity, and so on) configurations that can differ the performance of your setup from what is mentioned here. But you should run this test anyway to get the baseline statistics of your system.

Not all test cases can be stress tested using Cassandra's built-in stress tool. Based on what your application does, you may need to write your own stress test that represents your application's model behavior.

Another load test mechanism that is worth looking at is **Yahoo! Cloud Serving Benchmark (YCSB)**. You can read more on YCSB at `https://github.com/ brianfrankcooper/YCSB/wiki/Getting-Started`. It is a framework with which you can add a database interface as a plugin and run a load against it. Cassandra is one of the many databases that it supports out of the box. Details of this tool are out of the scope of this book, but you can easily learn how to use it from its excellent documentation on GitHub.

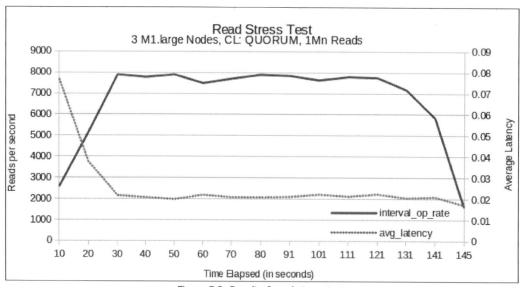

Figure 5.2: Result of read stress test

Performance tuning

With stress tests completed, you might have identified the key areas for improvement. The broadest area that you can categorize performance tuning into is the read and write performance area. But there may be worries such as the I/O contention (compaction tuning) on servers. Apart from these, there may be several external factors, for example, slow disk, shared resources (such as shared CPU), and connectivity issues. We are not going to discuss external factors here. The assumption is that you will have sufficient resources allocated to the Cassandra servers. This section will discuss various tweaks to get Cassandra performing the best that it can within the given resources.

Write performance

Cassandra writes are sequential; all it needs to do is to append to commit log and put in memory. There is not much that can be done internally to Cassandra settings to tweak writes. However, if disk writes are fast, and somehow I/O contentions can be lowered due to multiple things that happen in the Cassandra life cycle, such as flushing MemTable to disk, compaction, and writes to commit logs, it can boost the write performance.

So, having fast disks, and having commit logs and datafiles in separate dedicated hard disks directly attached to the system, will improve write throughput.

Read performance

Reading in Cassandra is rather complicated. It may need to read from the memory or from the hard drive, and it may need to aggregate multiple fragments of data from different SSTables, it may require to get data across multiple nodes, take care of tombstones, and validate, digest, and get tombstones back to the client. But the common pattern of increasing the read performance in Cassandra is the same as any other data system—caching: to keep the most frequent data in memory, minimize disk access, and keep search path/hops small on disk. Also, a fast network and lesser networks access as well as a low read consistency level may help.

Choosing the right compaction strategy

With each flush of a MemTable, an immutable SSTable gets created. So, with time, there will be numerous SSTables if their numbers are not limited by an external process. The main problem with this is slow read speed. A search may need to hop through multiple SSTables to fetch the requested data. The compaction process executes repeatedly to merge these SSTables into one larger SSTable, which has a cleaned-up version of the data that was scattered in fragments into different smaller SSTables littered with tombstones. This also means that compaction is pretty disk I/O intensive, so the longer and more frequently it runs, the more contention it will produce for other Cassandra processes that require to read from or write to the disc.

Cassandra provides two compaction strategies as of Version 1.1.11. A compaction strategy is a column family level setting, so you can set an appropriate compaction strategy for a column family based on its behavior.

Size tiered compaction strategy

This is the default strategy. The way it works is as soon as the `min_threadhold` (default value is 4) number of equal-sized SSTables are available, they get compacted into one big SSTable. As the compacted SSTables get bigger and bigger, it is rare that large SSTables gets compacted further. This leaves some very large SSTables and many smaller SSTables. This also means that row updates will be scattered in multiple SSTables and we will require more time to process multiple SSTables to get the fragments of a row.

With the occasional burst of I/O load during compaction, `SizeTieredCompactionStrategy` is a good fit where rows are inserted and never mutated. This will ensure that all the bits of rows are in one SSTable. This is a write and I/O friendly strategy.

Leveled compaction

`LeveledCompactionStrategy` is a relatively new introduction to Cassandra, and the concepts are taken from Google's LevelDB project. Unlike size tiered compaction, this has many small and fixed sized SSTables grouped into levels. Within a level, the SSTables do not have any overlap. Leveled compaction works in such a way that for most cases, a row will require to access just one SSTable. This is a big advantage over the size tiered version. It makes `LeveledCompactionStrategy` a better choice for reading heavy column families. Updates are favored in level compaction as it tries to spread rows as low as possible.

The downside of leveled compaction is high I/O. There is no apparent benefit if data is of write-once type. It's because in that case, even with the size tiered strategy, the data is going to stay in one SSTable.

Anyone coming from the traditional database world who has ever worked on scaling up read requests and speeding up data retrievals knows that caching is the most effective way to speed up the reads. It prevents database hits for the data that is already fetched (in the recent past) for the price of extra RAM that the caching mechanism uses to store the data temporarily. So, you have a third-party caching system such as Memcached that manages it for you. The nasty side of third-party caching mechanisms is the whole managing-the-distributed-cache part. It may intrude into the application code.

Cassandra provides an inbuilt caching mechanism that can be really helpful if your application requires heavy read capability. There are two types of caches in Cassandra, row cache and key cache. Refer to the following figure:

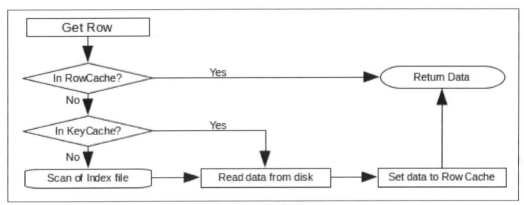

Figure 5.3: How caching works

Row cache

Row cache is true caching in the sense that it caches a complete row of data and returns immediately without touching the hard drive. It is fast and complete. Row cache stores data off heap (if JNA is available), which means it will be unaffected by the garbage collector.

Cassandra is capable of storing really large rows of data with about 2 billion columns in it. This means that the cache is going to take up as much space, which may not be what you wanted. So, while row cache is generally good to boost the read speed, it is best suited for not-so-large rows. So, you can cache the users column family in row cache, but it will be a bad idea to have the `users_browsing_history` or `users_click_pattern` column family in a row cache.

Key cache

Key cache is to store the row keys in memory. Key caches are default for a column family. It does not take much space but it boosts performance to a large extent (but less than the row cache). As of Cassandra Version 1.1.11, it assigns a minimum of 100 MB or 5 percent of the JVM heap memory to the key cache.

Key caches contain information about the location of the row in SSTables, so it's just one disk seek to retrieve the data. This simplifies the process of looking through a sampled index and then scanning the index file for the key range. Since it does not take up as much space as a row cache, you can have a large number of keys cached in a relatively small amount of memory.

Cache settings

The general rule of thumb is, for all normal purposes, a key cache is good enough. You may tweak a key cache to stretch its limits. You'd buy more for a little increase in the key cache settings. Row caching, on the other hand, needs a little thinking to do. A good fit data for row cache is same as a good fit data for a third-party caching mechanism; the data should be read mostly, and mutated occasionally. Rows with a smaller number of columns are better suited. Before you go ahead with cache tweaking, you may want to check the current cache usage. You can use jConsole as discussed in *Chapter 7, Monitoring*, to see the cache hit. In jConsole, the cache statistics can be obtained by expanding the org.apache.cassandra.db menu. It shows the cache hit rate and the number of hits and the cache size for a particular node and column family.

Cache settings are mostly global as of Version 1.1.11. The settings can be altered in cassandra.yaml. At column family level, the only choices that you have are what cache type to use or if you should use any cache at all. The options are: all, keys_only, rows_only, and none. The all option is to use both caches; the none option is to use none of the two. Here is an example:

```
CREATE COLUMN FAMILY rowcachedCF WITH COMPARATOR = UTF8Type AND
CACHING = rows_only;
```

Here are the caching specific settings in cassandra.yaml:

- key_cache_size_in_mb: By default, this is set to 100 MB or 5 percent of the heap size. To disable it globally, set it to zero.

- key_cache_save_period: The time after which the cache is saved to disk to avoid a cold start. A cold start is when a node starts afresh and gets marred by lots of requests; with no caching at the time of start, it will take some time to get a cache loaded with the most requested keys. During this time, responses may be sluggish.

The caches are saved under a directory as described by the `saved_caches_directory` setting in the `.yaml` file. We configured this during the cluster deployment in *Chapter 4, Deploying a Cluster*. The default value for this setting is 14,400 seconds:

- `key_cache_keys_to_save`: Number of keys to save. It is commented to store all the keys. In general, it is okay to let it be commented.

- `row_cache_size_in_mb`: Row caching is disabled by default by setting this attribute to zero. Set it to an appropriate positive integer. It may be worth taking a look at `nodetool -h <hostname> cfstats` and taking the row mean size and the number of keys into account.

- `row_cache_save_period`: Similar to `key_cache_save_period`, this saves the cache to the saved caches directory after the prescribed time. Unlike key caches, row caches are bigger, and saving to disk is an I/O expensive task to do. Compared to the fuss of saving a row cache, it does not give proportional benefit. It is okay to leave it as zero, that is, disabled.

- `row_cache_keys_to_save`: Same as `key_cache_keys_to_save`.

- `row_cache_provider`: Out of the box, Cassandra provides two mechanisms to enable a row cache:

   ◦ `SerializingCacheProvider`: A modern cache provider that stores data off-heap. It is faster and has a smaller memory footprint than the other implementation. It is the default cache provider and it is preferred to read-heavy and mutate-light types of environment, which is where caching shines, anyway. Being off-heap means a smaller JVM heap, which means faster garbage collection and hence smaller GC pauses.

   ◦ `ConcurrentLinkedHashCacheProvider`: In JVM heap caching, its performance is low than the other cache mechanism. It performs better for update-heavy cases with its update feature in place.

- You can plug in your own cache provider by putting a `.jar` or `.class` file in Cassandra's installation's `lib` directory and mentioning a fully-qualified class name as `row_cache_provider`. The class must implement `org.apache.cassandra.cache.IRowCacheProvider`.

Enabling compression

Column family compression is a very effective mechanism to improve read and write throughput. As you might expect, (any) compression leads to a compact representation of data at the cost of some CPU cycles. Enabling compression on a column family makes the disk representation of the data (SSTables) terse. That means efficient disk utilization, lesser I/O, and a little extra burden to the CPU. In case of Cassandra, the tradeoff between I/O and the CPU, due to compression, almost always yields favorable results. The cost of CPU performing compression and decompression is less than what it takes to read more data from a disc.

Compression setting is done column family wise; if you do not mention any compression mechanism, `SnappyCompressor` is applied to the column family by default. Here is how you assign a compression type:

```
# Create column family with compression settings
CREATE COLUMN FAMILY compressedCF
WITH compression_options =
{
 'sstable_compression':'SnappyCompressor',
 'chunk_length_kb':64
};
```

Let's see what compression options we have:

- `sstable_compression`: This parameter specifies which compressor is used to compress a disk representation of an SSTable when a MemTable is flushed. Compression takes place at the time of flush. As of Cassandra Version 1.1.11, it provides two compressors out of the box: `SnappyCompressor` and `DeflateCompressor`.

 Cassandra Version 1.2.2+ has another compressor named `LZ4Compressor`. LZ4 is 50 percent faster than Snappy compression. If you think that it may worth reading more about it, read this JIRA ticket https://issues.apache.org/jira/browse/CASSANDRA-5038

- `SnappyCompressor` is faster to deflate, but less effective in terms of compression when compared to `DeflateCompressor`. This means that `SnappyCompressor` will take up a little extra space, but it will have higher read speed.

- Like everything else in Cassandra, compressors are pluggable. You can write your own compressor by implementing `org.apache.cassandra.io.compress.ICompressor`, compiling the compressor, and putting the `.class` or `.jar` files in the `lib` directory. Provide the fully-qualified class name of the compression as `sstable_compression`.

- `chunk_length_kb`: Chunk length is the smallest slice of the row that gets decompressed during reads. Depending on the query pattern and the median size of the rows, this parameter can be tweaked in such a way that it is big enough to not have to deflate multiple chunks, but it should be small enough to not have to decompress excessive unnecessary data. Practically, it is hard to guesstimate this. The most common suggestion is to keep it as 64 KB if you do not have any idea.

- Compression can be added, removed, or altered anytime during the lifetime of a column family. In general, compression always boosts performance and it is a great way to maximize the utilization of disk space. Compression gives double to quadruple reduction in data size when compared to an uncompressed version. So, you should always set a compression to start with; it can be disabled pretty easily:

```
# Disable Compression
UPDATE COLUMN FAMILY compressedCF
WITH compression_options = null;
```

It must be noted that enabling compression may not immediately halve the space used by SSTables. The compression is applied to the SSTables that get created after the compression is enabled. With time, as compaction merges SSTables, older SSTables get compressed.

Tuning the bloom filter

Accessing a disk is the most expensive task. Cassandra thinks twice before needing to read from a disk. The bloom filter can help to identify which SSTables may contain the row that the client has requested. But the bloom filter, being a problematic data structure, yields false positives (refer to *Chapter 1*, *Quick Start*). The more the false positives, the more the SSTables need to be read before realizing whether the row actually exists in the SSTable or not.

False positive ratio is basically the probability of getting a true value from the bloom filter of an SSTable for a key that does not exist in it. In simpler words, if the false positive ratio is 0.5, chances are that 50 percent of the time you end up looking into an index file for the key, but it is not there. So, why not set the false positive ratio to zero; never have to make a disk touch without being 100 percent sure. Well, it comes with a cost—memory consumption. If you remember from *Chapter 1*, *Quick Start*, the smaller the size of the bloom filter, the smaller the memory consumption; the more the likelihood of the collision of hashes, the higher the false positive. So, as you decrease the false positive value, your memory consumption shoots up. So, we need a balance here.

The default value of the bloom filter false positive ratio is set to 0.000744. To disable the bloom filter, that is, to allow all the queries to SSTable—all false positive— this ratio needs to be set to 1.0. You may need to bypass the bloom filter by setting the false positive ratio to 1 if you have to scan all SSTables for data mining or other analytical applications.

Here is how you can create a column family with false positive chance as 0.01:

```
# Create column family with false positive chance = 0.01
CREATE COLUMN FAMILY myCFwithHighFP
WITH bloom_filter_fp_chance = 0.01;
```

You may alter the false positive chance on an up-and-running cluster without any need to reboot. But the false positive chance is applied only to the newer SSTables— created by means of flush or via compaction.

You can always see the bloom filter chance by running the `describe` command in `cassandra-cli` or by running a `nodetool` request for `cfstats`. Node tool displays the current ratio too.

```
# Incassandra-cli
describe myCFwithHighFP;
ColumnFamily: myCFwithHighFP
[-- snip -]
Bloom Filter FP chance: 0.01
[-- snip --]
```

In case you want to force the new value of false positive across all nodes, you need to execute `upgradesstable` on the column family via `nodetool`.

```
# enforcing new settings to all the sstables of a CF
$ /opt/cassandra/bin/nodetool -h 10.147.171.159 \
upgradesstablesmyKeyspacemyCFwithHighFP
```

More tuning via cassandra.yaml

`cassandra.yaml` is the hub of almost all the global settings for the node or the cluster. It is well documented, and you can learn very easily by reading this documentation. Listed here are some of those properties from Cassandra Version 1.1.11 and short descriptions of them. It is suggested that a reader should refer `cassandra.yaml` of his version of Cassandra and read the details there.

index_interval

Each SSTable is accompanied by a primary index that tells you which row is where (offset) in the SSTable. It is inefficient to read a primary index from a disk to seek from SSTables; moreover, if the bloom filter was false positive, it is a waste of computational power. Cassandra keeps the sampled index values in memory, which is a subset of the primary index. A sampled index is created by choosing one entry out of all `index_interval` entries from the primary index. This means that the smaller the `index_interval`, the larger the sampled index, the larger the memory usage, the lesser the disk lookups, the better the read performance.

The default is 128. It is suggested to use between the values 128 and 512. To avoid storing too many samples (that overshoots memory) or too few samples (so that samples do not provide much leverage compared to directly reading from the primary index), you may use a decent default index interval with a larger key cache size to get a much better performance than `index_interval` alone.

commitlog_sync

As we know from *Chapter 1, Quick Start*, Cassandra provides durable writes by the virtue of appending the new writes to the commit logs. This is not entirely true. To guarantee that each write is made in such a manner that a hard reboot/crash does not wash off any data, it must be fsync'd to the disk. Flushing commit logs after each write is detrimental to write performance due to slow disk seeks. Instead of doing that, Cassandra periodically (by default, `commitlog_sync: periodic`) flushes the data to the disk after an interval described by `commitlog_sync_period_in_ms` in milliseconds. But Cassandra does not wait for the commit logs to synchronize; it immediately acknowledges the write. This means that if a heavy write is going on and a machine crashes, you will lose at the most the data written in the `commitlog_sync_period_in_ms` window. But you should not really worry; we have a replication factor and consistency level to help recover this loss, unless you are unlucky enough that all the replicas die in the same instant.

> `fsync()` transfers (flushes) all modified in-core data of (that is, modified buffer cache pages for) the file referred to by the file descriptor `fd` to the disk device (or other permanent storage device) so that all changed information can be retrieved even after the system crashed or was rebooted. Read more on `http://linux.die.net/man/2/fsync`.

The `commitlog_sync` method gives high performance at some risk. To someone who is paranoid about data loss, Cassandra provides a guarantee write option, set `commitlog_sync` to batch mode. In the batch mode, Cassandra accrues all the writes to go to the commit logs and then fsyncs after `commitlog_sync_batch_window_in_ms`, which is usually set to a smaller value such as 50 milliseconds. This avoids the problem of flushing to disk after every write, but the durability guarantee forces the acknowledgement to be done only after the flush is done or the batch window is over; whichever is sooner. This means the batch modes will always be slower than the periodic modes.

For most practical cases, the default value periodic and default `fsync()` period of 10 seconds will do just fine.

column_index_size_in_kb

This property tells Cassandra to add a column index if the size of a row (serialized size) grows beyond the KBs mentioned by this property. In other words, if the row size is 314 KB and `column_index_size_in_kb` is 64 KB, there will be a column index with at least five entries, each containing the start and the finish column name in the chunk and its offset and width.

So, if the row contains many columns (wide rows) or you have columns with really large values, you may want to up the default. This has a con. For large column indexes in KB, Cassandra will need to read at least this much amount of data; even a single column with small rows and small values needs to be read. On the other hand, too small value for this property, large index data will need to be read at each access. The default is okay for most cases.

commitlog_total_space_in_mb

The commit log file is memory mapped. This means the file takes the address space. Cassandra flushes any unflushed MemTable that exists in the oldest mmap'd commit log segment to disk. Thinking from the I/O point of view, it does not make sense to keep this property small, because the total space of smaller commit logs will be filled up quickly, requiring frequent writes to the disk and higher disk I/O. On the other hand, we do not want commit logs to hog all the memory. Note that the data that was not flushed to the disk in the event of a shutdown is replayed from the commit log. So, the larger the commit log, the more the replay time will take upon restart.

The default for 32-bit JVM is 32 MB and for 64-bit JVM is 1024 MB. You may tune it based on the memory availability on the node.

Tweaking JVM

Cassandra runs in **JVM (Java Virtual Machine)**—all the threading, memory management, processes, and the interaction with underlying OS is done by Java. Investing time to optimize JVM settings to speed up Cassandra operations pays off. We will see that the general assumptions, such as setting Java, heap too high to eat up most of the system's memory, and may not be a good idea.

Java heap

If you look into `conf/cassandra-env.sh`, you will see nicely written logic such as does the following: `max(min(1/2 ram, 1024MB),min(1/4 ram, 8GB)`. This means that the max heap depends on the system memory as Cassandra chooses a decent default, which is:

- Max heap = 50 percent for a system with less than 2 GB of RAM
- Max heap = 1 GB for 2 GB to 4 GB RAM
- Max heap = 25 percent for a system with 4 GB to 32 GB of RAM
- Max heap = 8 GB for 32 GB onwards RAM

The reason to not go down with large heap is the garbage collection that does not do well for more than 8 GB. High heaps may also lead to poor page caches of the underlying operating system. In general, the default serves good enough. In case you choose to alter the heap size, you need to edit `cassandra-env.sh` and set `MAX_HEAP_SIZE` to the appropriate value.

Garbage collection

Further down `cassandra-env.sh`, you may find the garbage collection setting:

```
# GC tuning options
JVM_OPTS="$JVM_OPTS -XX:+UseParNewGC"
JVM_OPTS="$JVM_OPTS -XX:+UseConcMarkSweepGC"
JVM_OPTS="$JVM_OPTS -XX:+CMSParallelRemarkEnabled"
JVM_OPTS="$JVM_OPTS -XX:SurvivorRatio=8"
JVM_OPTS="$JVM_OPTS -XX:MaxTenuringThreshold=1"
JVM_OPTS="$JVM_OPTS -XX:CMSInitiatingOccupancyFraction=75"
JVM_OPTS="$JVM_OPTS -XX:+UseCMSInitiatingOccupancyOnly"
JVM_OPTS="$JVM_OPTS -XX:+UseTLAB"
```

Cassandra, by default, uses the **concurrent mark and sweep garbage collector (CMS GC)**. It performs garbage collection concurrently with the execution of Cassandra and pauses for a very short while. This is a good candidate for high performance applications such as Cassandra. With a concurrent collector, a parallel version of the young generation copying collector is used. And thus, we have UseParNewGC, which is a parallel copy collector that copies surviving objects in young generation from Eden to Survivor spaces and from there to old generation—it is written to work with concurrent collectors such as CMS GC.

Further more, CMSParallelRemarkEnabled reduces the pauses during the remark phase.

The other garbage settings do not impact garbage collection significantly. However, low values for CMSInitiatingOccupancyFraction may lead to frequent garbage collection, because concurrent collection starts if occupancy of the tenured generation grows above the initial occupancy. CMSInitiatingOccupancyFraction sets the percentage of current tenured generation size.

If you decide to debug the garbage collection, it is a good idea to use tools such as JConsole in order to look into how frequent garbage collection takes place, CPU usage, and so on. You may also want to uncomment the GC logging options in cassandra-env.sh to see what's going on beneath.

> If you decide to increase Java heap size over 6 GB, it may be interesting to switch the garbage collection settings too. **Garbage First Garbage Collector (G1 GC)** is shipped with Oracle Java 7 update 4+. It is claimed to work reliably on larger heap sizes. Also, it is suggested that applications currently running on CMS GC will be benefited by G1 GC in more ways than one. (Read more about G1 GC on http://www.oracle.com/technetwork/java/javase/tech/g1-intro-jsp-135488.html.)

Other JVM options

Compressed **Ordinary Object Pointers (OOPs)**: In 64-bit JVM, OOPs normally have the same size as the machine pointer, that is, 64-bit. This causes a larger heap size requirement on a 64-bit machine for the same application when compared to the heap size requirement on a 32-bit machine. Compressed OOP options help to keep the heap size smaller on 64-bit machines. (Read more about compressed OOPs on http://docs.oracle.com/javase/7/docs/technotes/guides/vm/performance-enhancements-7.html#compressedOop.)

It is generally suggested to run Cassandra on Oracle Java 6. Compressed OOPs are supported and activated by default from Java SE Version 6u23+. For earlier releases, you need to explicitly activate this by passing the `-XX:+UseCompressedOops` flag.

Enable **Java Native Access (JNA)**: Please refer to *Chapter 3, Design Patterns* for specific information regarding how to install the JNA library for your operating system. JNA gives Cassandra access to native OS libraries (shared libraries, DLLs). Cassandra uses JNA for off-heap row caching that does not get swapped and in general gives favorable performance results on reads and writes. If no JNA exists, Cassandra falls back to on-heap row caching, which has a negative impact on performance. JNA also the helps while taking backups; snapshots are created with help of JNA which would have taken much longer with fork and Java.

Scaling horizontally and vertically

We will see scaling in more detail in *Chapter 6, Managing a Cluster – Scaling*, Node Repair, and Backup, but let's discuss scaling in context of performance tuning. As we know, Cassandra is linearly horizontally scalable. So, adding more nodes in Cassandra will result in a proportional gain in performance. This is called horizontal scaling.

The other thing that we have observed is that Cassandra reads are memory and disk speed bound. So, having larger memory, allocating more memory to caches, and dedicated and fast spinning hard discs (or solid state drives) will boost the performance. Having high processing power with multi-core processors will help compression, decompression, and garbage collection to run more smoothly. So, having a beefy server will help improve overall performance. In today's cloud age, it is economical to use lots of cheap and low-end machines than to use a couple of expensive but high I/O, high CPU, and high memory machines.

Network

Cassandra, like any other distributed system, has network as one of the important aspects that can vary performance. Cassandra needs to make calls across networks for both reads and writes. A slow network can therefore be a bottleneck for the performance. It is suggested to use a gigabit network and redundant network interfaces. In a system with more than one network interface, it is recommended to bind `listen_address` for clients (Thrift) to one network interface card and `rpc_address` to another.

Summary

Starting with the stress test, we got a sense of how good a given Cassandra setup will do under an artificially standardized load. This may or may not reflect the particular use case that you are planning to use Cassandra for. You may tweak the stress test parameters to get closer to your test case. But if needed, you should simulate a load that represents the load condition that you are expecting on Cassandra. This will give you a basis of what to look out for when tuning. It will be helpful to keep some profiling running at OS level to gauge which resource is being depleted—things such as `jConsole`, `nodetool cfstats`, and `tpstats`, and Linux commands such as `iostats`, `vmstats`, `top`, `df`, and `free` can help to look through what's getting heated up or if everything is okay. We will see these tools in more detail in *Chapter 6, Managing a Cluster - Scaling*, Node Repair, and Backup.

Now that we have some idea of how our system is performing and what might need some tweaking, we can go ahead and make step-by-step changes. You may find that probably most of the defaults are good enough and that you only need to change a couple of them, which is better than just going and turning all the knobs and not knowing what affected the performance.

The production demands, sometimes, to not leave enough time to tweak various bits of Cassandra and wait to see how it affects the performance. The easiest thing to do in such scenarios is to throw in more servers on a quick call. This is the best way to up the performance. But once things come back to normal, it may be worth investing some time in analyzing the settings on the nodes to ensure that they are serving the best they can from the given hardware.

In the next chapter, we will see different ways to tackle everyday DevOps problems—how to scale up when traffic is high, how to replace a dead node, and other issues. In a later chapter, we will see how to keep tabs on various performance statistics. We will see that the learning in this and in the next couple of chapters comes to help when troubleshooting is an issue.

6
Managing a Cluster – Scaling, Node Repair, and Backup

As a system grows, or an application gets matured, or the cloud infrastructure starts to warn of failure of the underlying hardware, or probably you have got hit by the TechCrunch effect, you may need to do one of these things: repair, backup, or scale up/down. Or, perhaps, the management decides to have another data center set up just for analysis of data (maybe using Hadoop) without affecting the user's experience for which the data is served from the existing data center. These tasks come as an integral part of a system administrator's day job. Fortunately, all these tasks are fairly easy in Cassandra and there is a lot of documentation available for it.

In this chapter, we will go through Cassandra's built-in DevOps tool and the discuss on scaling a cluster up and shrinking it down. We will also see how one can replace a dead node or just remove it, and let other nodes bear the extra load. Further, we will briefly see backup and restoration. We will observe how Cassandra tried its best to accommodate the changes, but most of the operations leave the cluster unbalanced — in the sense that tokens to each machine are not uniformly distributed. The load balancing section shows how easy it is to rebalance the cluster.

Although most of the tasks are mechanical and really simple to automate, it may be a burden to maintain a large cluster. The last section briefly introduces Priam, a Java-based web application, to simplify many operational tasks.

 TechCrunch Effect is basically sudden surge of traffic to your website when the popular technical news website http://techcrunch.com features your company/application. It is generally referred to indicate the tsunami of traffic that comes via all the PR sources.

Scaling

Adding more nodes to Cassandra (scaling up) or shrinking the number of nodes (scaling down) is a pretty straightforward task. In a smaller and moderate-sized Cassandra cluster setup (say, fewer than 25 nodes), it can be easily managed by doing the tasks manually. But in larger clusters, the whole process can be automated by writing appropriate shell script to perform the task.

Adding nodes to a cluster

Cassandra is one of the purest distributed systems where all the nodes are identical. So, adding a new node is just a matter of launching a Cassandra service with almost the same parameters as any other machine in the ring. In a cloud environment such as Amazon Web Services, it is a pretty common practice to have a machine image of Cassandra that contains the blueprint of a Cassandra node. Each time you have to add a node to the cluster, you launch the AMI, tweak a couple of parameters that are specific to the node, and done. It is as simple as that.

To add a new node to the cluster, you need to have a Cassandra setup that has:

- **Setup node's identity**: Edit `cassandra.yaml` to set the following appropriately:
    - `cluster_name`: It is the same as the other nodes in the cluster where this node is joining in.
    - `listen_address`: Set it to the IP or the hostname where other nodes connect the Cassandra service on this node to. Be warned that leaving this field empty may not be a good idea. It will assume `listen_address` is the same as the hostname, which may or may not be correct. In Amazon EC2, it is usually just right.
    - `broadcast_address`: It may be needed to set for a multi data center Cassandra installation.

- **Seed node**: Each node must know the seed node to be able to initialize the gossip (refer to the *Gossip* section of *Chapter 2, Cassandra Architecture,* for gossip), learn about the topology, and let other nodes know about itself.

- **Initial token**: It is the data range this node is going to be responsible for. One can just leave the initial token and Cassandra will assign the token by choosing the middle of a token range of the most loaded node. This is the fastest way to make a lopsided cluster. The nodes should be well balanced.

Apart from these settings, any customization in other nodes `cassandra.yaml` should be made into new nodes configuration.

Now that the node is ready, here are the steps to add new nodes:

1. **Initial tokens**: Depending on the type of partitioner that you are using for the key distribution, you will need to recalculate the initial tokens for each node in the system (refer to the *Initial token* section of *Chapter 4, Deploying a Cluster,* for initial token calculation). This means older nodes are going to have different data sets than they originally owned. However, there are a couple of smart tricks in the initial token assignment.

    i. **N-folding the capacity**: If you are doubling, triplicating, or increasing the capacity N times, you'll find that the initial token generated includes older initial tokens. Say, for example, you had a 3-node cluster with initial tokens as 0, t/3, and 2t/3. If you decide to triple the capacity by adding six more nodes, the new tokens should be 0, t/9, ...t/3, ...2t/3, and... 8t/9. The trick here is to leave the tokens that are already in use in the existing cluster, and assign the rest of the nodes with the remaining tokens. This saves extra move commands to adjust the tokens. You just launch the new nodes and wait till data streams out to all the nodes.

    ii. **Rebalance later**: This is the most common technique among those who have started with Cassandra. The idea is not to bother about imbalance. You can just launch new nodes. Cassandra will assign it with a token value, that is, the middle value of the highest loaded node. This, as expected, does a pretty decent job in removing hotspots from the cluster (and many times this is what you want when you are adding a new node). Once the data streaming between the nodes is done, the cluster may or may not be perfectly balanced. You may want to load balance now. (Refer to the *Load Balancing* section in this chapter.)

    iii. **Right token to right node**: This is the most complex but the most common case. Usually, you do not go for doubling or quadrupling the cluster. It is more like you are asked to add two new nodes. In this case, you calculate the tokens for the new configuration, edit the new nodes' `cassandra.yaml`, and set initial tokens to them (no specific choice). You start them and move the data around the nodes so that the nodes comply with the new initial tokens that we calculated. (We'll see how to do this later in this chapter.)

2. **Start a new node**: With the initial token assigned or not assigned to the new nodes, we should start the nodes one by one. It is recommended to have a pause of at least two minutes between two consecutive nodes start. These two minutes are to make sure that the other nodes know about this new node via gossip.

3. **Move data**: If adding a new node has skewed the data distributed in the cluster, we may need to move the data around in such a way that each node has equal share of the token range. This can be done using `nodetool`. You need to run `nodetool move NEW_INITIAL_TOKEN` on each node.

4. **Cleanup**: Move does not really move the data from one machine to another; it copies the data instead. This leaves nodes with unused old data. To clean this data, execute `nodetool cleanup` on each node.

Following is a demonstration adding of a node into a 3-node cluster, that is, the expansion of a 3-node cluster into a 4-node cluster.

Ring status: Use `nodetool -h HOSTNAME ring` to see the current ring distribution.

```
$ /opt/cassandra/bin/nodetool -h 10.99.9.67 ring
Address           Effective-Ownership    Token
                                         113427455640312821154458202477256070485
10.99.9.67        66.67%                 0
10.147.171.159    66.67%                 67137278201564105772291012386280352420
10.114.189.54     66.67%                 134274556403128211544582024772560704850
# Some columns are removed from the result to fit the width
```

The previous sample looks pretty balanced with three nodes and a replication factor of 2.

New tokens: Adding additional nodes is going to split the token range into four. Instead of calculating the tokens manually, we'll let the tools provided by Cassandra do it for us. Let's see what they are.

```
$ /opt/cassandra/tools/bin/token-generator 4

DC #1:
   Node #1:    0
   Node #2:    42535295865117307932921825928971026432
   Node #3:    85070591730234615865843651857942052864
   Node #4:    127605887595351923798765477786913079296
```

> **A couple of things**: Be aware that token numbers are partitioner dependent and in this case it was `RandomPartitioner`. The other thing is if you see the old and new tokens, you will realize that the first node is not going to be touched. It is already set to the correct value. Also, it will be profitable in the old node, 2. The old node 3 gets assigned to the token values of node 2 and node 3 in the new configuration. This way we'll minimize data movement across the nodes (streaming). The new node will have the initial token as described by node 4 in the previous result.

Start the new node: Edit `cassandra.yaml` of the new node to set the appropriate value of the cluster name, initial token, seed node, listen address, and any other customization as per the environment (such as broadcast address, snitch, security, datafile, and so on). Now, start the node by issuing the `cassandra` command or starting the Cassandra service. Wait for a couple of minutes as the new node gets introduced with the cluster. The cluster now looks pretty lopsided:

```
$ /opt/cassandra/bin/nodetool -h 10.99.9.67 ring
```

```
Address           EO*      Token
                           127605887595351923798765477786913079296
10.99.9.67        33.33%   0
10.147.171.159    58.33%   56713727820156410577229101238628035242
10.114.189.54     66.67%   113427455640312821154458202477256070485
10.166.54.134     41.67%   127605887595351923798765477786913079296
*EO = Effective ownership
```

Move tokens: Let's balance the nodes by moving data around. We need not touch `Node #1` and `Node #4`. We need to move data from `Node #2` and `Node #3`. They are the ones with wrong tokens. Here is how:

```
# Move data on Node #2
$ /opt/cassandra/bin/nodetool -h 10.147.171.159 move 42535295865117307932
921825928971026432
```

```
# Cassandra is still unbalanced.
# Move data on Node #3
$ /opt/cassandra/bin/nodetool -h 10.114.189.54 move 85070591730234615865 8
43651857942052864
```

This is a blocking operation. That means you will need to wait till the process finishes. In a really large cluster with huge data, it may take some time to move the data. Be patient. This operation moves data. It heavily burdens the network and the data size on disks may change. So, it is not ideal to do this task when your site is running at peak traffic. Perform this task at a relatively slow traffic time.

It may be useful to watch streaming statistics on the node by using nodetool `netstats`. Here is an example of how that looks (sampled every one second):

```
$ for i in {1..300} ; do  /opt/cassandra/bin/nodetool -h 10.114.189.54
netstats; sleep 1; done
```

```
Mode: NORMAL

Not sending any streams.

Not receiving any streams.
```

Pool Name	Active	Pending	Completed
Commands	n/a	0	1371882
Responses	n/a	0	7871820

```
Mode: MOVING

Not sending any streams.

Not receiving any streams.
```

Pool Name	Active	Pending	Completed
Commands	n/a	0	1371882
Responses	n/a	0	7871823

```
[-- snip --]

Mode: MOVING

Streaming to: /10.99.9.67
```

/mnt/cassandra-data/data/Keyspace1/Standard1/Keyspace1-Standard1-hf-1-
Data.db sections=1 progress=8126464/20112794 – 40%

/mnt/cassandra-data/data/Keyspace1/Standard1/Keyspace1-Standard1-hf-2-
Data.db sections=1 progress=0/15600228 - 0%

```
Not receiving any streams.
```

Pool Name	Active	Pending	Completed
Commands	n/a	0	1371882
Responses	n/a	0	7871925

```
Mode: NORMAL

Not sending any streams.

Not receiving any streams.
```

Pool Name	Active	Pending	Completed
Commands	n/a	0	1371882
Responses	n/a	0	7871934

After the move is done, the balancing is done. The latest cluster now looks much better:

```
$ /opt/cassandra/bin/nodetool -h 10.99.9.67 ring
```

Address	EO*	Token
		127605887595351923798765477786913079296
10.99.9.67	50.00%	0
10.147.171.159	50.00%	42535295865117307932921825928971026432
10.114.189.54	50.00%	85070591730234615865843651857942052864
10.166.54.134	50.00%	127605887595351923798765477786913079296

```
*EO = Effective-Ownership
```

Cleanup: Now that everything is done and there is relatively low traffic on the database, it is a good time to clean the useless data from each node.

```
$ /opt/cassandra/bin/nodetool -h 10.114.189.54 cleanup
$ /opt/cassandra/bin/nodetool -h 10.99.9.67 cleanup
$ /opt/cassandra/bin/nodetool -h 10.147.171.159 cleanup
$ /opt/cassandra/bin/nodetool -h 10.166.54.134 cleanup
```

Now, we are done with adding a new node to the system.

Removing nodes from a cluster

It may not always be desired to have a high number of nodes up all the time. It adds to the cost and maintenance overheads. In many situations where one has scaled up to cope with a sudden surge in the traffic (for high I/O) or to avoid a hotspot for a while, it may be required to retire some machines and come back to the normal operation mode. Another reason to remove a node is hardware or communication failure, like a dead node that needs to be ejected out of the ring.

Removing a live node

Removing a live node is to stream the data out of the node to its neighbors. The command to remove a live node is `nodetool decommission`. That's all. You are done with removing a live node. It will take some time to stream the data and you may need to rebalance the cluster.

Here is what decommissioning a node looks like. Assume that the ring is the same as when we added one node to a 3-node cluster. The following command will show the process of decommissioning a live node:

```
$ /opt/cassandra/bin/nodetool -h 10.166.54.134 decommission
```

This will decommission the node at 10.166.54.134. It is a blocking process, which means the **command-line interface (CLI)** will wait till the decommissioning gets done. Here is what netstats on the node looks like:

```
$ for i in {1..300} ; do  /opt/cassandra/bin/nodetool -h 10.166.54.134
netstats; sleep 1; done
```

```
Mode: NORMAL

Not sending any streams.

Not receiving any streams.


Pool Name      Active    Pending        Completed

Commands       n/a       0              7

Responses      n/a       0              139736

Mode: LEAVING

Not sending any streams.

Not receiving any streams.


Pool Name      Active    Pending        Completed

Commands       n/a       0              7

Responses      n/a       0              139784

Mode: LEAVING


Streaming to: /10.99.9.67

/mnt/cassandra-data/data/Keyspace1/Standard1/Keyspace1-Standard1-hf-10-
Data.db sections=1 progress=9014392/9014392 - 100%

/mnt/cassandra-data/data/Keyspace1/Standard1/Keyspace1-Standard1-hf-9-
Data.db sections=1 progress=0/33779859 - 0%

/mnt/cassandra-data/data/Keyspace1/Standard1/Keyspace1-Standard1-hf-8-
Data.db sections=1 progress=0/7298715 - 0%
```

```
Streaming to: /10.147.171.159
/mnt/cassandra-data/data/Keyspace1/Standard1/Keyspace1-Standard1-hf-9-
Data.db sections=1 progress=15925248/53814752 - 29%
```

```
Not receiving any streams.
```

Pool Name	Active	Pending	Completed
Commands	n/a	0	7
Responses	n/a	0	139886

```
Mode: DECOMMISSIONED
Not sending any streams.
Not receiving any streams.
```

Pool Name	Active	Pending	Completed
Commands	n/a	0	7
Responses	n/a	0	139967

Obviously, it leaves the ring imbalanced:

```
$ /opt/cassandra/bin/nodetool -h 10.99.9.67 ring
```

Address	EO*	Token
		85070591730234615865843651857942052864
10.99.9.67	75.00%	0
10.147.171.159	75.00%	42535295865117307932921825928971026432
10.114.189.54	50.00%	85070591730234615865843651857942052864

```
*EO=  Effective-Ownership
```

Removing a dead node

Removing a dead node is similar to decommissioning except for the fact that data is streamed from replica nodes to other nodes instead of streaming from the node that is being replaced. The command to remove a dead node from the cluster is:

```
$ nodetool -h HOSTNAME removetoken TOKEN_ASSIGNED_TO_THE_NODE
```

So, if you've decided to remove a node that owned a token, 85070591730234615865 843651857942052864, you just run:

```
$ nodetool -h 10.99.9.67 removetoken 85070591730234615865843651857942052
864
```

It has a similar effect on the ring as `nodetool decommission`. But `decommission` or `disablegossip` cannot be used with a dead node. It may require moving/rebalancing the cluster tokens after this.

> It must be noted that decommissioning or removing a token does not remove the data from the node that is being removed from the system. If you plan to reuse the node, you must clean the data directories manually.

Replacing a node

Once in a while, a dead node needs to be replaced. This means you just wanted an exact replacement instead of just removal. Here are the steps:

1. Note down the dead node's token.
2. Set the new node's initial token as the dead node's token minus one. This node is going to own the new data, so you must make sure that the data directories are empty to avoid any conflict.
3. Configure `cassandra.yaml` appropriately. Similar to the way we did when adding a new node. (Refer to the *Adding nodes to a cluster* section in this chapter.)
4. Let the bootstrap complete and see the node appear in the `nodetool ring` listing.
5. Perform a `nodetool repair` for each keyspace for integrity.
6. Perform `nodetool removetoken` for the old node.

Let us see this in action. The example cluster here has three nodes and a replication factor of 2. One of the nodes is down. We will replace it with a new node.

Here is what the current ring looks like:

```
$ bin/nodetool -h 10.99.9.67 ring

Address            Status   EO*       Token
                                      113427455640312821154458202477256
070484
10.99.9.67         Up       66.67%    0
10.147.171.159     Up       66.67%    567137278201564105772291012386280
35242
10.114.189.54      Down     66.67%    113427455640312821154458202477256
070484

# * EO stands for Effective-ownership
```

As you can see, we need to replace the third node, `10.114.189.54`. We fired up a new machine, installed Cassandra, altered `cassandra.yaml` to match the cluster specifications, and set up the listen address and data directory. We also made sure that the data directories (commit log, saved caches, and data) are blank. Since this node is going to replace a node with token 113427455640312821154458202477256070484, we are setting the new node's `initial_token` as 113427455640312821154458202477256070483. By default `auto_bootstrap` is true, which is good.

```
# cassandra.yaml on replacement node

initial_token: 113427455640312821154458202477256070483
```

We start the Cassandra service on the node. Looking at the logs, it seems it has got all the information it needed:

```
# Cassandra log, joining the cluster with dead-node
...
 INFO 08:30:34,841 JOINING: schema complete

 INFO 08:30:34,842 JOINING: waiting for pending range calculation

 INFO 08:30:34,842 JOINING: calculation complete, ready to bootstrap

 INFO 08:30:34,843 JOINING: getting bootstrap token

 INFO 08:30:34,849 Enqueuing flush of Memtable-
LocationInfo@2039197494(36/45 serialized/live bytes, 1 ops)

 INFO 08:30:34,849 Writing Memtable-LocationInfo@2039197494(36/45
serialized/live bytes, 1 ops)

 INFO 08:30:34,873 Completed flushing /mnt/cassandra-data/data/system/
LocationInfo/system-LocationInfo-hf-6-Data.db (87 bytes) for commitlog
position ReplayPosition(segmentId=1371630629459, position=30209)

 INFO 08:30:34,875 JOINING: sleeping 30000 ms for pending range setup

 INFO 08:30:43,856 InetAddress /10.114.189.54 is now dead.

 INFO 08:31:04,875 JOINING: Starting to bootstrap...

 INFO 08:31:05,685 Finished streaming session 4 from /10.147.171.159

 INFO 08:31:09,108 Finished streaming session 3 from /10.99.9.67

 INFO 08:31:10,613 Finished streaming session 1 from /10.99.9.67

 INFO 08:31:10,622 Finished streaming session 2 from /10.147.171.159

...
```

Now that the new node has joined, the `nodetool ring` still does not seem to be right.

```
$ bin/nodetool -h 10.99.9.67 ring
```

```
Address        Status  EO*     Token
                               113427455640312821154458202477256070484
10.99.9.67     Up      33.33%  0
10.147.171.159 Up      66.67%  56713727820156410577229101238628035242
10.166.54.134  Up      66.67%  113427455640312821154458202477256070483
10.114.189.54  Down    33.33%  113427455640312821154458202477256070484
```

```
# * EO stands for Effective-ownership
```

This means we need to remove the dead node from the cluster. But before we go ahead and remove the node, let's just repair the keyspaces to make sure that the nodes are consistent.

```
$ bin/nodetool -h 10.99.9.67 repair Keyspace1
```

```
[2013-06-19 08:40:55,336] Starting repair command #1, repairing 2 ranges
for keyspaceKeyspace1
```

```
[2013-06-19 08:41:01,297] Repair session f4e1f830-d8bb-11e2-0000-
23f6cbfa94fd for range (113427455640312821154458202477256070484,0]
finished
```

```
[2013-06-19 08:41:01,298] Repair session f86bbb30-d8bb-11e2-0000-
23f6cbfa94fd for range (113427455640312821154458202477256070483,1134274
55640312821154458202477256070484] failed with error java.io.IOException:
Cannot proceed on repair because a neighbor (/10.114.189.54) is dead:
session failed
```

```
[2013-06-19 08:41:01,298] Repair command #1 finished
```

```
$ bin/nodetool -h 10.99.9.67 repair mytest
```

```
[2013-06-19 08:41:25,867] Starting repair command #2, repairing 2 ranges
for keyspacemytest
```

```
[2013-06-19 08:41:26,377] Repair session 0712f3b0-d8bc-11e2-0000-
23f6cbfa94fd for range (11342745564031282115445820247725 6070484,0]
finished


[2013-06-19 08:41:26,377] Repair session 075ea2b0-d8bc-11e2-0000-
23f6cbfa94fd for range (11342745564031282115445820247725 6070483,1134274
55640312821154458202477256070484] failed with error java.io.IOException:
Cannot proceed on repair because a neighbor (/10.114.189.54) is dead:
session failed


[2013-06-19 08:41:26,377] Repair command #2 finished
```

Now, let's remove the dead node. We will use the same technique of `nodetool`
`removetoken` as we did in the *Removing a dead node* section in this chapter. The
cluster looks good after removal.

```
# Remove dead node
$ bin/nodetool -h 10.99.9.67 removetoken 1134274556403128211544582024 7725
6070484


# Ring status
$ bin/nodetool -h 10.99.9.67 ring


Address         Status   EO*      Token
                                  1134274556403128211544582024 77256070483
10.99.9.67       Up      66.67%   0
10.147.171.159   Up      66.67%   56713727820156410577229101238628035242
10.166.54.134    Up      66.67%   1134274556403128211544582024 77256070483


# * EO stands for Effective-ownership
```

If, for some reason, you are unable to perform the replacement using the previous
method, there is an alternative approach. Here are the steps to replace a node with a
new one:

1. Set the new (replacement) node's IP the same as the one that died.
2. Configure `cassandra.yaml` appropriately.
3. Set `initial_token` the same as the token assigned to the dead node. Start
    the substitute node.

The cluster will assume that the dead node came alive. Run `nodetool repair` on all the keyspaces. This will stream the data to the new node.

In Cassandra 1.0 and onwards, a dead node can be replaced with a new node by the property `cassandra.replace_token=<Token>`. Set this property using the `-D` option while starting Cassandra. Make sure the data directories are empty on the new node and run a `nodetool repair` after the node is up.

The two alternative approaches (inserting a node with a new token versus replacing the node with the same token) have different perspectives of how the fix is made. The former approach inserts a node between the dead node and the previous node. We leave just one token to the dead node. This one token gets assigned to the node next to the dead node when we remove the dead node from the ring. The latter approach, however, is like saying the dead node came back to life but lost its memory. So, the replica nodes fill it in. There is no specific preference on which method one should prefer. Choose the one convenient to you.

Backup and restoration

Cassandra provides a simple backup tool to take a backup and incremental snapshots: `nodetool snapshot`. The snapshot command flushes MemTables to the disk and creates a backup by creating a hard link to SSTables (SSTables are immutable).

 Hard link is a directory entry associated with a file data on a filesystem. It can roughly be assumed as an alias to a file that refers to the location where data is stored. It is unlike a soft link that just aliases filenames, not the actual underlying data.

These hard links stay under the data directory, which is placed under `<keyspace>/<column_family>/snapshots`.

The general plan to take a backup of a cluster roughly follows the steps described:

1. **Take a snapshot**: Take a snapshot of each node one by one. The snapshot command provides an option to specify whether to back up the whole keyspace or just the selected column families.

2. **Move to a safe location**: Taking a snapshot is just half of the story. To be able to restore the database at a later point, you need to move these snapshots to a location that cannot be affected by the node's hardware failure or the node's unavailability. One of the easiest things to do is to move the data to a network-attached storage. To AWS users, it is fairly common to back up the snapshots in the S3 bucket.

3. **Clean the snapshots**: Once you are done with backing the snapshots up, you need to clean them. `nodetool clearsnapshot` cleans all the snapshots on a node.

It is important to understand that creating snapshots creates hard links to the datafiles. These datafiles do not get deleted when they get obsolete, because they are saved for backup. This extraneous disk can be avoided by `clearsnapshot` after the snapshots are copied to a different location.

For really large datasets, it may be hard to take a daily backup of the entire keyspace. Plus, it is expensive to transfer large data over a network to move the snapshots to a safe location. You can take a snapshot at first, and copy it to a safe location. Once this is done, all we need to do is move the incremental data. This is called incremental backup. To enable incremental backup to a node, you need to edit `cassandra.yaml` and set `incremental_backups: true`. This will cause the creation of hard links in the backup's directory under the data directory.

So, you have snapshots with incremental backup, and you have a backup of all the SSTables created after the snapshot is taken. Incremental backups have the same problem as snapshots. They are hard links; they delete obsolete datafiles that are not to be deleted. It is recommended to run `clearsnapshot` before a new snapshot is created and make sure that the backup's directory has no incremental backup.

Taking a backup is just half the story. Backups are meaningful when they are restored in case of node replacement or perhaps to launch a whole new cluster from the backup data of another cluster. There is more than one way to restore a node. We will see two approaches here. The first is to just paste the appropriate files to the appropriate location. Here are the suggested steps:

1. Shut down the node to restore. Clean the `.db` files for the column family from the data directory. It is located under `<data_directoy>/<keyspace>/<column_family>`. Do not delete anything other than the `.db` files. Also, delete the commit logs from the commit log directory.

2. From the backup, take the snapshot directory that you wanted to replace. Paste the content of everything in that snapshot directory to the data directory mentioned in the previous step.

3. If you have enabled incremental backup, you may want to take them into account too. You need to paste all the incremental backup taken from your backup (it is situated under `<data_directory>/<keyspace>/<column_family>/backups`) to the data directory, the same as we did with snapshots in the previous step.

4. Restart the node.

A couple of things to note:

If you are restoring the complete cluster, shut down the cluster while restoring, and restore the nodes one by one.

1. Once the restoration process is done, execute `nodetool repair`.
2. If you are trying to restore on a completely new machine that has no idea about the keyspace that is being restored, it may be worth checking the schema for the keyspace and the column family that you wanted to restore. The schema can be queried by executing `show schema;` in the Cassandra-cli console. You may need to create them to be able to get the restoration working.

Using Cassandra bulk loader to restore the data

An alternative technique to load the data to Cassandra is using the `sstableloader` utility. It can be found under the `bin` directory of the Cassandra installation. This tool is especially useful when the number of nodes and the replication strategy is changed, because unlike the copy method, it streams appropriate data parts to appropriate nodes, based on the configuration.

Assuming that you have `-Index.db` and `-Data.db` files with you, here are the steps to use `sstableloader`:

1. Check the node's schema. If it does not have the keyspaces and the column families that are being restored, create the appropriate keyspaces and the column families.
2. Create a directory with the same name as the keyspace that is being loaded. Inside this directory, all the column families' data (the `.db` files) that are being restored should be kept in a directory with the name same as the column family name. For example, if you are restoring a column family `myCF` in keyspace `mykeyspace`, all the `mykeyspace-myCF-hf-x-Data.db` and `mykeyspace-myCF-hf-x-Index.db` (where x is an integer) should be placed within a directory structure: `mykeyspace/myCF/`.
3. Finally, execute `bin/sstableloadermykeyspace`.

Cassandra bulk loader simplified the task to an extent that one can just store the backup in the exact same directory structure as required by `sstableloader` and whenever a restoration is required just download the backup directory and execute `sstableloader`.

It can be observed that the backup step is very mechanical and can easily be automated to take a daily backup using the Cron job and the shell script. It may be a good idea to `clearsnapshot` once in a while, and take a snapshot from then on.

Backup

Coming from the traditional database, one thinks that data backup is an essential part of data management. Data must be backed up daily, stored in a hard disk, and stored in a safe place. This is a good idea. It gets harder and inefficient to achieve this as the data size grows to terabytes. With Cassandra, you may set up a configuration that makes it really hard to lose data. A setup with three data centers in Virginia (US East), California (US West), and Tokyo (Japan), where data is replicated across all three data centers, you will seldom need to worry about data. If you are the nervous type, you may have a Cron job backing up the data from one of the data centers, at every time interval up to which you may take a risk. With this setup, in the rare event of the two US data centers going down, you can serve the users without any repercussions. Things will catch up as soon as the data centers come back up.

Load balancing

A balanced Cassandra cluster is one where each node owns an equal number of keys. This means when you query `nodetool ring`, a balanced cluster will show the same percentage for all the nodes under the `Owns` or `Effective Ownership` columns. If the data is not uniformly distributed between the keys, even with equal ownership you will see some nodes are more occupied by the data than others. We use `RandomPartitioner` or `Murmur3Partitioner` to avoid this sort of lopsided cluster.

Anytime a new node is added or a node is decommissioned, the token distribution gets skewed. Normally, one always wants to have Cassandra fairly load balanced to avoid hotspots. Fortunately, it is very easy to load balance. Here is the two-step load balancing process.

1. Calculate the initial tokens based on the partitioner that you are using. It can be manually generated by equally dividing the token range for a given partitioner among the number of nodes. Or, you can use `tools/bin/token-generator` to generate tokens for you. For example, the following snippet generates the tokens for two data centers with each having three nodes:

```
$ tools/bin/token-generator 3 3
DC #1:
  Node #1:  0
  Node #2:  56713727820156410577229101238628035242
  Node #3:  113427455640312821154458202477256070484
```

```
DC #2:

  Node #1:   169417178424467235000914166253263322299

  Node #2:   55989722784154413846455963776007251813

  Node #3:   112703450604310824423685065014635287055
```

2. Please note that these tokens are generated for `RandomPartitioner`. That means it is good for default Cassandra 1.1.x, but not for default Cassandra 1.2.x or higher. Cassandra 1.2.x and higher uses `Murmur3Partitioner` as default. Murmur has a different key range.

3. Now that we have tokens, we need to call:

```
bin/nodetool -h <node_to_move> move <token_number>
```

The trick here is to assign a new token to a node that is closest to it. This will allow faster balancing as there will be less data to move. Live example of how load balancing is done is covered under the topic *Adding nodes to a cluster* in this chapter, where we add a node to the cluster, which makes the cluster lopsided. We finally balance it by moving tokens around.

It is actually very easy to write a shell or Python script that takes the ring and then balances it automatically. For someone using `RandomPartitioner`, there is a GitHub project, Cassandra-Balancer (`https://github.com/tivv/cassandra-balancer`), which calculates the tokens for a node and moves the data. So, instead of writing one of your own you can just use this groovy script. Execute on each node, one by one, and you are done.

Priam – managing large clusters on AWS

Cassandra is probably the best example of out-of-bound success of the community-driven open source project. Netflix contributes heavily to Cassandra projects. Netflix's cluster management tool, Priam, simplifies the administration of large clusters over Amazon Web Service's EC2 cloud platform. Unfortunately, detailed discussion on Priam is out of the scope of this book. The wiki page of the project is not extensive either.

Priam is a Java-based web application, primarily for the following tasks:

- Token assignment
- Backup and restoration
- Configuration management
- API to query Cassandra metrics

As an advice, for a small cluster setup (say, under 25 nodes), it is suggested to stick with simple automation based on `nodetool` and perhaps a shell or Python script. It will keep the administration simple. Priam requires too many parameters to set it up and perhaps it is more work for smaller clusters than to manage it manually.

More information about Priam, setup, and scaling procedures can be learned from its GitHub page: `https://github.com/Netflix/Priam/wiki`.

Summary

So we know how to move around data and manage Cassandra instances to handle the production situations. Cassandra provides simple one-liner commands to perform various complicated maintenance tasks to make life easy. Scaling up, scaling down, removing live or dead nodes, and load balancing are pleasantly simple and can be automated based on your configuration using scripts. Backups fall in the same category, but restoration can be a bit tricky. With the Cassandra data model, built-in replication, and support for multiple data center setup, one may configure Cassandra such that it may never need a backup. Also, for really large databases, it may be impractical to siphon out data instead of using replication. It may make sense to back up in a case where the database is not very large and one uses a replication factor of 1. In such a case, going down a node may cause loss of data. However, $RF=1$ is a bad idea in production setup and backup can just restore the data until the latest backup is made.

Priam gives a decent option to move on from the nodetool-based mechanism to a more sophisticated tool. If you are just starting out, or have a small cluster, it is not worth the effort it takes to configure Priam. It is a good suggestion for large cluster owners. Moreover, Priam is built to support the AWS infrastructure and tied to the AWS configuration. So, it may not be useful to everyone. One may consider DataStax's OpsCenter for such tasks. We will discuss OpsCenter in the next chapter.

This chapter gives you enough knowledge to tackle an infrastructure issue. Now, you, as an operations person, need to keep a watch on how things are doing without losing your sleep and waking up from nightmares. The next chapter will walk you through the various ways to monitor and recognize problems, and troubleshoot the Cassandra infrastructure in detail.

7
Monitoring

Monitoring is the key to provide reliable service. For a distributed software, monitoring becomes more important and more complex. Fortunately, Cassandra has an excellent tool built-in for it. It is called `nodetool`. Apart from this, there are third-party tools to monitor Cassandra.

The purpose of monitoring is to be able to catch a problem before or as soon as it happens and resolve it. So, this chapter will be a mix of monitoring, management (comes with monitoring tools), and very quick troubleshooting tips. It gets you familiarized with the JMX interface that Cassandra provides and then moves on to accessing it via JConsole. Cassandra's `nodetool`—the application to monitor and administer Cassandra—is discussed in detail. Further, DataStax OpsCenter (community version), which is an excellent web-based tool that stores performance history, is discussed. Nagios is another tool that can be used to not only monitor Cassandra but also the complete infrastructure with heterogeneous components. Nagios is a veteran monitoring tool. It is a pretty simple, intuitive, extendable, and robust tool. It provides monitoring along with e-mail notification.

Cassandra JMX interface

Cassandra has a powerful JMX interface to monitor almost all of its aspects. **Java Management Extension (JMX)** is a standard part of Java SE (standard edition) 5.0 and onward. It provides a standard interface to manage and monitor resources such as applications, devices, JVM settings, and services. The way JMX technology manages and monitors a resource is called **Managed Beans (MBeans)**. JMX defines standard connectors that enable us to access JMX agents remotely. With this introductory JMX knowledge, let's see what Cassandra offers us to control or monitor almost all of its aspects using JMX.

This discussion is sufficient to get you to work with JMX in the context of Cassandra. Learn more about it at `http://docs.oracle.com/javase/tutorial/jmx/TOC.html`.

Cassandra exposes JMX MBeans in different packages. These are:

- The `org.apache.cassandra.internal` package: This package includes MBeans that inform us about internal operations. So, you can view the status of AntiEntropy, FlushWriter, gossip, hinted handoff, response stage, migration and stream stages, pending range calculation, and commit log archival. Other than getting internal status statistics, there is not much that can be done with these MBeans.

- The `org.apache.cassandra.db` package: This is probably the most interesting MBean package. It includes vital metrics and actionable operational items. MBeans gives statistics and commands for the following database components: cache management, column family, commit log, compaction control, hinted handoff management, storage service (general ring statistics and operations), and storage proxy (client read/write statistics).

- The `org.apache.cassandra.net` package: This package contains statistics on network communication within the cluster. It has some interesting Mbeans such as FailureDetector, gossip, inter-node messaging, and data stream status.

- The `org.apache.cassandra.request` package: One can view pending and completed tasks at different stages. The stages listed under this package are: mutation stage, read repair stage, read stage, replicate on write stage, and read response stage.

- The `org.apache.cassandra.metrics` package: It includes statistics about client read and write. Specifically, the number of requests that are timed out and those that have thrown `UnavailableException`, that is, not enough replicas available to satisfy the operation with the given consistency level or, maybe, many replicas are down.

Cassandra is designed around **Staged Event Driven Architecture (SEDA)**. At very high levels, it chunks a task into multiple stages, each having their own thread pool and event queue. To read more about SEDA visit `http://www.eecs.harvard.edu/~mdw/proj/seda`.

Accessing MBeans using JConsole

JConsole is a built-in utility in JDK 5+. You can access it from `$JAVA_HOME/bin/jconsole`. It is a JVM monitoring tool and allows you to access MBeans in the Java application to which JConsole is connected to. It allows you to monitor the CPU, memory, thread pools, heap information, and other important JVM-related things.

To peek into the insides of Cassandra, launch JConsole. The GUI shows two options to connect to—**Local Process** and **Remote Process**. If you are running JConsole on the same machine as Cassandra, you will see the option to connect to Cassandra in the drop-down under the **Local Process** radio button. However, it is not recommended to run JConsole on the same machine as Cassandra. This is because JConsole takes a large amount of system resources and can hamper Cassandra's performance. So, unless you just want to test Cassandra on your local machine, it may not be a good idea to have Cassandra and JConsole running on the same machine.

The JConsole summary tab is shown in the following screenshot:

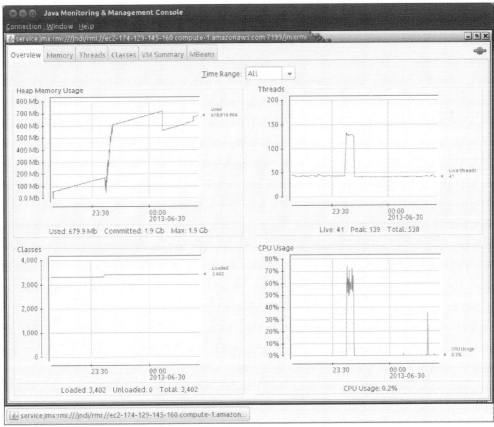

Figure 7.1: JConsole summary tab

To connect to a remote machine, you need to select the **Remote process** radio button and fill in the URL of the Cassandra node. The format is:

```
# CASSANDRAHOST is address of remote Cassandra node
  service:jmx:rmi:///jndi/rmi://CASSANDRAHOST:7199/jmxrmi
```

If you have a firewall or port blocking the Cassandra node, you may face some issues in connection.

AWS Users: It requires some work to get JConsole connected to your Cassandra instance running within EC2 from outside the security group without compromising its security. The suggested way is to connect via an SSH tunnel. Setting up an SSH tunnel is outside the scope of this book. You may refer to articles online. One of the online articles for using an SSH tunnel to connect to JConsole is: http://simplygenius.com/2010/08/jconsole-via-socks-ssh-tunnel.html.

 You may want to add your local machine's external IP to Cassandra's security group and open all the TCP ports (0 to 65535) to it. By doing this, you are compromising the security of the server. It is not a recommended way to get around this problem. Remember to remove this entry once you are done with the JConsole task.

In case you have a server set up with different internal and external IPs, you may need to configure an RMI hostname. Open `config/cassandra-env.sh`, and add the `hostname` parameter for JMX as part of `JVM_OPTS` in the following manner:

```
JVM_OPTS="$JVM_OPTS -Djava.rmi.server.hostname=174.129.145.160"
JVM_OPTS="$JVM_OPTS -Dcom.sun.management.jmxremote.port=$JMX_PORT"
JVM_OPTS="$JVM_OPTS -Dcom.sun.management.jmxremote.ssl=false"
JVM_OPTS="$JVM_OPTS -Dcom.sun.management.jmxremote.authenticate=false"
```

Amazon Web Services (AWS) users may need to put a public DNS name provided for the Cassandra node. Once you are connected to the node, you can see an overview of the JVM on that node; see Figure 7.1. Look through the tabs and analyze them more closely. Interestingly, you can see a spike in the memory usage, CPU usage, and thread counts. This is the duration in which a sample stress was running.

To execute various JMX operations provided via JConsole, you will need to switch to the **MBeans** tab. Expand the various menu items in the bar on the left-hand side of the screen. The interesting ones are under **org.apache.cassandra.***. For example, you can clear the value of hinted handoff for a node that is dead before the configured timeout (`max_hint_window_in_ms`) for that node arrives (see Error! Reference source not found.).

As a matter of taste, some people prefer VisualVM over JConsole. VisualVM does not provide JMX support out of the box. However, it is fairly easy to add a VisualVM-MBeans plugin to enable such functionality. VisualVM combines JConsole, jstat, jinfo, jstack, and jmap. This is available in versions starting from JDK 6 and can be accessed at $JDK_HOME/bin/jvisualvm.

Details on VisualVM are outside the scope of this book, but you can learn about them at https://visualvm.java.net/jmx_connections.html.

Cassandra nodetool

The nodetool utility is a command-line utility that comes out of the box with Cassandra. You can access it from $CASSANDRA_HOME/bin/nodetool. It communicates with JMX to perform operational and monitoring tasks exposed by MBeans. It is much easier to use than JConsole. We have already seen a bit of nodetool in the previous chapter. The nodetool utility is a great tool for administration and monitoring. The following section will discuss some of the useful functionalities of nodetool. Most of the nodetool commands are obvious and can be easily learned by reading the help text. Unfortunately, there is no help option, but it prints help messages anyway.

The following screenshot shows how to invoke methods via JConsole:

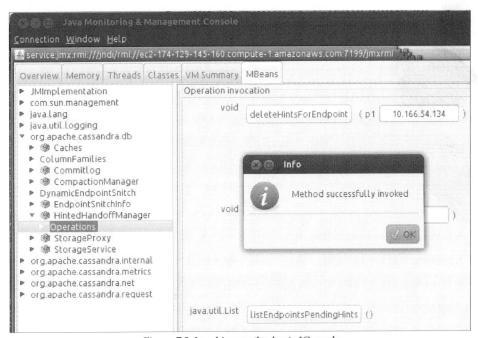

Figure 7.2: Invoking methods via JConsole

The standard way to execute any command on a Cassandra node using `nodetool` is as follows:

```
nodetool -h CASSANDRA_HOST [-p JMX_PORT -u JMX_USERNAME -pw JMX_PASSWORD]
COMMAND
```

In general, you do not need to provide `JMX_PORT`, `JMX_USERNAME`, and `JMX_PASSWORD` unless you've explicitly configured them. The following sections discuss the `COMMAND` keyword in the previous command.

Monitoring with nodetool

The `nodetool` utility provides some of the basic, yet very informative, statistics of Cassandra. This is often used to take a quick glance at how Cassandra is doing and to monitor it. This section will introduce you to some of the interesting commands that `nodetool` offers to monitor Cassandra.

cfstats

`cfstats` stands for column family statistics; it comprises details about every significant statistic regarding all the column families in the ring and across all the keyspaces. Executing `cfstats` looks like the following code (all these are per-node data):

```
$ bin/nodetool -h 'hostname' cfstats
Keyspace: Keyspace1
  Read Count: 74426
  Read Latency: 0.1452843092467686 ms.
  Write Count: 333208
  Write Latency: 0.035750168063191756 ms.
  Pending Tasks: 0
    Column Family: Standard1
    SSTable count: 2
    Space used (live): 110260160
    Space used (total): 110260160
    Number of Keys (estimate): 333312
    Memtable Columns Count: 0
    Memtable Data Size: 0
    Memtable Switch Count: 7
    Read Count: 74426
```

```
Read Latency: 0.145 ms.
Write Count: 333208
Write Latency: NaN ms.
Pending Tasks: 0
Bloom Filter False Positives: 56
Bloom Filter False Ratio: 0.00101
Bloom Filter Space Used: 625888
Compacted row minimum size: 311
Compacted row maximum size: 372
Compacted row mean size: 372
...
----------------
...
```

A few important statistics are as follows:

- **Read Latency** and **Write Latency**: These provide the average time elapsed in performing these operations. It may be nice to look at if you see the throughput is slow.

- **Read Count** and **Write Count**: These can provide a general idea of how frequently a column family is accessed. It may be an indicator of how busy a column family is.

- **Pending Tasks**: Lots of pending tasks are an indication of an overloaded node. Maybe one should look into rebalancing the cluster or, probably, adding more machines or improving the node's hardware.

- **Space Used** (**live** and **total**): The live statistic represents the space used by the SSTables in use. The `total` statistic is the total space used by the SSTable. The total statistic is always greater than or equal to the live statistic due to the existence of deleted, but yet-to-be-removed, data. All these data are in bytes (just bytes, not kilobytes or megabytes).

- **Number of Keys** and **Maximum Row Size**: This can help you to estimate a rough size for the row cache for the column family, if you decide to use it.

netstats

The `netstats` command is to view the network statistics (streaming information) of the node within the ring. This is a very useful tool, especially during maintenance work, such as moving, repairing, removing the node (decommission), or starting up a new one.

The following snippet shows various stages of the node as provided by `netstats` while a node is being decommissioned:

```
$ bin/nodetool -h 10.147.171.159 netstats
Mode: LEAVING
Not sending any streams.
Not receiving any streams.
Pool Name    Active    Pending        Completed
Commands         n/a          0                0
Responses        n/a          0             1410


$ bin/nodetool -h 10.147.171.159 netstats
Mode: LEAVING
Streaming to: /10.166.54.134
/mnt/cassandra-data/data/Keyspace1/Standard1/Keyspace1-Standard1-hf-9-
Data.db sections=1 progress=6898944/6898944 - 100%
/mnt/cassandra-data/data/Keyspace1/Standard1/Keyspace1-Standard1-hf-8-
Data.db sections=1 progress=0/97061952 - 0%
Not receiving any streams.
Pool Name    Active    Pending        Completed
Commands         n/a          0                0
Responses        n/a          0             1412


$ bin/nodetool -h 10.147.171.159 netstats
Mode: DECOMMISSIONED
Not sending any streams.
Not receiving any streams.
Pool Name    Active    Pending        Completed
Commands         n/a          0                0
Responses        n/a          0             1507
```

ring and describering

The `ring` command is the most frequently used command. It shows you all the members in the ring and the tokens they are assigned to. It also shows their individual percentage ownership, which can help you determine if the ring is lopsided.

```
$ bin/nodetool -h 10.147.171.159 ring
```

Address	DC	Rack	Status	State	Load	Owns	Token
							11342745564
							03128211544
							58202477256
							070483
10.99.9.67	us-east	1b	Up	Normal	97.45 MB	33.33%	0
10.147.171.159	us-east	1b	Up	Normal	105.23 MB	33.33%	56713727820
							15641057722
							91012386280
							35242
10.166.54.134	us-east	1b	Up	Normal	96.99 MB	33.33%	11342745564
							03128211544
							58202477256
							070483

ring [<Keyspace>] is usually just sufficient, but using the describering [<Keyspace_name>] command,, makes the output look like the following output:

```
$ bin/nodetool -h 10.147.171.159 describering Keyspace1
Schema Version:b8d7527e-85a5-37ef-86b1-35ef9e64af15
TokenRange:
  TokenRange(
  start_token:0,
  end_token:56713727820156410577229101238628035242,
  endpoints:[10.147.171.159],
  rpc_endpoints:[10.147.171.159],
  endpoint_details:[
   EndpointDetails(
    host:10.147.171.159,
    datacenter:us-east,
    rack:1b)
  ])
```

```
TokenRange(
start_token:5671372782015641057722910123862803524 2,
end_token:11342745564031282115445820247725607048 3,
endpoints:[10.166.54.134],
rpc_endpoints:[10.166.54.134],
endpoint_details:[
 EndpointDetails(
   host:10.166.54.134,
   datacenter:us-east,
   rack:1b)
])
TokenRange(
start_token:1134274556403128211544582024772560704 83,
end_token:0,
endpoints:[10.99.9.67],
rpc_endpoints:[10.99.9.67],
endpoint_details:[
 EndpointDetails(
   host:10.99.9.67,
   datacenter:us-east,
   rack:1b)
])
```

tpstats

`tpstats` stands for thread pool statistics. This is an important measure of how much pressure the node is bearing at a given instant. You can see task counts that are running, pending, completed, and blocked in various stages. The rule of thumb is that more pending tasks indicate a performance bottleneck. The following command-line output shows the result of a `tpstats` usage:

```
$ bin/nodetool -h 10.147.171.159 tpstats
Pool Name          Active Pending Completed Blocked ATB*
ReadStage          0      0       74426     0       0
```

RequestResponseStage	0	0	815033	0	0
MutationStage	0	0	333235	0	0
ReadRepairStage	0	0	0	0	0
ReplicateOnWriteStage	0	0	0	0	0
GossipStage	0	0	1096434	0	0
AntiEntropyStage	0	0	60	0	0
MigrationStage	0	0	5	0	0
MemtablePostFlusher	0	0	18	0	0
StreamStage	0	0	0	0	0
FlushWriter	0	0	18	0	0
MiscStage	0	0	0	0	0
PendingRangeCalculator	0	0	6	0	0
commitlog_archiver	0	0	0	0	0
AntiEntropySessions	0	0	2	0	0
InternalResponseStage	0	0	9	0	0
HintedHandoff	0	0	3	0	0

Message type	Dropped
RANGE_SLICE	0
READ_REPAIR	0
BINARY	0
READ	0
MUTATION	0
REQUEST_RESPONSE	0

*ATB = All time blocked

It also displays various types of message drops that happen due to various reasons. These message drops may or may not be significant to you. A message to a node that does not get processed within the limits of rpc_timeout_in_ms (cassandra. yaml) is dropped so that the coordinator node does not keep waiting. This means the coordinator node will get a timeout response for executing a request made to the node. For example, a read request may get a couple of timeouts, but the user will get the data as long as there are sufficient replicas that return valid responses for the request such that the consistency level of the query is satisfied. For a write or mutate request, this means that the node that has timed out is in an inconsistent state. It will get fixed either during a read repair or an anti-entropy repair. If you get lots of dropped messages, it may be worth investigating what is going on in the node.

One may relate thread pools getting backed up to dropping messages in **tpstats:** there are more tasks that can be processed by the threads within timeout limits.

compactionstats

The `compactionstats` command shows the compaction process running in the instant. Compaction is a CPU and I/O-intensive task. It may temporarily increase used disk space. So, it may be a good idea to check if any compaction is running if there is no obvious indication from other monitoring statistics but you suddenly see high I/O, CPU, or space consumption.

```
$ bin/nodetool -h 10.147.171.159 compactionstats
pending tasks: 0
Active compaction remaining time :        n/a
```

info

The `info` command prints an overall bird's-eye view of the node's health. This command can be used to get a quick summary of the node. Some of the labels, such as heap size and recent cache hit rate, may give you some sense of how the node is doing.

```
$ bin/nodetool -h 10.147.171.159 info
Token             : 56713727820156410577229101238628035242
Gossip active     : true
Thrift active     : true
Load              : 105.23 MB
Generation No     : 1372274081
Uptime (seconds)  : 344212
Heap Memory (MB)  : 613.87 / 1844.00
Data Center       : us-east
Rack              : 1b
Exceptions        : 0
Key Cache         : size 3095424 (bytes), capacity 96468960 (bytes), 18981
hits, 74562 requests, 0.254 recent hit rate, 14400 save period in seconds
Row Cache         : size 0 (bytes), capacity 0 (bytes), 0 hits, 0
requests, NaN recent hit rate, 0 save period in seconds
```

Administrating with nodetool

We have seen some usage of `nodetool` while setting up the Cassandra cluster in *Chapter 4, Deploying a Cluster,* and during various maintenance tasks in *Chapter 6, Managing a Cluster.* We will see some more administrative tooling in this section.

drain

The `drain` command makes the node stop listening from other nodes and clients. It flushes all the data to SSTables. No more write commands are processed. This is a handy tool if you want to safely shut down Cassandra to upgrade it.

```
# Drain the data to SSTables
$ bin/nodetool -h 10.147.171.159 drain


# can't connect to it.
$ bin/cassandra-cli -h 10.147.171.159
org.apache.thrift.transport.TTransportException: java.net.
ConnectException: Connection refused
  at org.apache.thrift.transport.TSocket.open(TSocket.java:183)
```

decommission

We have seen `decommission` during node removal in the *Removing nodes from cluster* section in *Chapter 6, Managing a Cluster.* Decommissioning is a way to remove a live node from the cluster. It streams all the data that it has to a replica node or a node that will be responsible for the data after the node that is being decommissioned dies.

move

Decommissioning or adding a new node usually imbalances the cluster. To reassign a different token ID to a node, you need to execute the following command:

```
$ bin/nodetool -h NODE_IP_TO_CHANGE_TOKEN move NEW_TOKEN
```

Like `decommission`, the `move` command streams data off the node. These may create large network traffic and affect performance temporarily. These tasks should be done during the time the application is relatively free. Refer to *Chapter 6, Managing a Cluster,* for more on `move`.

removetoken

To completely remove a node from a ring, the `removetoken` command is used. We have seen it earlier in the *Removing a dead node* section in *Chapter 6, Managing a Cluster*. Once `removetoken` is executed, the key range that the *to-be-removed* node holds gets streamed to the other node that now owns the responsibility for that key range. This streaming is done from other replicas of the node.

The `removetoken` command provides three options:

- `removetoken <token>`: Removes the specified token
- `removetoken force`: Forces pending token removal operations to occur
- `removetoken status`: Displays the status of this operation

repair

Nodetool's `repair` command performs pretty useful maintenance tasks. It helps the cluster avoid returning data from the dead (the re-appearance of deleted data). It is highly recommended to run repair periodically on the whole cluster to avoid *forgotten* deletes. The time period between two consecutive repairs should be less than the value assigned to `gc_grace_seconds` (configured per column family, the default is 10 days).

Hinted handoff is useful only as long as there is no hardware failure that lasts more than the value assigned to `max_hint_window_in_ms`. So, it is generally a good idea to set up a cron job for your production machines that executes `nodetool repair` for all the nodes.

The way *forgotten* deletes come back can be explained with an example. Let's say you have two nodes, A and B, with the data X replicated between them. If you issue a delete action with `CL.ONE` when B is down, the client will get success, and hinted handoff will make a note to resend the request to B when it comes back. If, unfortunately, B does not come back before hinted handoff is cleared, `GCGraceSeconds` wipes the data from node A. Now, if B comes back to life, Cassandra will treat the deleted row as a new row that is not replicated to A (it will be copied to A during read repair). Running a node repair has no way of fixing the problem, now that `GCGraceSeconds` have been exceeded.

`nodetool repair` has the following format:

```
nodetool -h HOSTNAME repair [Keyspace] [cfnames] [-pr]
```

So, repair can be executed for a node or a given keyspace or a list of column families. There is an interesting option called primary range, denoted by -pr. The primary range option just repairs the range that the node owns. Without the primary range option, however, the command forces Cassandra to repair the node as well as all the replicas. So, if you are planning to repair a whole cluster, you should use the -pr switch; otherwise, you are duplicating the task RF times. The following are the scenarios for the repair command:

- **Periodic repair**: Periodic repair should be executed on every node periodically within gc_grace_seconds, normally within 10 days. Running the repair weekly, timed at a relatively low traffic zone, is a good idea. Periodic repair is suggested to be executed with the -pr option.

- **Outage**: When a node goes down long enough to get hinted handoff, since the node may have been deleted, repair should be executed. Note that you should not use the -pr option in this case.

A typical complete node repair looks as follows:

```
$ bin/nodetool -h 10.99.9.67 repair

[2013-07-01 06:44:46,768] Nothing to repair for keyspace 'system'

[2013-07-01 06:44:46,776] Starting repair command #3, repairing 1 ranges
for keyspace Keyspace1

[2013-07-01 06:44:46,777] Repair session b83f6b80-e219-11e2-0000-
23f6cbfa94fd for range (113427455640312821154458202477256070483,0]
finished

[2013-07-01 06:44:46,777] Repair command #3 finished

[2013-07-01 06:44:46,795] Starting repair command #4, repairing 2 ranges
for keyspace mytest

[2013-07-01 06:44:47,828] Repair session b84251b0-e219-11e2-0000-
23f6cbfa94fd for range (0,113427455640312821154458202477256070483]
finished

[2013-07-01 06:44:47,842] Repair session b8924670-e219-11e2-0000-
23f6cbfa94fd for range (113427455640312821154458202477256070483,0]
finished

[2013-07-01 06:44:47,842] Repair command #4 finished
```

upgradesstable

This command rebuilds SSTables. It is generally used during upgrades or during the compression ratio changes.

snapshot

The nodetool snapshot we have seen earlier while taking a backup (refer to *Chapter 6, Managing a Cluster*) basically creates hard links for SSTables in the snapshots folder, to be used to restore the node. There is a command to remove the snapshot; it is called `clearsnapshot`. The command has the following options:

```
# Create snapshot
nodetool -h CASSANDRA_HOST snapshot [Keyspaces...] -cf [columnfamilyName]
-t [snapshotName]
```

```
# Remove snapshots
nodetool -h CASSANDRA_HOST clearsnapshot [Keyspaces...] -t [snapshotName]
```

There are more commands that `nodetool` provides that we have not discussed here. In general, we have discussed the commands that you will find frequently. The rest of the commands can be learned from the help text provided by `nodetool`. The `nodetool` documentation can be found online.

>
> Nodetool documentation on Apache Cassandra wiki:
> `http://wiki.apache.org/cassandra/NodeTool`.
> The relatively newer documentation on DataStax:
> `http://www.datastax.com/docs/1.1/references/nodetool`.

DataStax OpsCenter

DataStax (`http://www.datastax.com`) is the leading company that provides commercial support for Cassandra. At the time of writing of this book, DataStax claimed to employ more than 90 percent of Cassandra committers. DataStax provides an easy-to-use, web-based utility—OpsCenter—that is little more than a GUI wrapper over Cassandra's JMX instrumentation. OpsCenter provides a clean, simple, and intuitive interface to manage and monitor a Cassandra cluster. This section will briefly go over OpsCenter.

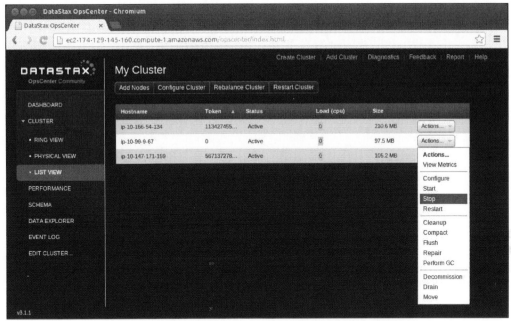

Figure 7.3: DataStax OpsCenter Cluster View and Actionable Items

DataStax provides two versions of OpsCenter: an enterprise version and a community version. The enterprise version has more features, official support, and is paid. The community version can be downloaded and used for free in a production environment. You may download and evaluate the enterprise version for free for development purposes. In this section, we will briefly go over installing, configuring, monitoring, and administrating a single data center, 3-node cluster using OpsCenter's community version.

OpsCenter Features

OpsCenter is a superset of `nodetool`. It provides all the functionality of `nodetool`, displays metrics in an intuitive way, and also provides administrative tooling beyond the default toolset that comes with Cassandra. The following is a short list of features:

- **Centralized view of all the clusters**: Options to visualize a cluster in different modes: ring view, list view, and view by data centers.

- **Manage cluster configuration**: Edit and update cluster-wide configuration from the web console.

- **Visualize performance**: OpsCenter actually stores the performance history over time. This can help you visualize performance in various time windows: 20 minutes, hourly, daily, weekly, and monthly.

- **Add a new node**: On your local cluster, you can ask OpsCenter to add another node by providing the node address and credentials (of a sudoer), and choosing the appropriate DataStax package, which is basically Cassandra and OpsCenter packaged in a user-friendly way by DataStax.

- OpsCenter's enterprise edition has more advanced features, as follows:

  - New cluster addition from GUI
  - Downloadable diagnostic information
  - Single-click cluster rebalancing
  - Multiple cluster management
  - Alerts and e-mail notification

 If you are on AWS EC2, OpsCenter allows you to automatically add a new node to your existing cluster. This node is basically an instance of DataStax AMI with the appropriate Cassandra version that you have chosen.

Installing OpsCenter and an agent

OpsCenter installation comprises two parts: installation of the OpsCenter web interface on one machine and installation of agents on each Cassandra node. The web interface and nodes communicate with one an other to be able to display information.

Prerequisites

- **Java 6**: The machines where you are planning to install a web interface or agents must have Java 6; or any version that is specifically not lower than version 1.6.0_19. Java 7 is not recommended. The version can be checked for as follows:

```
$ java -version
java version "1.6.0_34"
Java(TM) SE Runtime Environment (build 1.6.0_34-b04)
Java HotSpot(TM) 64-Bit Server VM (build 20.9-b04, mixed mode)
```

- **Python 2.6+**: The web interface is Python-based and utilizes the Twisted package. Python's recommended version is 2.6+. It may or may not work with Python 3. Use the following command to find out the version of Python installed on your computer:

```
# yes, UPPERCASE V
$ python -V
Python 2.6.8
```

- **sysstat**: sysstat is a bundle of system monitoring utilities. It provides statistics about CPU usage, memory usage, space monitoring, I/O activity information, network statistics, and some other data about system resources. The presence of this can be checked by executing the following command:

```
# iostat is one the utilities in sysstat. V is uppercase.
$ iostat -V
sysstat version 9.0.4
(C) Sebastien Godard (sysstat <at> orange.fr)
```

If it is not already installed, use the following commands depending on your Linux distribution:

```
# CentOS or RHEL like systems
sudo apt-get install sysstat


# Ubuntu or Debian like systems
yum install sysstat
```

- **OpenSSL**: OpenSSL is an optional component. OpsCenter uses a secure connection to communicate within the OpsCenter web interface and agents by default. If you are just testing OpsCenter, you are running within a secure internal network, or there is no appropriate OpenSSL implementation for the platform, you may just avoid this step by adding the following lines in `$OPSCENTER_HOME/conf/opscenterd.conf`:

```
[agents]
use_ssl = false
```

You will also need to update the agent's `conf/address.yaml` file using:

```
use_ssl: 0
```

In case you want SSL to be enabled, make sure you have the correct OpenSSL version installed for your platform.

```
$ openssl version
OpenSSL 1.0.1e-fips 11 Feb 2013
```

DataStax provides the following compatibility list for OpenSSL with OpsCenter:

Version	Operating System
0.9.8	CentOS 5.x, Debian, Mac OS X, Oracle Linux 5.5, RHEL 5.x, SuSe Enterprise 11.x, Ubuntu, and Windows
1.0.0	CentOS 6.x, Oracle Linux 6.1, and RHEL 6.x

In case you have the 1.0.0 version on an operating system that requires version 0.9.8 for OpsCenter to work, installing a 0.9.8 version may solve the problem. It may not be ideal to have two versions of OpenSSL. The following code shows how a server with CentOS 5.x with the 1.0.0 version was fixed (OpsCenter requires version 0.9.8). Please note that this may not be an ideal solution and it can potentially break some other functionality.

```
$ yum install openssl098e

# Bad practice!
$ sudo ln -s /usr/lib64/libssl.so.0.9.8e \
  /usr/lib64/libssl.so.0.9.8
$ sudo ln -s /usr/lib64/libcrypto.so.0.9.8e \
  /usr/lib64/libcrypto.so.0.9.8
```

Running a Cassandra cluster

You need to have a running Cassandra cluster that can communicate with OpsCenter's web interface machine.

Installing OpsCenter from Tarball

DataStax provides different binaries packaged specifically for different operating systems. One may download an RPM package, a Deb package, or an MSI (Windows) package based on what operating system one is using. In this section, we will use the Tarball archive because it works across several platforms (Linux, Mac OS X).

View all the download options for OpsCenter Community
Edition at `http://planetcassandra.org/Download/`
`DataStaxCommunityEdition`.

1. **Download and untar:**

   ```
   # Download latest OpsCenter
   $ wget \
    http://downloads.datastax.com/community/opscenter.tar.gz
   # Untar
   $ tar -xzf opscenter.tar.gz
   ```

2. **Edit** `conf/opscenterd.conf` **and insert the appropriate hostname,
   OpsCenter's port number, and SSL setting (if required):**

   ```
   # vi conf/opscenterd.conf
   [webserver]
   port = 80
   interface = 10.147.171.159 #IP of OpsCenter machine
   [agents]
   use_ssl = false
   ```

3. **Start the OpsCenter web server:**

   ```
   # Use -f to start in foreground
   $OPSCENTER_HOME/bin/opscenter


   # In the command above, $OPSCENTER_HOME is just a reference
   # to the OpsCenter installation location.
   ```

If the web server starts without any error, you should be able to access OpsCenter
from your browser. Make sure the security settings allow the port mentioned in
`opscenterd.conf`. When no agent is added, it will ask you to create a new cluster or
join an existing cluster. This is the time to set up agents on each Cassandra node.

Setting up an OpsCenter agent

The ways OpsCenter works is that there are agents that the web interface of OpsCenter talks to. These agents collect data points and send commands to the nodes. See the following figure:

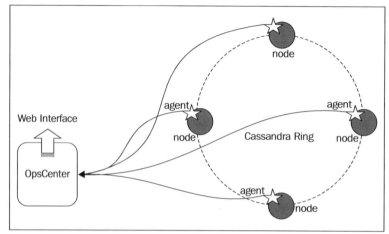

Figure 7.4: OpsCenter in action

An agent is available within the OpsCenter directory under the `agent` directory. You need to set up the agent and then copy the agent directory to all other nodes. Then, start the agents. The following are the steps to set up the agent:

1. Go to the agent's directory:

   ```
   cd $OPSCENTER_HOME/agent
   ```

2. Set up the agent:

   ```
   bin/setup OPSCENTER_IP
   ```

   Here, `OPSCENTER_IP:` is the address of the machine hosting OpsCenter.

   This updates the `$AGENT_HOME/conf/address.yaml` file.

3. If you have SSL disabled, add `use_ssl: 0`:

   ```
   # address.yaml
   stomp_interface: "10.147.171.159"
   use_ssl: 0
   ```

4. Once this is done and the agent directory is copied across all nodes, start the agents on each node by executing the following command:

```
# Execute this from agent directory, user -f for foreground
$ bin/opscenter-agent
```

5. After OpsCenter and the agents are up, open OpsCenter in the browser, click on **Join existing cluster**, and provide the node IPs (data of a single node should be sufficient).

Monitoring and administrating with OpsCenter

OpsCenter exposes all the functionality of JMX via a web console. This means everything that we were able to do using `nodetool`, we can do with OpsCenter. Most of the node-level administrative options are available by clicking on the node (under the cluster view menu) and then clicking on the **Action** button.

For cluster-wide operations, there are menus under the cluster view page. You can add a node, change the configuration file cluster-wide, and perform a rolling restart of the cluster. In the paid version, you can create a cluster, add more than one cluster to OpsCenter, download information to diagnose a problem, and generate reports.

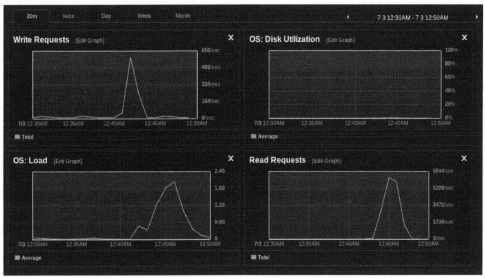

Figure 7.5: A subset of monitoring options by OpsCenter

OpsCenter provides a plethora of attributes to keep a tab on. It covers Cassandra-specific attributes like read/write requests, pending tasks in different stages, row and key cache hit rate; column family-specific statistics like pending read and writes, SSTables' size and count, and so on; and operating system resource-specific statistics such as CPU, memory, disk usage, network, and some more. Basically, a superset of monitoring options is provided by nodetool. To add more plots to the **Performance** screen, you need to click on the **Add Graph** button and select the appropriate graph. To make this setting permanent, save this plot setting by choosing **Save as...** from the drop-down menu next to the **Performance Metrics** heading.

Other features of OpsCenter

Apart from operational tasks, OpsCenter can be pretty useful to add, remove, or modify keyspaces. The **Schema** screen provides options to play with keyspaces and column families.

Another interesting feature is the **Data Explorer** screen. This provides a visually pleasing interface to browse keyspace and column families. You can also search within a column family by the row key.

OpsCenter provides security features; it allows us to enable SSL for the OpsCenter web console, a simple authentication mechanism for OpsCenter. Advanced configuration and setup is outside the scope of this book; refer to the official DataStax documentation for this at `http://www.datastax.com/docs/opscenter/index`.

Nagios – monitoring and notification

Nagios (`http://www.nagios.org`) is an open source monitoring and notification utility. It enables users to monitor various resources, such as CPU, memory, disk usage, network status, reachability, HTTP status, testing web page rendering, and various checks using Nagios-compatible sensors. There is a giant list of Nagios plugins that covers the monitoring of almost all popular services and software. The best thing with Nagios is its plugin architecture. You can write a simple plugin for custom resource monitoring. So, effectively, anything where its state can be measured, can be monitored via Nagios. This section will discuss, very briefly, Nagios setup and how it can be enabled to monitor system resources and Cassandra.

Installing Nagios

Nagios ships in different packages, such as DIY, student, professional, and business, based on a number of features and support; you may visit the Nagios website and choose one based on your needs. With the number of free plugins, the Nagios free version is generally a good option. In this section, we will see how to install and configure the Nagios free version (from the source) on a CentOS machine. These instructions should work on any RHEL variant. For Ubuntu- or Debian-like environments, you may need to look for an `apt-get` equivalent of the `yum` commands in the script. Based on your Linux distribution, the Nagios distribution can be installed from additional repositories. It may or may not be the latest and greatest among Nagios, but it eases a lot of installation hassles. We use tarball installation for this book to keep things generic.

Prerequisites

The Nagios server (PHP-based) has some dependencies to be fulfilled before you can start installing it.

- **PHP**: You will need to have a PHP processor to run Nagios. Check its availability using the following command:

  ```
  $ php -v
  PHP 5.3.26 (cli) (built: Jun 24 2013 18:08:10)
  Copyright (c) 1997-2013 The PHP Group
  Zend Engine v2.3.0, Copyright (c) 1998-2013 Zend Technologies
  ```

  If PHP does not exist, install it.

  ```
  $ sudo yum install php
  ```

- **httpd**: The Apache httpd web server serves as the frontend to a PHP-based Nagios web application. To check whether you have httpd or not, execute the following command:

  ```
  $ httpd -v
  Server version: Apache/2.2.24 (Unix)
  Server built:   May 20 2013 21:12:45
  ```

  If httpd does not exist, install it.

  ```
  $ sudo yum install httpd
  ```

- **GCC compiler**: Check for the installed version of GCC compiler using the following command:

```
$ gcc -v
Using built-in specs.
COLLECT_GCC=gcc
COLLECT_LTO_WRAPPER=/usr/libexec/gcc/x86_64-amazon-linux/4.6.3/
lto-wrapper
Target: x86_64-amazon-linux
Configured with: ../configure --prefix=/usr --mandir=/usr/
share/man --infodir=/usr/share/info --with-bugurl=http://
bugzilla.redhat.com/bugzilla --enable-bootstrap --enable-shared
--enable-threads=posix --enable-checking=release --with-system-
zlib --enable-__cxa_atexit --disable-libunwind-exceptions
--enable-gnu-unique-object --enable-linker-build-id --enable-
languages=c,c++,objc,obj-c++,,fortran,ada,go,lto --enable-
plugin --disable-libgcj --with-tune=generic --with-arch_32=i686
--build=x86_64-amazon-linux
Thread model: posix
gcc version 4.6.3 20120306 (Red Hat 4.6.3-2) (GCC)
```

  Install it, if it does not exist:

```
$ sudo yum install gcc glibc glibc-common
```

- **GD graphics library**: GD is a dynamic graphics development library to generate various formats of dynamically generated images. Unfortunately, there is no quick way to see GD installation. To install GD Library, execute the following command:

```
$ yum install gd gd-devel
```

Preparation

Before we jump into installing Nagios, we need to set up a user account and a group for Nagios.

```
$ sudo -i
$ useradd -m nagios
$ passwd nagios
$ groupadd nagcmd
$ usermod -a -G nagcmd nagios
$ usermod -a -G nagcmd apache
```

Installation

Nagios installation can be divided into four parts: installing Nagios, configuring Apache httpd, installing plugins, and setting up Nagios as a service.

Installing Nagios

The following are the steps to install Nagios from tarball:

1. Download tarball from the Nagios download page and untar it:

   ```
   $ wget http://prdownloads.sourceforge.net/sourceforge/nagios/
   nagios-3.5.0.tar.gz
   ```

   ```
   $ tar xzf nagios-3.5.0.tar.gz
   ```

2. Install Nagios from the source:

   ```
   $ cd nagios
   $ ./configure –with-command-group=nagcmd
   $ make all
   $ sudo make install \
       install-base \
       install-cgis \
       install-html \
       install-exfoliation \
       install-config \
       install-init \
       install-commandmode \
       fullinstall
   ```

3. Nagios is installed now. Update the contact details before you move to the next step:

   ```
   $ sudo vi /usr/local/nagios/etc/objects/contacts.cfg
   define contact{
    contact_name nagiosadmin       ; Short name of user
    use            generic-contact ; Inherit default values
    alias          Nagios Admin    ; Full name of user
    email          YOUR_EMAIL_ID   ; *SET EMAIL ADDRESS*
   }
   ```

Configuring Apache httpd

1. Set Apache httpd with the appropriate Nagios configuration:

```
$ sudo make install-webconf

/usr/bin/install -c -m 644 sample-config/httpd.conf /etc/httpd/
conf.d/nagios.conf

*** Nagios/Apache conf file installed ***
```

2. Set the password for the Nagios web console for the user `nagiosadmin`:

```
$ sudo htpasswd -c /usr/local/nagios/etc/htpasswd.users
nagiosadmin
```

3. Restart Apache httpd:

```
$ sudo service httpd restart
```

Installing Nagios plugins

1. Download and untar Nagios plugins from the Nagios website's plugins page, `http://www.nagios.org/download/plugins/` using the following commands:

```
$ wget http://prdownloads.sourceforge.net/sourceforge/nagiosplug/
nagios-plugins-1.4.16.tar.gz

$ tar xzf nagios-plugins-1.4.16.tar.gz
```

2. Install the plugin:

```
$ cd nagios-plugins-1.4.16

$ ./configure --with-nagios-user=nagios –with-nagios-group=nagios

$ make

$ make install
```

> Warning! If you get an error such as `check_http.c:312:9:`
> `error: 'ssl_version' undeclared (first use in this`
> `function)` while trying to execute `./configure` or `make`, your
> system probably lacks the `libssl` library. To resolve this issue,
> execute the following commands:
>
> On RHEL- or CentOS-like systems:
>
> `yum install openssl-devel -y`
>
> On Debian- or Ubuntu-like systems:
>
> `sudo apt-get install libssl-dev`

3. Re-run `./configure`, then `make clean`, then `make`.

Setting up Nagios as a service

Everything is set; let's set Nagios as service:

```
$ sudo chkconfig --add nagios
$ sudo chkconfig nagios on
```

Check if the default configuration is good to go and start the Nagios service:

```
# Check configuration file
$ sudo /usr/local/nagios/bin/nagios -v /usr/local/nagios/etc/nagios.cfg
[-- snip --]
Website: http://www.nagios.org
Reading configuration data...
   Read main config file okay...
Processing object config file '/usr/local/nagios/etc/objects/commands.
cfg'...
[-- snip --]
Processing object config file '/usr/local/nagios/etc/objects/localhost.
cfg'...
   Read object config files okay...
Running pre-flight check on configuration data...
[-- snip --]
Total Warnings: 0
Total Errors:   0
Things look okay - No serious problems were detected during the pre-
flight check
```

```
# Start Nagios as a service
$ sudo service nagios start
```

Now you are ready to see the Nagios web console. Open the `http://NAGIOS_HOST_ADDRESS/nagios` URL in your browser. You should be able to see the Nagios home page with a couple of default checks on the Nagios host.

Nagios plugins

Nagios' power comes from a lot of plugin libraries available for it. There are sufficient default plugins provided as a part of the base package to perform decent resource monitoring. For advanced or non-standard monitoring, you will have to either download it from somewhere, such as the Nagios plugins directory or GitHub, or you will have to write a plugin of your own. Writing a custom plugin is very simple. There are only two requirements: the plugin should be executable via command prompt, and the plugin should return with the following exit values:

- `0` implying OK state
- `1` implying warning state
- `2` implying critical state
- `3` implying unknown state

This means you are free to choose your programming language and tooling. As long as you follow these two specifications, your plugin can be used in Nagios.

Nagios plugins directory:

  `http://exchange.nagios.org/directory/Plugins`

Nagios plugins projects on GitHub:

  `https://github.com/search?q=nagios+plugin&type=Repo`
  `sitories&ref=searchresults`

Nagios plugins for Cassandra

There are a few Cassandra-specific plugins in the Nagios plugins directory. There is a promising project on GitHub, namely, Nagios Cassandra Monitor (`https://github.com/dmcnelis/NagiosCassandraMonitor`); it seems a little immature, but worth evaluating. In this subsection, we will use a JMX-based plugin that is not Cassandra-specific. We will use this plugin to connect to Cassandra nodes and query heap usage. This will tell us about two things: whether or not it can connect to Cassandra (which can be treated as an indication of whether or not the Cassandra process is up) and what the heap usage is.

The following are the steps to get the JMX plugin installed. All these operations take place on the Nagios machine and not on Cassandra nodes.

1. Download the plugins from `http://exchange.nagios.org/directory/Plugins/Java-Applications-and-Servers/check_jmx/details`.

2. Untar and navigate to the `libexec` directory:

   ```
   $ tar xvzf check_jmx.tgz
   $ cd check_jmx/nagios/plugin/
   $ sudo cp check_jmx jmxquery.jar /usr/local/nagios/libexec/
   ```

3. Assign them proper ownership and run a test:

   ```
   $ cd /usr/local/nagios/libexec/
   $ sudo chown nagios:nagios check_jmx jmxquery.jar
   ```

4. Replace `10.99.9.67` with your Cassandra node:

   ```
   $ ./check_jmx -U
   service:jmx:rmi:///jndi/rmi://10.99.9.67:7199/jmxrmi -O java.
   lang:type=Memory -A HeapMemoryUsage -K used -I HeapMemoryUsage -J
   used -vvvv -w 4248302272 -c 5498760192

   JMX OK HeapMemoryUsage.used=1217368912{committed=1932525568;init=1
   953497088;max=1933574144;used=1217368912}
   ```

Executing remote plugins via an NRPE plugin

NRPE is a plugin to execute plugins on remote hosts. One may think of it as OpsCenter and its agents (see the following figure). With NRPE, Nagios can monitor remote host resources, such as memory, CPU, disk, network, and can execute any plugin on a remote machine.

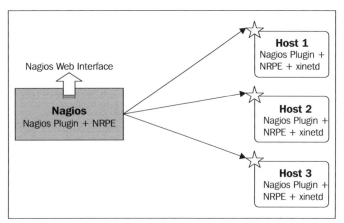

Figure 7.6: Nagios with NRPE plugin in action

NRPE installation has to be done on the Nagios machine as well as all the other machines where we want to execute a Nagios plugin locally, for example, to monitor the CPU usage.

Installing NRPE on host machines

First, you need to create a `nagios` user and a `nagios` group and set the user with a password as discussed in the *Preparation* subsection in this chapter. After that, install the Nagios plugin as mentioned in the *Installing Nagios plugins* section in this chapter. Now you may proceed to the NRPE installation.

1. Install `xinetd` if it does not already exist:

   ```
   $ sudo yum install xinetd
   ```

2. Download the NRPE daemon and plugin from the NRPE Nagios page at `http://exchange.nagios.org/directory/Addons/Monitoring-Agents/NRPE--2D-Nagios-Remote-Plugin-Executor/details` and install them:

   ```
   # Download and untar NRPE
   $ wget http://downloads.sourceforge.net/project/nagios/nrpe-2.x/
   nrpe-2.14/nrpe-2.14.tar.gz
   $ tar xvzf nrpe-2.14.tar.gz


   # make and install daemon and plugin, configure xinetd
   $ cd nrpe-2.14
   $ ./configure
   $ make all
   $ sudo make install-plugin
   $ sudo make install-daemon
   $ sudo make install-daemon-config
   $ make install-xinetd
   ```

3. After this, you need to make sure each host machine accepts requests coming from Nagios. For this, you need to edit `/etc/xinetd.d/nrpe` to add the Nagios host address to it. In the following code snippet below, you need to replace `NAGIOS_HOST_ADDRESS` with the actual Nagios host address:

   ```
   # edit /etc/xinetd.d/nrpe
   only_from = 127.0.0.1 NAGIOS_HOST_ADDRESS


   # edit /etc/services append this
   nrpe      5666/tcp              # NRPE
   ```

4. Restart and test if xinet is functional:

```
# Restart xinetd
$ sudo service xinetd restart
Stopping xinetd:    [FAILED]
Starting xinetd:    [  OK  ]


# Check if it's listening
$ netstat -at | grep nrpe
tcp    0    0 *:nrpe    *:*    LISTEN
# Check NRPE plugin
$ /usr/local/nagios/libexec/check_nrpe -H localhost
NRPE v2.14


# Try to invoke a plugin via NRPE
$ /usr/local/nagios/libexec/check_nrpe -H localhost -c check_load


OK - load average: 0.01, 0.04, 0.06|load1=0.010;15.000;30.000;0;
load5=0.040;10.000;25.000;0; load15=0.060;5.000;20.000;0;
```

Now we have the machine ready to be monitored via NRPE.

Installing NRPE plugin on a Nagios machine

Installing NRPE plugin on a Nagios machine is a subset of the task that we did for the remote host machine. All you need to do is install the NRPE plugin and nothing else. The following are the steps:

```
$ wget http://downloads.sourceforge.net/project/nagios/nrpe-2.x/nrpe-
2.14/nrpe-2.14.tar.gz
$ tar xvzf nrpe-2.14.tar.gz
$ cd nrpe-2.14
$ ./configure
$ make all
$ sudo make install-plugin


# Test if plugin is working, you should replace 10.99.9.67
# with one of the machine's address with NRPE + xinetd
$ /usr/local/nagios/libexec/check_nrpe -H 10.99.9.67
NRPE v2.14
```

Setting things up to monitor

In this section, we will talk about how to set up CPU, disk, and Cassandra monitoring. However, the detail is enough to enable you to set up any Nagios plugin and configure monitoring.

Monitoring CPU and disk space: These are the tests that need to be executed on remote machines. So, we may need to configure NRPE configuration to allow those plugins to be executed remotely. This configuration is stored in /usr/local/ nagios/etc/nrpe.cfg. If you do not find the plugin that you wanted to execute or you want to change the parameters to be passed to the plugin, this is the place; to achieve that, use the following set of commands:

```
# edit /usr/local/nagios/etc/nrpe.cfg
command[check_users]=/usr/local/nagios/libexec/check_users -w 5 -c 10


command[check_load]=/usr/local/nagios/libexec/check_load -w 15,10,5 -c
30,25,20


command[check_hda1]=/usr/local/nagios/libexec/check_disk -w 20% -c 10% -p
/dev/hda1
[-- snip --]


#custom commands *add your commands here*


# EC2 ephemeral storage root disk
command[check_sda1]=/usr/local/nagios/libexec/check_disk -w 20% -c 10% -p
/dev/sda1
```

Have a look at the following screenshot:

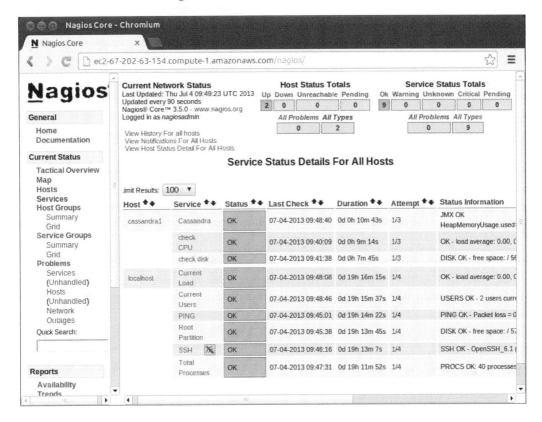

Figure 7.7: Nagios interface monitoring local and remote resources

As you can see, we have a CPU check (check_load) and a disk check already provided by the default configuration. However, if I wanted to monitor the /dev/sda1 device for space availability, I would add a new check, check_sda1, for this.

Setting up a JMX monitor: For Cassandra, we want to check the JVM heap usage via JMX. Since this executes on the local machine (Nagios) to connect to the JMX service on the remote machine, we do not need to use NRPE for this. So, we have nothing to do here.

Updating configuration: The best part of Nagios is its configuration. With a little trick and grouping, you can make a fine configuration that can scale to hundreds of machines. All configurations in Nagios are text-based with JSON-ish syntax. You can have files organized in whichever way you want and let Nagios know where the files are. For this particular case, the `/usr/local/nagios/etc/objects/cassandrahosts.cfg` file is created. This file houses all the information related to monitoring. The following code is what it looks like (see the comments in bold):

```
# A machine to be monitored
# DEFINE ALL CASSANDRA HOSTS HERE

define host{
        use                     linux-server
        host_name               cassandra1
        alias                   Cassandra Machine
        address                 10.99.9.67
        }


# create logical groupings, manageable, saves typing
# HOST GROUP TO COLLECTIVELY CALL ALL CASSANDRA HOSTS

define hostgroup{
        hostgroup_name  cassandra_grp
        alias           Cassandra Group
        members         cassandra1  ;this is CSV of
                                    ;hosts defined above

        }


# A service defines what command to execute on what hosts
# MONITORING SERVICES

# A service that executes locally
#Check Cassandra on remote machines

define service{
        use                     generic-service
        hostgroup_name          cassandra_grp
        service_description     Cassandra
        check_command           check_cas ;defined below
        }


# A service that gets executed remotely via NRPE
# check disk space status
```

```
define service{
  use                 generic-service
  hostgroup_name      cassandra_grp
  service_description check disk
  check_command       check_nrpe!check_sda1
  }

# check CPU status
define service{
  use                 generic-service
  hostgroup_name      cassandra_grp
  service_description check CPU
  check_command       check_nrpe!check_load
  }

# A command is a template of a command line call, here:
#    $USER1$ is plugin directory, nagios/libexec
#    $HOSTADRRESS$ resolves to the address defined in
#    host block above, hosts are chosen from the service that
#    calls this command

# define custom commands
# check JVM heap usage using JMX,
# warn if > 3.7G, mark critical if > 3.85G

define command {
        command_name check_cas
        command_line $USER1$/check_jmx -U service:jmx:rmi:///
jndi/rmi://$HOSTADDRESS$:7199/jmxrmi -O java.lang:type=Memory -A
HeapMemoryUsage -K used -I HeapMemoryUsage -J used -vvvv -w 3700000000
-c 3850000000
        }
```

Letting Nagios know about the new configuration: We have created a new
configuration file that Nagios does not know about. We need to register it
in /usr/local/nagios/etc/nagios.cfg; append the following line to this file:

```
#custom file *ADD YOUR FILES HERE*
cfg_file=/usr/local/nagios/etc/objects/cassandrahosts.cfg
```

Test the configuration and you are done.

```
$ sudo /usr/local/nagios/bin/nagios -v /usr/local/nagios/etc/nagios.cfg
Nagios Core 3.5.0
[-- snip --]
```

```
Reading configuration data...

    Read main config file okay...

Processing object config file '/usr/local/nagios/etc/objects/commands.
cfg'...

Processing object config file '/usr/local/nagios/etc/objects/contacts.
cfg'...

Processing object config file '/usr/local/nagios/etc/objects/timeperiods.
cfg'...

Processing object config file '/usr/local/nagios/etc/objects/templates.
cfg'...

Processing object config file '/usr/local/nagios/etc/objects/
cassandrahosts.cfg'...

Processing object config file '/usr/local/nagios/etc/objects/localhost.
cfg'...

    Read object config files okay...

Running pre-flight check on configuration data...

[-- snip --]

 Total Warnings: 0

Total Errors:   0

Things look okay - No serious problems were detected during the pre-
flight check
```

Restart Nagios by executing `sudo service nagios restart`.

Monitoring and notification using Nagios

Nagios has built-in support to send mails whenever an interesting event, such as
a warning, an error, or a service coming back to the OK state, occurs. By default, it
uses the `mail` command, so if your mail is configured correctly, you should see mails
when you execute the following command:

```
# substitute YOUR_EMAIL_ADDRESS with your email id.
/usr/bin/printf "%b" "Hi Nishant, \nthis is Nagios." | /bin/mail -s
"Nagios test mail" YOUR_EMAIL_ADDRESS
```

If this does not reach your mail box or the spam folder, you should check your
configuration. If you do not have the mail utility installed already, execute the
following command:

```
# mail utility on RHEL like OS
$ sudo yum install mailx
```

```
# On Ubuntu or Debian derivatives
$ sudo apt-get install mailutils
```

If you are not happy with the mailing option or want to change the mailer to send mail via a specific mail provider like Gmail, you should dig into the plugins directory or GitHub to find appropriate alternatives.

Nagios provides a pretty intuitive GUI—a web-based console that immediately highlights anything that is wrong with any service or host. Apart from displaying the immediate state, Nagios also stores the history of monitored events. There are many reporting capabilities that provide a complete infrastructure status overview. One can easily generate a histogram that states the performance of a service. Refer to the following diagram:

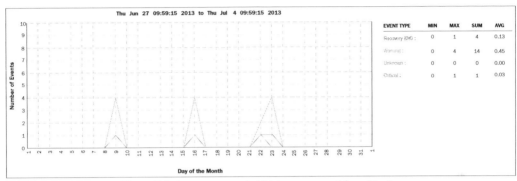

Figure 7.8: An auto generated histogram report from Nagios

There are many reporting options; options to disable the alerts during a scheduled downtime of infrastructure. It may be worth playing around the Nagios GUI to learn about the various options.

Cassandra log

Last, but not least, Cassandra log is a good tool for monitoring what is going on inside Cassandra. However, monitoring the logfile is an extremely non-scalable option. So, if you are starting with anything fewer than five Cassandra machines, you may consider occasionally looking into their logfiles. The most common use of the Cassandra log is to perform the postmortem for a failure when you do not have any other monitoring and reporting mechanism in place.

The location of the `log4j` log can be found out from Cassandra's `conf/log4j-server.properties` file:

 # This has been altered during installation

`log4j.appender.R.File=/mnt/cassandra-logs/system.log`

As long as you view this file filled with lines, starting with INFO, you may think the system has been behaving alright. Lines with WARN may or may not be interesting.

For example, it is OK to have some WARNs in the system as shown in the following system:

```
INFO [MemoryMeter:1] 2013-05-24 12:31:39,099 Memtable.java
   (line 213) CFS(Keyspace='Keyspace1', ColumnFamily='Standard1')
   liveRatio is 1.0 (just-counted was 1.0).
   calculation took 3ms for 325 columns
WARN [MemoryMeter:1] 2013-05-24 12:31:39,135 Memtable.java
   (line 197) setting live ratio to minimum of 1.0
   instead of 0.8662032831217121
```

But, some warnings may be a definite sign of danger and should be fixed to avoid a catastrophe (it may not be a big deal if you have RF and CL set properly).

```
# May be a future crash due to lack of disk space
WARN [CompactionExecutor:45] 2013-05-24 17:34:03,709
   CompactionTask.java (line 82) insufficient space to compact all
   requested files SSTableReader(path='/mnt/cassandra-
   data/data/Keyspace1/Standard1/Keyspace1-Standard1-hf-34-
   Data.db'), SSTableReader(path='/mnt/cassandra-
   data/data/Keyspace1/Standard1/Keyspace1-Standard1-hf-35-
   Data.db'), SSTableReader(path='/mnt/cassandra-
   data/data/Keyspace1/Standard1/Keyspace1-Standard1-hf-28-
   Data.db')
```

An ERROR should always be attended to. It usually answers buts and whys about Cassandra behavior, points out incorrect configuration, tells you about what to do next, and what to change in the read/write pattern.

```
# oh snap! Dave was right about horizontal scaling.
ERROR [FlushWriter:7] 2013-05-24 17:35:21,617 AbstractCassandraDaemon.
java (line 132) Exception in thread Thread[FlushWriter:7,5,main]
java.lang.RuntimeException: Insufficient disk space to flush 71502048
bytes
[-- snip --]
WARN [CompactionExecutor:46] 2013-05-24 17:35:26,871 FileUtils.
java (line 116) Failed closing IndexWriter(/mnt/cassandra-data/data/
Keyspace1/Standard1/Keyspace1-Standard1-tmp-hf-42)
java.io.IOException: No space left on device
```

Cassandra logs are great. If you find yourself looking too frequently into it, you probably need a better monitoring mechanism. Also, if you feel like getting blinded by the abundance of information, you may change the log a level up from INFO to WARN in the `log4j-server.properties` file. It is suggested not to turn on the DEBUG mode, unless you are editing the Cassandra code base and debugging the changes. It may lead to lots of I/O activity and may affect the performance.

Enabling Java Options for GC Logging

JVM options provide a nice way to monitor Java applications. It is not specific to Cassandra. One may set various -XX options as part of arguments when starting the Java application. In Cassandra, these options can be enabled by uncommenting the lines with –xx. The following is the list of the options:

```
# GC logging options -- uncomment to enable
# JVM_OPTS="$JVM_OPTS -XX:+PrintGCDetails"
# JVM_OPTS="$JVM_OPTS -XX:+PrintGCDateStamps"
# JVM_OPTS="$JVM_OPTS -XX:+PrintHeapAtGC"
# JVM_OPTS="$JVM_OPTS -XX:+PrintTenuringDistribution"
# JVM_OPTS="$JVM_OPTS -XX:+PrintGCApplicationStoppedTime"
# JVM_OPTS="$JVM_OPTS -XX:+PrintPromotionFailure"
# JVM_OPTS="$JVM_OPTS -XX:PrintFLSStatistics=1"
# JVM_OPTS="$JVM_OPTS -Xloggc:/var/log/cassandra/gc-'date +%s'.log"


# If you are using JDK 6u34 7u2 or later you can enable GC log
rotation
# don't stick the date in the log name if rotation is on.
# JVM_OPTS="$JVM_OPTS -Xloggc:/var/log/cassandra/gc.log"
# JVM_OPTS="$JVM_OPTS -XX:+UseGCLogFileRotation"
# JVM_OPTS="$JVM_OPTS -XX:NumberOfGCLogFiles=10"
# JVM_OPTS="$JVM_OPTS -XX:GCLogFileSize=10M"
```

It is pretty obvious what these options do. In case you wanted to enable some of these options, the following table shows what they mean:

Option	Description
-XX:+PrintGCDetails	Prints more details at garbage collection.
-XX:+PrintGCDateStamps	Prints GC events with the date and time rather than with a timestamp that we get using -XX:+PrintGCTimeStamps.
-XX:+PrintHeapAtGC	Prints detailed GC information, including heap occupancy before and after GC.

Option	Description
`-XX:+PrintTenuring Distribution`	Prints tenuring age information.
`-XX:+PrintGC ApplicationStoppedTime`	Prints the net time of every stop-the-world event.
`-XX:+PrintPromotion Failure`	Prints the size of the objects that fail promotion.
`-XX:PrintFLSStatistics=1`	Prints free list statistics for each young or old collection (FLS = Free List Space).

The rest of the options are for log location, log size, and rolling log counts.

Troubleshooting

We have learned cluster configuration, repairing and scaling, and, finally, monitoring. The purpose of all this learning is for you to keep the production environment up and running smoothly. You chose the right ingredients to set up a cluster that fits your need, but there may be node failures, high CPU usage, high memory usage, disk space issues, network failures, and, probably, performance issues with time. Most of this information you will get from the monitoring tool that you have configured. You will need to take necessary action depending on the problems that you are facing.

Usually, one goes about finding these issues via various tools that we've discussed in the past. You may want to extend the list of tools to include Linux tooling for investigation, such as `netstat` and `tcpdump` for network debugging' `vmstat`, `free`, `top`, and `dstat` for memory statistics; `perf`, `top`, `dstat`, and `uptime` for CPU; and `iostat`, `iotop`, and `df` for disk usage.

So, how would you know there is a problem? With a decent monitoring setup and a vigilant system-admin, the problems usually come to one's knowledge via alerts sent by the monitoring system. It may be a mail from OpsCenter or a critical message from Nagios or from your home-grown JMX-based monitoring system. Another way to see the issues is as performance degradation at a certain load. You may find that your application is acting weird or abnormally slow. You dig into the error and find out that the Cassandra calls are taking a really long time, more than expected. The other, and scarier, way the problems come to one's notice is on production. Things have been working decently in the test environment and you suddenly start seeing frequent garbage collection calls or the production servers start to scream, "Too many open files."

In many of the error scenarios, the solution is a simple one. For cases such as where AWS notifies an instance shutdown due to underlying hardware degradation, the fix is to replace the node with a new one. For a *disk full* issue, you may add either a new node or just more hard disks and add the location to the data directories setting in Cassandra — yaml. The following are a few troubleshooting tips. Most of these things you might have known from the previous chapters.

High CPU usage

High CPU usage can be associated with frequent garbage collections (GC). If you see a lot of GC call information in Cassandra logs and if they take longer than one second to finish, it means the system has loaded the JVM with the garbage collector.

The easiest fix is to add more nodes. Another option can be increasing the JVM heap size (adding more RAM, if required) and tweak the garbage collector setting for Cassandra.

Compaction is a CPU-intensive process; you may expect a spike during compaction. You should plan to perform a `nodetool compact` during relatively silent hours. The same goes for repair; execute `nodetool repair` during low load.

High memory usage

Before we dive into memory usage, it is useful to point out that providing a lot of RAM to the Java heap may not always help. We have learned in a previous chapter that Cassandra automatically sets the heap memory, which is good in most cases. If you are planning to override it, note that garbage collection does not do well beyond an 8 GB heap.

There are a couple of things you should check when debugging for high memory usage. Bloom filter's false positive ratio can lead to large memory usage. For smaller error rates in the Bloom filter, we need a larger memory. In case you find the Bloom filter to be the culprit and decide to increase the false positive ratio, remember that the recommended maximum value for the false positive value is `0.1`; performance starts to degrade after this. This may not be applicable to Cassandra 1.2 and onward where the Bloom filter is managed off-heap.

Continuing the subject of off-heap, another thing that you might want to look into is row caches. Row caches are stored off-heap, if you have the JNA installed. If there is no JNA, the row cache falls back onto the on-heap memory — adding to the used heap memory. It may lead to frequent GC calls.

High memory usage can be a result of pulling lots of rows in one go. Look into such queries. Cassandra 1.2 onward has a trace feature that can help you find such queries.

Hotspots

A hotspot in a cluster is a node or a small set of nodes that show abnormally high resource usage. In the context of Cassandra, it will be the nodes in the cluster that get abnormally high hits or show high resource usage compared to other nodes.

A poorly balanced cluster can cause some nodes to own a high number of keys. If the request for each key has equal probability, the nodes with the higher numbers of ownership will have to serve a high number of requests. Rebalancing the cluster may fix this issue.

Ordered partitioners, such as `ByteOrderedPartitioner`, usually have a hard time making sure that each key range has an equal amount of data, unless the data coming for each key range has the same probability. It is suggested that you rework the application to avoid dependency on key ordering and use `Murmur3Partitioner` or `RandomOrderPartitioner`, unless you have a very strong reason to depend on byte order partitioning. Refer to the *Partitioners* section in *Chapter 4, Deploying a Cluster*.

High-throughput-wide columns may cause a hotspot. We know that a row resides on one server (actually, on all the replicas). If we have a row that gets written to and/or read from at a really high rate, the node gets loaded disproportionately (and the other nodes are probably idle). A good idea is to bucket the row key. For example, assume you are a popular website; if you decide to document a live presidential debate by recording everything told by the candidates, host, and audiences and stream this data live, you allow users to scroll back and forth to see the past records. In this case, if you decide to use a single row, you are creating a hotspot. The ideal thing would be to break the row key into buckets like `<rowKey>:<bucket_id>` and round robin the buckets to store the data. Keys are being distributed across the nodes; now you have the load distributed on multiple machines. To fetch the data, you may want to `multiget slice` the buckets and merge them into the application. The merging should be fast because the rows are already sorted. Refer to the *High throughput rows and hotspots* section in *Chapter 3, Design Patterns*.

Another cause of hotspots can be wrong token assignment in a multi-data-center setup (refer to *Chapter 4, Deploying a Cluster*). If you have two nodes, A and B, in data center 1, and two nodes, B and C, in data center 2, you calculate equidistant tokens and assign them to A, B, C, and D in increasing order. It seems OK, but it actually makes node A and node C hotspots.

Ideally, one should assign alternate tokens in different data centers. So, A should get the first token, C should get the second, B the third, and D the fourth. If there are three data centers, pick one from each and assign increasing tokens, then go for the second, and so on.

OpenJDK may behave erratically

Linux distros ship with Open Java and OpenJDK. Cassandra does not officially support any variant of the JVM other than Oracle/Sun Java 1.6. Open Java may cause some weird issues, such as the GC pausing for very long and performance degradation. The safest thing to do is to remove Open Java and install the suggested version.

Disk performance

Amazon Web Services users often find **Elastic Block Storage (EBS)** lucrative to use from performance and reliability points of view. Unfortunately, it is a bad idea to use them.

EBS with Cassandra: It slows down the disk I/O speed. It can cause slow reads and writes. If you are using EBS, try comparing it with the instance store (ephemeral storage) with the RAID0 setup.

If you see **Too many open files** or any other resource-related issue, the first thing to check is `ulimit -a` to see all available system resources. You can edit this setting by editing `/etc/security/limits.conf` and setting it to the following recommended setting:

```
* soft nofile 32768
* hard nofile 32768
root soft nofile 32768
root hard nofile 32768
* soft memlock unlimited
* hard memlock unlimited
root soft memlock unlimited
root hard memlock unlimited
* soft as unlimited
* hard as unlimited
root soft as unlimited
root hard as unlimited
```

Slow snapshot

Creation of a snapshot for backup purposes is done by creating a hard link to SSTables. In the absence of JNA, it is done by using `/bin/ln` by fork and exec to create a hard link. This is observably slow with thousands of SSTables. So, if you are seeing an abnormally high snapshot time, check if you have the JNA configured.

Getting help from the mailing list

Cassandra is a robust and fault-tolerant software. It is possible that your production is running as expected while something is broken within. Replication and eventual consistency can help you to build a robust application on top of Cassandra, but it is important to keep an eye on monitoring statistics.

The tools that have been discussed in this and previous chapters should help you get enough information about what went wrong. You should be able to fix common problems using these tools. But sometimes it is a good idea to ask about a stubborn issue on the friendly Cassandra mailing list: `user@cassandra.apache.org`.

When asking a question on the mailing list, provide as many statistics as you can gather around the problem. Nodetool's `cfstats`, `tpstats`, and `ring` are common ways to get Cassandra-specific statistics. You may want to check the Cassandra logs, enable `JVM_OPTS` for GC-related statistics, and profile using Java `jhat` or JConsole. Apart from this, server specifications, such as memory, CPU, network, and disk stats provide crucial insights. Among other things, one may mention replication factor, compaction strategy, consistency level, and column family specifications as required.

Summary

Setting up proper monitoring of your infrastructure is the most recommended and the most disregarded suggestion to a development team, especially in startups where teams are small, resources are limited, and fast development is the only priority. It usually goes hand-in-hand with lethargy to go through a painfully long mechanical process to set up a system. The importance of monitoring is best understood when a failure that could have been avoided occurs at a critical hour. Monitoring is an important tool to show the reliability of a system.

With multiple tools in hand, you are knowledgeable to take your weapon of choice. Starting with JConsole, which enables you to view the status of Cassandra internals, the JVM, and you may tweak and control some parameters. It is a bit tricky to get it working. Plus, it is a resource hog. On the other hand, `nodetool` is a powerful utility. It can help you get the internal stats and performs many administrative tasks. However, it is a command-line tool. So, probably, the managers are not going to like this. Plus, it shows an instantaneous status. It is not meant to gather status. This is where OpsCenter comes into the picture. With really simple installation and the ability to store performance history and resource monitoring, it is hands-down the best option to monitor Cassandra. But, the free version does not have an alert mechanism, report generation, and some other options such as auto load balancing. The other downside of it is that it is a whole different system to monitor just Cassandra. If you have a heterogeneous system with application servers, RDBMS, a stand-alone application, and a website, you would probably want something that can monitor everything and you can see the complete picture in one place. Nagios and its plugins take over. It allows you to monitor almost anything that can be measured in at least OK and CRITICAL states. Unlike the community version of OpsCenter, Nagios provides a nice interface to generate reports and an in-built mailing alert mechanism. All these can be extended by custom-written plugins. Nagios is open source with a very large and enthusiastic community.

Choose a tool or a set of tools that fit your environment. In many cases, having Nagios to monitor Cassandra, CPU, memory, ping, and disk statistics is good enough. Others may want a dedicated monitoring and management tool such as OpsCenter. There are still others who just write a code that utilizes the JMX interface to monitor particular statistics. It is really up to you.

Cassandra is a big data store. What is the use of a big data store if you can't analyze it to extract interesting statistics? Fortunately, Cassandra provides hooks to smoothly integrate it with various Apache Hadoop projects like Hadoop MapReduce, Pig, and Hive. It can be used as a corpus store for Solr. Cassandra plays well with low latency stream processing tools such as Twitter Storm and can be seamlessly integrated with the Spark project (`http://spark-project.org`). The next chapter is all about using analytical tools with Cassandra.

8
Integration

Big Data is the latest trend in the technical community and industry in general. Cassandra and many other NoSQL solutions solve a major part of the problem: storage of a large amount of data set in a scalable manner while keeping the mutations and retrieval queries superfast. But this is just half the picture. A major part is processing. A database that provides better integration with analytical tools such as Apache Hadoop, Twitter Storm, Pig, Spark, and other platforms will be a preferable choice.

Cassandra provides native support to Hadoop MapReduce, Pig, Hive, and Oozie. It is a matter of tiny changes to get the Hadoop family up and working with Cassandra. There are a couple of independently developed projects that use Cassandra as storage. One of the most popular projects is Solandra. Solandra provides Cassandra integration with **Solr**. However, it does not magically enable you to test search in Cassandra. Cassandra serves just as a backend.

Third-party supports for Hadoop and Solr have taken Cassandra to the next step in terms of integration. Third-party proprietary tooling such as DataStax Enterprise edition for Cassandra makes it easy to work with Hadoop and actually text search Cassandra using Solr.

Cassandra is a very powerful database engine. We have seen its salient features as a single software entity. In this chapter we will see how Cassandra can be used as a data store for third-party software such as Hadoop MapReduce, Pig, and Apache Solr.

This chapter does not cover Cassandra integration with Hive and Oozie. To learn about Cassandra integration with Oozie, refer to:

`http://wiki.apache.org/cassandra/HadoopSupport#Oozie`

Hive can be integrated with Cassandra via independent projects such as `https://github.com/riptano/hive_old` on GitHub. But it seems deprecated, so it is suggested to not use it. There are ongoing efforts to bring Hive integration to Cassandra as its native part. If you are planning to use Cassandra with Hive, keep watch on this issue at:

`https://issues.apache.org/jira/browse/CASSANDRA-4131`

DataStax Enterprise editions have built-in Cassandra-enabled Hive MapReduce clients; you may want to check them out at:

`http://www.datastax.com/docs/datastax_enterprise3.0/`
`solutions/about_hive`

Using Hadoop

Hadoop is for data processing. So is Matlab, R, Octave, Python (NLTK and many other libraries for data analysis), and SAS, you may say. They are great tools, but they are good for data that can fit in memory. It means you can churn a couple of GBs to maybe 10s of GBs, and the rate of processing depends on the CPU on that machine, maybe 16 cores. This poses a big restriction. The data is no more in GB limits at Internet scale. In the age of billions of cell phones (an estimated 6.8 billion cell users at the end of 2012; source: `http://mobithinking.com/` `mobile-marketing-tools/latest-mobile-stats/a#subscribers`), we are generating a humongous amount of data every second (Twitter reports 143,199 Tweets per second; source: `https://blog.twitter.com/2013/new-tweets-` `per-second-record-and-how`) by checking in places, tagging photos, uploading videos, commenting, messaging, purchasing, dining, running (fitness apps monitor your activities), and many other activities that we do; we literally record events somewhere. It does not stop at organic data generation. A lot of data, a lot more than organic data, is generated by machines (`http://en.wikipedia.org/wiki/` `Machine-generated_data`). Web logs, financial market data, data from various sensors (including ones in your cell phone), machine part data, and many more are such examples. Health, genomics, and medical science have some of the most interesting Big Data corpus ready to be analyzed and inferred. To give you a glimpse of how big genetic data can be, we should check data from 1,000 genome projects (`http://www.1000genomes.org/`). This data is available for free (there are storage charges) to be used by anyone. The genome data for (only) 1,700 individuals makes a corpus of 200 terabytes. It is doubtful that any conventional in-memory computation tool such as R or Matlab can do it. Hadoop helps you process the data of that extent.

Hadoop is an example of distributed computing, so you can scale beyond a single computer. Hadoop virtualizes the storage and processors. This means you can roughly treat a 10-machine Hadoop cluster as one machine with 10 times the processing power and 10 times storage capacity than a single one. With multiple machines parallely processing the data, Hadoop is the best fit for large unstructured data sets. It can help you to clean data (data munging) and can perform data transformation too. HDFS provides a redundant distributed data storage. Effectively, it can work as your extract, transform, and load (ETL) platform.

Hadoop and Cassandra

In the age of Big Data analytics, there are hardly any data-rich companies that do not want their data to be extracted, evaluated, and inferred to provide more business inside. In the past, analyzing large data sets (structured or unstructured) that span terabytes or petabytes used to be expensive and a technically challenging task to a team; distributed computing was harder to keep track of, and hardware to support this kind of infrastructure was not financially feasible to everyone.

What changed the demography completely in favor of medium and small companies are a couple of things. Hardware prices dropped down to earth. Memories and processing powers of computing units increased dramatically at the same time. Hardware on demand came into the picture. You can spend about 20 dollars to rent about a 100 virtual machines with quad-core (virtual) processors, 7.5 GB RAM, and 840 GB of ephemeral storage (you can plug in gigantic network-attached storages that are permanent) from Amazon Web Services for one hour. There are multiple vendors that provide this sort of cloud infrastructure. However, the biggest leap in making Big Data analysis commonplace is the availability of extremely high, quality free, and open source solutions that abstract the developers from managing distributed systems. These software made it possible to plug in various algorithms and use the system as a black box to take care of getting the data, applying the routines, and returning the results. Hadoop is the most prominent name in this field. Currently, it is the de-facto standard of Big Data processing.

 At the time of writing this book, this is the specification of an AWS M1.large machine. The pricing estimate is based on the hourly price of on-demand instances at USD 0.24 per hour.

Hadoop deserves a book of its own. If you wanted to learn about Hadoop, you may want to refer to Yahoo!'s excellent tutorial on this subject (`http://developer.yahoo.com/hadoop/tutorial/index.html`). This section will give a simplistic introduction to Hadoop, which is by no means complete. If you are already familiar with Hadoop, you may skip this section.

Introduction to Hadoop

Apache Hadoop is an open source implementation of two famous white papers from Google: **Google File System (GFS)** (`http://research.google.com/archive/gfs.html`) and **Google MapReduce** (`http://research.google.com/archive/mapreduce.html`). Vanilla Hadoop consists of two modules: **Hadoop Distributed File System (HDFS)** and **MapReduce (MR)**. HDFS and MR are implementations of GFS and Google MapReduce, respectively. One may consider HDFS as a storage module and MapReduce as a processing module.

HDFS – Hadoop Distributed File System

Let's start with an example. Assume you have 1 TB of data to read from a single machine with a single hard disk. Assuming the disk read rate is 100 MBps, it will take about 2 hours and 45 minutes to read the file. If you could split this data over 10 hard disks and read them all in parallel, it would have decreased the read time by 10 — more or less. From a layman's perspective, this is what HDFS does; it breaks the data into fixed sized blocks (default is 64 MB) and distributes them over a number of slave machines.

HDFS is a filesystem that runs on top of a regular filesystem. Production installations generally have **ext3** filesystems running beneath HDFS. By distributing data across several nodes, the storage layer can scale to a very large virtual storage that scales linearly. To provide reliability to store data, the data is stored with redundancy. Each block is replicated three times by default. HDFS is architected in such a way that each data block gets replicated to different servers and if possible on different racks. This saves data from disk, server, or complete rack failure. In the event of a disk or a server failure, data is replicated to a new location to meet the replication factor. If this reminds you of Cassandra, or any other distributed system, you are on the right track. But as we will see very soon, unlike Cassandra, HDFS has a single point of failure due to its master-slave design.

Despite all these good features, HDFS has a few shortcomings too.

1. HDFS is optimized for streaming. This means that there is no random access to a file. It may not utilize the maximum data transfer rate.

2. **NameNode** (discussed later) is a single point of unavailability for HDFS.

3. HDFS is better suited for large files.

4. The append method is not supported by default. However, one can change the configuration to allow the append method.

Data management

HDFS uses the master-slave mechanism to distribute data across multiple servers. The master node is usually backed by a powerful machine so that it does not fail. The slave machines are data nodes; these are commodity hardware. The reason of master nodes being beefy machines is that it is a single point failure. If the master node (that is, the NameNode) goes down, the storage is down—unlike the Cassandra model. To load the data to HDFS, the client connects to the master node and sends an upload request. The master node tells the client to send parts of data to various data nodes. Note that data does not stream through the master node. It just directs the client to appropriate data nodes and maintains the metadata about the location of various parts of a file.

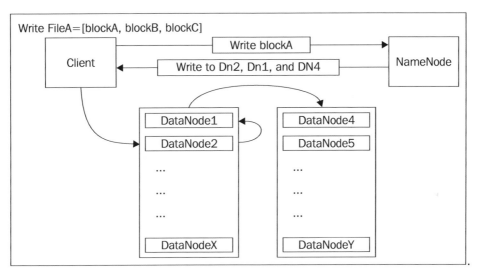

Figure 8.1: Client makes a request to NameNode to write a block. NameNode returns the nodes where the block is to be written. Client picks one DataNode from the nodes list in the previous step and forwards to other nodes

There are two processes one needs to know about to understand how the data is distributed and managed by HDFS.

NameNode

NameNode process is the one that runs on a master server. Its job is to keep metadata about the files that are stored in the data nodes. If the NameNode is down, the slaves have no idea how to make sense of the block stored. So, it is crucial to have NameNode on redundant hardware. In general, in a Hadoop cluster, there is just one master NameNode.

DataNodes

DataNodes are the slaves. They are the machines that actually contain the data. The DataNode process manages the data blocks on the local machine. DataNodes keep on checking with the master node as in a sort of heartbeat. This enables the master to replicate the data if one of the slaves dies.

Data never goes via NameNode. DataNodes are the ones responsible for streaming the data out.

NameNode and DataNodes work in harmony to provide a scalable and giant virtual filesystem that is oblivious to the underlying hardware or the operating system. The way data read or write takes place is as follows:

1. Client makes a write request for a block of a file to the master, the NameNode server.

2. NameNode returns a list of servers that the block is copied to (in a replicated manner, a block is copied at many places as replication is configured).

3. Client makes an is-ready request to one of the to-be-written-on DataNodes. This node forwards the request to the next node, which will forward it to the next, until all the nodes to write the data on acknowledge OK.

4. On receipt of the OK message, a client starts to stream the data to one of the data nodes that internally streams the data to the next replica node and so on.

5. Once the block gets written successfully, slaves notify the master. The slave connected to the client returns a success.

6. Figure 8.1 shows the data flow when a Hadoop client (CLI or Java) makes a request to write a block to HDFS.

Hadoop MapReduce

MapReduce or MR is a very simple concept once you know it. It is algorithm 101: divide and conquer. The job is broken into small independent tasks and distributed across multiple machines; the result gets sorted and merged together to generate the final result. The ability to distribute a large computational burden over multiple servers into a small computational load over multiple servers enables a Hadoop programmer to have effectively limitless CPU capability for data analysis. MR is the processing part of Hadoop; it virtualizes the CPU. Figure 8.2 depicts this process.

As an end user, you need to write a Mapper and a Reducer for the tasks you need to get done. The Hadoop framework performs the heavy lifting of getting data from a source and splitting it into maps of keys and values based on what the data source is. It may be a line from a text file, a row from a relational database, or a key-value from the Cassandra column family. These maps of key-value pairs (indicated as Input key-val pairs in the next figure) are forwarded to the Mapper that you have provided to Hadoop. Mapper performs unit tasks of the key-value pair; for example, for a word count task, you may want to remove punctuations, split the words by whitespace, iterate in this split array of words, forward key as an individual word, and set value as one. These make the intermediate key-value pair, as indicated in the next figure.

These results are sorted by the key and forwarded to the Reducer interface that you provided. Reducers can use this property, that coming tuples have the same key. Understanding the last sentence is important to a beginner. What it means is that you can just iterate in the incoming iterator and do things such as group or count—basically reduce or fold the map by key.

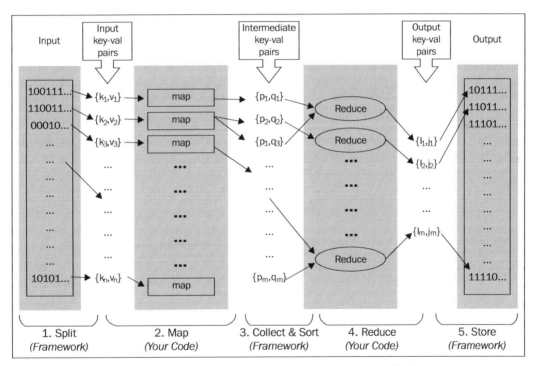

Figure 8.2: Hadoop MapReduce framework in action (simplified)

The reduced values are then stored in a storage of your choice that can be HDFS, RDBMS, Cassandra, or one of the many other storage options.

There are two main processes that you should know about in the context of Hadoop MapReduce.

JobTracker

Similar to NameNode, JobTracker is a master process that governs the execution of worker threads such as TaskTracker. Like any master-slave architecture, JobTracker is a single point of failure. So, it is advisable to have a robust hardware and redundancy built into the machine that has a JobTracker running.

JobTracker's responsibility includes estimating the number of Mapper tasks from the input split, for example, file splits from HDFS via `InputFormat`. It uses already configured values as numbers of Reducer tasks. Client application can use JobClient to submit jobs to JobTracker and inquire status.

TaskTracker

Like the DataNode in the case of HDFS, the TaskTracker is the actual execution unit of Hadoop. It creates a child JVM for Mapper and Reducer tasks. The maximum number of tasks (Mapper and Reducer tasks) can be set independently. TaskTracker may re-use the child JVMs to improve efficiency.

Reliability of data and process in Hadoop

Hadoop is a very robust and reliable architecture. It is meant to be run on commodity hardware and hence takes care of failure automatically. It detects failure of a task and retries the failed tasks. It is fault tolerant. A down DataNode is replicated (redundant) and a system heals by itself, in case of unavailability of a DataNode.

Hadoop allows servers to join the cluster or leave it without any repercussion. Rack-aware storage of data saves the cluster against disk failures, rack/machine power failure, and even a complete rack going down.

Figure 8.3 shows the famous schema of reliable Hadoop infrastructure using commodity hardware for slaves and heavy-duty servers (top of the rack) for the masters. Please note that these are physical servers as they are in the data centers. Later, when discussing using Cassandra as a data store, we will use a ring representation. Even in that case, the physical configuration may be the same as the one represented in Figure 8.3, but the logical configuration, as we have been seeing throughout this book, will be a ring-like structure to emphasize the token distribution.

Setting up local Hadoop

This section will discuss how to set up Hadoop 1.x on your local machine. At the time of this writing, Hadoop is transitioning from Version 1 to Version 2. Version 2 has disruptive changes and is presumably better than Version 1. HDFS is federated in the new version. The Apache documentation says this version scales the NameNode service horizontally using multiple independent NameNodes. This should ideally avoid single point of failure that NameNodes faced in the previous version. The other major improvement is in the new MapReduce frameworks, for example, MRNextGen, MRv2, and **Yet Another Resource Negotiator (YARN)**. More about the new version can be learned on the Apache website (What is YARN? `http://hadoop.apache.org/docs/current/hadoop-yarn/hadoop-yarn-site/YARN.html`). Here are the steps to get Hadoop Version 1 working on a Linux machine. To keep things generic, I have used a zipped download to install Hadoop. One may use a binary package for a specific platform without much change in instructions.

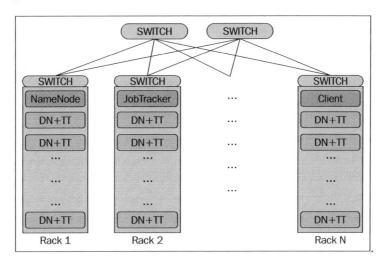

Figure 8.3: Hadoop Infrastructure: Heavy-duty master nodes at the top of the rack servers. Each rack has a rack switch. Slaves run DataNode and TaskTracker services. Racks are connected through 10GE switches. Note that not all racks will have a master server

Make sure you can add **secure shell (SSH)** to your local host using a key-based password-less login. If you can't, generate and set a key pair as described in the following command line:

```
# Generate key pair
$ ssh-keygen -t dsa -P '' -f ~/.ssh/id_dsa
Generating public/private dsa key pair.
Your identification has been saved in /home/ec2-user/.ssh/id_dsa.
Your public key has been saved in /home/ec2-user/.ssh/id_dsa.pub.
```

```
The key fingerprint is:
6a:dc:53:04:8a:52:50:9f:dd:2a:2e:99:04:86:41:f4 ec2-user@ip-10-147-
171-159
The key's randomart image is:
+--[ DSA 1024]----+
|+o.oo    .       |
| o.. o + o       |
|. +E. + . o      |
| . o     o       |
|    . . S .      |
|    . = + .      |
|     + = o       |
|      o  .       |
|                 |
+-----------------+
```

```
# Add public key to authorized_keys
$ cat ~/.ssh/id_dsa.pub >> ~/.ssh/authorized_keys
```

At this point, you should be able to add SSH to your machine by issuing
`ssh localhost`.

> You may need to install the SSH server if you do not have it installed already. In Ubuntu, execute this:
>
> **`sudo apt-get install openssh-server`**
>
> In RHEL variants, do this:
>
> **`yum install openssh-server`**

The first step is to download and extract Hadoop 1.x Version to a desired location:

```
# Download Hadoop
$ wget http://mirrors.gigenet.com/apache/hadoop/common/hadoop-1.1.2/
hadoop-1.1.2-bin.tar.gz


# Extract
$ tar xvzf hadoop-1.1.2-bin.tar.gz


# Create a soft link for easy access and updates without disrupting
PATH
$ ln -s hadoop-1.1.2 hadoop
$ cd hadoop
```

Let's assume the directory where the Hadoop tarball is extracted is $HADOOP_HOME. You need to configure Hadoop to get it working. We will perform the minimalistic configuration that gets Hadoop working in a pseudo-cluster mode where your single machine works as a master node with JobTracker and NameNode, and slave node with TaskTracker and DataNode. Remember, this is not a production-ready configuration.

Edit $HADOOP_HOME/conf/core-site.xml, and add the following:

```
<configuration>
<property>
<name>fs.default.name</name>
<value>hdfs://localhost:9000</value>
</property>
</configuration>
```

Edit $HADOOP_HOME/conf/hdfs-site.xml, and add the replication parameter for the data blocks:

```
<configuration>
<property>
<name>dfs.replication</name>
<value>1</value>
</property>
</configuration>
```

Edit $HADOOP_HOME/conf/mapred-site.xml, and set:

```
<configuration>
<property>
<name>mapred.job.tracker</name>
<value>localhost:9001</value>
</property>
</configuration>
```

Now, it is almost done. Except, you need to tell Hadoop where Java lives. Edit $HADOOP_HOME/conf/hadoop-env.sh and add an export statement for JAVA_HOME like this:

```
# The java implementation to use.  Required.
# export JAVA_HOME=/usr/lib/j2sdk1.5-sun
export JAVA_HOME=/opt/jdk
```

We are done. Next is testing the installation.

Testing the installation

Before we start testing the newly installed Hadoop, we need to format the NameNode to prepare the HDFS. We haven't provided any directory to HDFS, so it will default to /tmp, which may not survive a machine reboot.

```
$ bin/hadoop namenode -format

13/07/20 22:36:39 INFO namenode.NameNode: STARTUP_MSG:

/************************************************************

STARTUP_MSG: Starting NameNode

STARTUP_MSG:    host = marla/127.0.1.1

STARTUP_MSG:    args = [-format]

STARTUP_MSG:    version = 1.1.2

STARTUP_MSG:    build = https://svn.apache.org/repos/asf/hadoop/common/
branches/branch-1.1 -r 1440782; compiled by 'hortonfo' on Thu Jan 31
02:03:24 UTC 2013

************************************************************/

13/07/20 22:36:39 INFO util.GSet: VM type        = 64-bit

13/07/20 22:36:39 INFO util.GSet: 2% max memory = 17.77875 MB

13/07/20 22:36:39 INFO util.GSet: capacity        = 2^21 = 2097152 entries

13/07/20 22:36:39 INFO util.GSet: recommended=2097152, actual=2097152

13/07/20 22:36:40 INFO namenode.FSNamesystem: fsOwner=nishant

[-- snip --]

13/07/20 22:36:41 INFO common.Storage: Image file of size 113 saved in 0
seconds.

13/07/20 22:36:41 INFO namenode.FSEditLog: closing edit log: position=4,
editlog=/tmp/hadoop-nishant/dfs/name/current/edits

13/07/20 22:36:41 INFO namenode.FSEditLog: close success: truncate to 4,
editlog=/tmp/hadoop-nishant/dfs/name/current/edits

13/07/20 22:36:41 INFO common.Storage: Storage directory /tmp/hadoop-
nishant/dfs/name has been successfully formatted.

13/07/20 22:36:41 INFO namenode.NameNode: SHUTDOWN_MSG:

/************************************************************

SHUTDOWN_MSG: Shutting down NameNode at marla/127.0.1.1

************************************************************/
```

You may observe that the storage directory is set to /tmp/hadoop-nishant/dfs/ name by default. You may change it to a sensible location by editing configuration XML. But it will serve a purpose to demonstrate capability.

Let's start everything up and see if we are OK.

```
# Start all Hadoop services locally
$ bin/start-all.sh
startingnamenode, logging to /home/nishant/apps/hadoop-1.1.2/libexec/../
logs/hadoop-nishant-namenode-marla.out
localhost: starting datanode, logging to /home/nishant/apps/hadoop-1.1.2/
libexec/../logs/hadoop-nishant-datanode-marla.out
localhost: starting secondarynamenode, logging to /home/nishant/apps/
hadoop-1.1.2/libexec/../logs/hadoop-nishant-secondarynamenode-marla.out
startingjobtracker, logging to /home/nishant/apps/hadoop-1.1.2/
libexec/../logs/hadoop-nishant-jobtracker-marla.out
localhost: starting tasktracker, logging to /home/nishant/apps/
hadoop-1.1.2/libexec/../logs/hadoop-nishant-tasktracker-marla.out


# Test if all services are running
hadoop1$ jps
11816 DataNode
12158 JobTracker
11506 NameNode
12486 Jps
12408 TaskTracker
12064 SecondaryNameNode
```

jps is a built-in tool provided by Oracle JDK. It lists all the Java processes running on the machine. The previous snippet shows that all the Hadoop processes are up. Let's execute an example and see if things are actually working.

```
# Upload everything under conf directory to "in" directory in HDFS
$ bin/hadoop fs -put conf in


#View the contents (some columns and rows are omitted for brevity)
$ bin/hadoop fs -ls in
Found 16 items
-rw-r--r-- nishant supergroup  7457  /user/nishant/in/capacity-scheduler.
xml
-rw-r--r-- nishant supergroup  535  /user/nishant/in/configuration.xsl
[-- snip --]
-rw-r--r-- nishant supergroup  243  /user/nishant/in/ssl-client.xml.
example
```

```
-rw-r--r-- nishant supergroup  195  /user/nishant/in/ssl-server.xml.
example
-rw-r--r-- nishant supergroup  382  /user/nishant/in/taskcontroller.cfg
```

All set, so it's time to execute an example to it. We will run an example that greps all the words that match the dfs[a-z.]+ regular expression across all the files under the in folder and returns the counts in a folder called out.

```
# Execute grep example
$ bin/hadoop jar hadoop-examples-*.jar grep in out 'dfs[a-z.]+'
13/07/20 23:36:01 INFO util.NativeCodeLoader: Loaded the native-hadoop
library
13/07/20 23:36:01 WARN snappy.LoadSnappy: Snappy native library not
loaded
13/07/20 23:36:01 INFO mapred.FileInputFormat: Total input paths to
process : 16
13/07/20 23:36:02 INFO mapred.JobClient: Running job:
job_201307202304_0001
13/07/20 23:36:03 INFO mapred.JobClient:   map 0% reduce 0%
13/07/20 23:36:12 INFO mapred.JobClient:   map 12% reduce 0%
[-- snip --]
13/07/20 23:36:41 INFO mapred.JobClient:   map 87% reduce 20%
13/07/20 23:36:45 INFO mapred.JobClient:   map 100% reduce 29%
13/07/20 23:36:52 INFO mapred.JobClient:   map 100% reduce 100%
13/07/20 23:36:53 INFO mapred.JobClient: Job complete:
job_201307202304_0001
13/07/20 23:36:53 INFO mapred.JobClient: Counters: 30
[-- snip stats --]
13/07/20 23:37:12 INFO mapred.JobClient:      Reduce output records=3
13/07/20 23:37:12 INFO mapred.JobClient:      Map output records=3


# Result of the MapReduce execution
$ bin/hadoop fs -cat out/*
1  dfs.replication
1  dfs.server.namenode.
1  dfsadmin
```

Congratulations, you have just executed a job using MapReduce. It was a bit of a boring task. You could have executed the `grep` command on your Linux machine that runs much faster than this. But it gives a couple of important insights. One, that the configuration works, and the other is, it is not always the best thing to do everything using Hadoop; for some tasks it is better to use the tools that are best suited to them. We will see more on this when we discuss the cons of Hadoop later in this chapter.

Cassandra with Hadoop MapReduce

Cassandra provides built-in support for Hadoop. If you have ever written a MapReduce program, you will find out that writing a MapReduce task with Cassandra is quite similar to how one would write a MapReduce task for the data stored in HDFS. Cassandra supports input to Hadoop with `ColumnFamilyInputFormat` and output with `ColumnFamilyOutputFormat` classes, respectively. Apart from these, you will need to put Cassandra-specific settings for Hadoop via `ConfigHelper`. These three classes are enough to get you started. One other class that might be worth looking at is `BulkOutputFormat`. All these classes are under the `org.apache.cassandra.hadoop.*` package.

> To be able to compile the MapReduce code that uses Cassandra as a data source or data sink, you must have `cassandra-all.jar` in your classpath. You will also need to make Hadoop to be able to see jars in the Cassandra library. We will discuss this later in this chapter.

Let's understand the classes that we will be using to get Cassandra working for our MapReduce problem.

ColumnFamilyInputFormat

`ColumnFamilyInputFormat` is an implementation of `org.apache.hadoop.mapred.InputFormat` (or `mapreduce` in newer API). So, its implementation is dictated by the `InputFormat` class specifications. Hadoop uses this class to get data for the MapReduce tasks. It describes how to read data from column families into the Mapper instances.

The other job of ColumnFamilyInputFormat (or any implementation of InputFormat) is to fragment input data into small chunks that get fed to map tasks. Cassandra has ColumnInputSplit for this purpose. One can configure the number of rows per InputSplit via ConfigHelper.setInputSplitSize. But there is a caveat. It uses multiple get_slice_range queries for each InputSplit, so, as Cassandra documentation says, a smaller value will build up call overhead; on the other hand, too large a value may cause out-of-memory issues. Larger values are better for performance, so if you are planning to play with this parameter do some calculation based on median column size to avoid memory overflow. Trial and error can be handy. The default split size is 64 x 1024 rows.

ColumnFamilyOutputFormat

OutputFormat is the mechanism of writing the result from MapReduce to a permanent (usually) storage. Cassandra implements Hadoop's OutputFormat, that is, ColumnFamilyOutputFormat. It enables Hadoop to write the result from the reduce task as column family rows. It is implemented such that the results are written, to the column family, in batches. This is a performance improvement and this mechanism is called lazy write-back caching.

ConfigHelper

ConfigHelper is a gateway to configure Cassandra-specific settings for Hadoop. It is a pretty plain utility class that validates the settings passed and sets into Hadoop's org.apache.hadoop.conf.Configuration instance for the job. This configuration is made available to the Mapper and the Reducer.

ConfigHelper saves developers from inputting a wrong property name because all the properties are set using a method; any typo will appear at compile time. It may be worth looking at JavaDoc for ConfigHelper. Here are some of the commonly used methods:

- setInputInitialAddress: It can be a hostname or private IP of one of the Cassandra nodes.

- SetInputRpcPort: It will set the RPC port address if it has been altered from default. If not set, it uses default thrift port 9160.

- setInputPartitioner: It will set the appropriate partitioner according to the underlying Cassandra storage setting.

- SetInputColumnFamily: It will set the column family details to be able to pull data from.

- `SetInputSlicePredicate`: It will set the columns that are pulled from the column family to provide Mapper to work on.

- `SetOutputInitialAddress`: It will set the address of the Cassandra cluster (one of the nodes) where the result is being published; it is usually similar to `InputInitialAddress`.

- `SetOutputRpcPort`: It will set the RPC port to cluster where the result is stored.

- `SetOutputPartitioner`: It is the partitioner used in the output cluster.

- `SetOutputColumnFamily`: It will set the column family details to store results in.

Since Version 1.1, Cassandra added support to wide-row column families, bulk loading, and secondary indexes.

Wide-row support

Earlier, having multimillions of columns was a problem in Cassandra Hadoop integration. It was pulling a row per call limited by `SlicePredicate`. Version 1.1 onward, you can pass the wide-row Boolean parameter as true, as shown in the following snippet:

```
ConfigHelper.setInputColumnFamily(
conf,
keyspace,
inCF,
true// SET WIDEROW = TRUE
);
```

When wide row is true, the rows are fed to the Mapper one column at a time that is, you will iterate column by column.

Bulk loading

`BulkOutputFormat` is another utility that Cassandra provides to improve the write performance of jobs that result in large data. It streams the data in binary format, which is much quicker than inserting one by one. It uses `SSTableLoader` to do this. Refer to `SSTableLoader` in the Using Cassandra bulk loader to restore the data section in *Chapter 6, Managing a Cluster – Scaling*, Node Repair, and Backup.

```
Job job = new Job(conf);
job.setOutputFormatClass(BulkOutputFormat.class);
```

Secondary index support

One can use secondary index when pulling data from Cassandra to pass it on to the job. This is another improvement. It makes Cassandra shift the data and pass only the relevant data to Hadoop, instead of Hadoop burning the CPU cycles to weed out the data that is not going to be used in the computation. It lowers the overhead of passing extra data to Hadoop. Here is an example.

```
IndexExpression electronicItems =
        new IndexExpression(
            ByteBufferUtil.bytes("item_category"),
            IndexOperator.EQ,
            ByteBufferUtil.bytes("electronics")
        );

IndexExpression soldAfter2012 =
        new IndexExpression(
             ByteBufferUtil.bytes("sell_year"),
             IndexOperator.GT,
             ByteBufferUtil.bytes(2012)
        );

ConfigHelper.setInputRange(conf, Arrays.asList(electronicItems,
soldAfter2012));
```

The previous code returns the rows that fall in the electronics category and were sold after the year 2012.

Cassandra and Hadoop in action

So, with more than enough (rather boring) theory, we are ready to get some excitement. In this section, we will do a word count of a book. It will be more interesting than the grep example.

In this example we load Lewis Carroll's novel *Alice in Wonderland* (http://en.wikipedia.org/wiki/Alice%27s_Adventures_in_Wonderland) in Cassandra. To prepare this data, we read the text file line by line and store 500 lines in one row. The row names are formatted as row_1, row_2, and so on and the columns in each row have names such as col_1, col_2, and so on. Each row has at most 500 columns and each column has one line from the file.

To avoid noises, we have removed punctuations from the lines during the load. We could certainly do the noise reduction in the MapReduce code, but we wanted to keep it simple. What follows is the code and its explanation. It is suggested to download the code either from the author's GitHub account or from the publisher's website. Keep it handy while reading this chapter. The code is eventually compiled and submitted to Hadoop MapReduce to execute the compiled `jar` file. We use the Maven command `mvn clean install` to compile and create a `jar` file. If you are unaware of Maven or are new to Java, you can compile the files using appropriate dependencies or `jar` files in the classpath. Refer to the `pom.xml` file in the project to know what `jar` files you need to compile the example in Java.

Assuming that we have data ready in Cassandra to run MapReduce on it, we will write Mapper, Reducer, and a `main` method. Here is the Mapper:

```
public static class WordMapper
extends Mapper<ByteBuffer, SortedMap<ByteBuffer, IColumn>, Text,
IntWritable>{
    private static final IntWritable ONE = new IntWritable(1);
    private Text word = new Text();

    @Override
    protected void map(ByteBuffer key,
                       SortedMap<ByteBuffer, IColumn> cols,
                       Context context)
    throws IOException, InterruptedException {

      //Iterate through the column values
      for(IColumn col: cols.values()){
        String val = ByteBufferUtil.string(col.value());
        StringTokenizer tokenizer = new StringTokenizer(val);

            while (tokenizer.hasMoreTokens()) {
                word.set(tokenizer.nextToken());
                context.write(word, ONE);
            }
        }
      }
    }
}
```

This is what our Mapper looks like. To a person who has some experience in writing MapReduce programs, this does not deviate much from a regular Mapper. A couple of things to note:

1. Cassandra feeds a sorted map to Mapper. This is sorted by column name and it is basically column-name, column-value pair.

2. The key is of type `ByteBuffer` and it is the row key.

3. Use `org.apache.cassandra.utils.ByteBufferUtil` to convert `ByteBuffer` to meaningful types.

4. If you want to process column by column, loop through the columns sorted map.

5. Write out the output that you want this Mapper to forward to Reducer. The values that you write to context is sorted and grouped by the framework and forwarded to the Reducer.

6. Now that we have done the basic task of splitting the text in each column and forwarding them with key as word and value as one, in order to count each word, we need to get all the words that were forwarded by Mapper at one place so that we can just iterate in the grouped key-value pairs of word and 1, and update a counter until all the occurrences of that word exhausts. Here is what our Mapper looks like:

```
public static class WordReducer
extends Reducer<Text, IntWritable, ByteBuffer, List<Mutation>>{

        @Override
        protected void reduce(Text key,
                              Iterable<IntWritable> values,
                              Context context)
        throws IOException, InterruptedException {
                int sum = 0;
                for(IntWritable value: values){
                        sum = sum + value.get();
                }

                Column col = new Column();
                col.setName(ByteBufferUtil.bytes("count"));
                col.setValue(ByteBufferUtil.bytes(sum));
                col.setTimestamp(System.currentTimeMillis());

                Mutation mutation = new Mutation();
                mutation.setColumn_or_supercolumn(new
ColumnOrSuperColumn());
                mutation.getColumn_or_supercolumn().setColumn(col);
                context.write(
                        ByteBufferUtil.bytes(key.toString()),
                        Collections.singletonList(mutation)
                    );
        }
}
```

Reducer is a little more interesting than Mapper. It is because we are doing two things. One, we are counting the number of grouped elements that come to Reducer. From our Mapper, we know that it is grouped by word. So at the end of looping through the values, we will get the number of instances of that word. The second thing that we are doing here is storing this value to Cassandra. Instead of outputting the result to HDFS, we store it in Cassandra with row key as word, and we add a column named `count` that will hold the value that we just obtained in the previous step. You can see that there is no environment-specific configuration done here; we just instruct what to store in Cassandra and how, and we are done. So, the question arises, where do we set all the environment-specific and Cassandra-specific settings? The answer is in the `main` method. Here is what the `main` method for this particular example looks like. But in any Cassandra-based Hadoop project, it will not vary much.

```
public class CassandraWordCount extends Configured implements Tool {

  [-- snip --]

  public int run(String[] args) throws Exception {
    Job job = new Job(getConf(), "cassandrawordcount");
    job.setJarByClass(getClass());

// Anything you set in conf will be available to Mapper and Reducer
    Configuration conf = job.getConfiguration();

// set mapper and reducer
    job.setMapperClass(WordMapper.class);
    job.setReducerClass(WordReducer.class);

// Cassandra Specific settings for ingesting CF
    ConfigHelper.setInputInitialAddress(conf, Setup.CASSANDRA_HOST_
ADDR);
    ConfigHelper.setInputRpcPort(conf, String.valueOf(Setup.CASSANDRA_
RPC_PORT));
    ConfigHelper.setInputPartitioner(conf, RandomPartitioner.class.
getName());
    ConfigHelper.setInputColumnFamily(conf, Setup.KEYSPACE, Setup.
INPUT_CF);

    SliceRange sliceRange = new SliceRange(
                ByteBufferUtil.bytes(""),
                ByteBufferUtil.bytes(""),
                false,
                Integer.MAX_VALUE);
    SlicePredicate predicate = new SlicePredicate()
```

```
                     .setSlice_range(sliceRange);
       ConfigHelper.setInputSlicePredicate(conf, predicate);

       job.setInputFormatClass(ColumnFamilyInputFormat.class);


   //  Cassandra specific output setting
       ConfigHelper.setOutputInitialAddress(conf, Setup.CASSANDRA_HOST_
   ADDR);
       ConfigHelper.setOutputRpcPort(conf, String.valueOf(Setup.
   CASSANDRA_RPC_PORT));
       ConfigHelper.setOutputPartitioner(conf, RandomPartitioner.class.
   getName());
       ConfigHelper.setOutputColumnFamily(conf, Setup.KEYSPACE, Setup.
   OUTPUT_CF);

   //  set output class types
       job.setOutputKeyClass(ByteBuffer.class);
       job.setOutputValueClass(List.class);
       job.setOutputFormatClass(ColumnFamilyOutputFormat.class);

       job.setMapOutputKeyClass(Text.class);
       job.setMapOutputValueClass(IntWritable.class);

   //  verbose
       job.waitForCompletion(true);
       return 0;
   }

   public static void main(String[] args) throws Exception{
     ToolRunner.run(new Configuration(), new CassandraWordCount(),
   args);
     System.exit(0);
   }

 }
```

All right, lots of things, but nothing that we do not know about. Starting from the
main method, we provide an instance of our main class and any parameter that is
passed from the command-line interface and we kick off ToolRunner. ToolRunner
executes the run method, where all the settings for environment and Cassandra are.
We also tell where our Mapper and producer for this job are.

We tell Hadoop how to pull data from Cassandra by providing SlicePredicate
where we pull a complete row by not setting the start column name, the end column
name, and setting the count to two billion. One may want to modify and just set
wide row to true and achieve the same without worrying about SlicePredicate.

Executing, debugging, monitoring, and looking at results

To execute this example, compile the code and create a `jar` file. Add any required external libraries or dependency to the classpath or edit `conf/hadoop-env.sh` and add the location of the jars. One of the hard requirements to get all this Cassandra-related stuff running is to have the Cassandra library directory in Hadoop's classpath. To do that, edit `$HADOOP_HOME/conf/hadoop-env.sh` and update the classpath like this:

```
$ conf/hadoop-env.sh
# Extra Java CLASSPATH elements.Optional.
# export HADOOP_CLASSPATH=
export HADOOP_CLASSPATH=/home/nishant/apps/cassandra11/lib/*:$HADOOP_CLASSPATH
```

Make sure Hadoop and Cassandra are completely up and running. To execute your MapReduce program, submit the `jar` file to Hadoop with the appropriate classpath, if needed, and the fully qualified class name of the main class.

```
$ bin/hadoop jar materingcassadra-0.0.1-SNAPSHOT.jar \
in.naishe.mc.CassandraWordCount
```

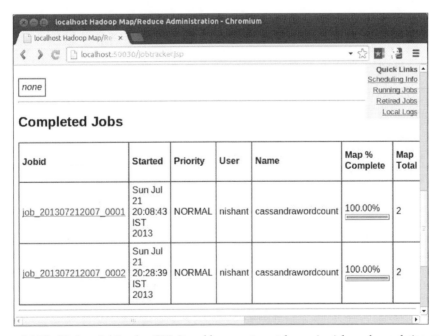

Figure 8.4: The Hadoop JobTracker GUI. It enables users to watch running jobs and completion; most importantly, you can see logs, system outs, and system error streams by drilling into job IDs

Hadoop provides a pretty simple web-based GUI to monitor and view debug logs, system out stream messages, and system error stream messages. One can monitor the status of a running, failed, or previously run job details. By default, this portal is available at the following URL: `http://JOBTRACKER_ADDRESS:50030`. So, if you are running everything locally, the address will be `http://localhost:50030`. The preceding figure shows a screenshot of the page. You can click on a job link and view details. On the job detail page, you can see logs for Mapper or Reducer processes.

As per our Reducer configuration, the results can be accessed from Cassandra from the appropriate column family. You may observe the result there. So, as expected, you will find `the` in highest use, and there are a decent number of references to `Alice`, `Hatter`, and `Cat`.

```
cqlsh:testks> select * from resultCF where key = 'the';
 KEY   | count
-------+-------
 the   | 1664

cqlsh:testks> select * from resultCF where key = 'Alice';
 KEY   | count
-------+-------
 Alice |   377

cqlsh:testks> select * from resultCF where key = 'Hatter';
 KEY    | count
--------+-------
 Hatter |    54

cqlsh:testks> select * from resultCF where key = 'Cat';
 KEY | count
-----+-------
 Cat |    23
```

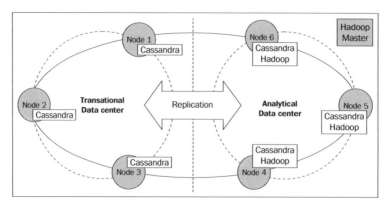

Figure 8.5: Typical setup for analytics with Cassandra and Hadoop

Hadoop in Cassandra cluster

The production version of Hadoop and Cassandra combination needs to go into a separate cluster. The first obvious issue is you probably wouldn't want Hadoop to keep pulling Cassandra nodes, hampering Cassandra performance to end users. The general pattern to avoid this is to split the ring into two data centers. Since Cassandra automatically and immediately replicates the changes between data centers, they will be in sync always. What's more, you can assign one of the data centers as a transactional with a higher replication factor and the other as an analytical data center with a replication factor of 1. The analytical data center is the one used by Hadoop without affecting the transactional data center a bit.

Now, you do not really need to have two physically separated data centers to make this configuration work. Remember `NetworkTopologyStrategy`? (Refer to the NetworkTopologyStrategy section in *Chapter 4, Deploying a Cluster*.) You can tweak Cassandra thinking there are two data centers by just assigning the nodes that you wanted to use for analytics in a different data center. You may need to use `PropertyFileSnitch` and specify the details about data centers in a `cassandra-toplogy.properties` file. So, your keyspace creation looks something like this:

```
createkeyspacemyKeyspace
withplacement_strategy = 'NetworkTopologyStrategy'
andstrategy_options = {TX_DC : 2, HDP_DC: 1};
```

The previous statement defines two data centers: `TX_DC` for transactional purposes and `HDP_DC` for Hadoop to do analytics. A node in a transactional data center has a snitch configured like this:

```
# Transaction Data Center
192.168.1.1=TX_DC:RAC1
192.168.1.2=TX_DC:RAC1

192.168.2.1=TX_DC:RAC2

# Analytics Data Center
192.168.1.3=HDP_DC:RAC1

192.168.2.2=HDP_DC:RAC2
192.168.2.3=HDP_DC:RAC2

# For new/unknown/unassigned nodes
default=TX_DC:RAC1
```

We are mostly done setting up machines. A couple of things to remember:

- Install TaskTracker and DataNode processes on each node in an analytical data center.

- Do not have a node that has Cassandra running on it and has running services for TaskTracker and DataNode. Use a separate robust machine to install the master services, such as JobTracker and NameNode.

- Make sure `conf/hadoop-env.sh` has all the `jar` files that need to execute the MapReduce program as a part of the `HADOOP_CLASSPATH` variable.

- With all these configurations, your Cassandra cluster should be ready to serve analytical results to all the concerned people.

Cassandra filesystem

Configuring Hadoop backed by Cassandra may give the illusion that we are replacing HDFS, because we take data from Cassandra and dump the results into it. It is not true. Hadoop still needs NameNode and DataNodes for various activities such as storing intermediate results, `jar` files, and static data. So, essentially, you are backed by no **single point of failure (SPOF)** database but you are still bounded by SPOFs such as NameNode and JobTracker.

DataStax, a leading company in professional support for Cassandra, provides a solution to it. Its enterprise offering of Cassandra DataStax Enterprise product has a built-in **Cassandra File System (CFS)**, which is HDFS compatible. CFS smartly uses Cassandra as an underlying storage. What this gives to an end user is simplicity in configuration and no need to have DataNode, NameNode, and secondary NameNode running.

More detail about CFS is out of the scope of this book. You may read more about CFS on the DataStax blog, Cassandra File System Design, at `http://www.datastax.com/dev/blog/cassandra-file-system-design`.

Integration with Pig

Configuring Hadoop with Cassandra in itself is quite some work. Writing verbose and long Java code to do something as trivial as word count is a turn-off to a high-level user like a data analyst. Wouldn't it be nice if we had a SQL-like interpreter that converts commands to MapReduce programs for us? Pig is exactly that tool.

Hadoop does not only support Java but also MapReduce programs can be written more concisely in multiple languages such as Scala, Python, C++ (Pipes), R, and many adapter languages.

Pig provides a SQL-like language called Pig Latin. One can write complex MapReduce programs using Pig Latin. You can create a set of intermediate variables that are a result of an operation and it can be used in subsequent operations, in the same way a stored procedure in RDBMS would. Finally, the output of an operation can be displayed on a screen or can be stored in a permanent storage such as HDFS or Cassandra.

Installing Pig

Pig installation is very simple; what is hard is getting it to work with Hadoop and Cassandra nicely. To install Pig, just download the latest version of Pig and untar it.

```
$ wget http://www.eng.lsu.edu/mirrors/apache/pig/pig-0.11.1/pig-
0.11.1.tar.gz
$ tar xvzf pig-0.11.1.tar.gz
$ ln -s pig-0.11.1 pig
```

Lets call this directory `$PIG_HOME`. Ideally, you should just execute `$PIG_HOME/bin/pig` and the Pig console should start to work given that your Cassandra and Hadoop are up and working. Unfortunately, it does not. Documentation, at the time of writing, is not adequate to configure Pig. To get Pig started, you need to do the following:

1. Set Hadoop's installation directory as a `HADOOP_PREFIX` variable.

2. Add all the `jar` files in the Cassandra `lib` directory to `PIG_CLASSPATH`.

3. Add `udf.import.list` to the Pig options variable, `PIG_OPTS`, in this way:

    ```
    export PIG_OPTS="$PIG_OPTS -Dudf.import.list=org.apache.cassandra.
    hadoop.pig";
    ```

4. Set one of the Cassandra nodes' address, Cassandra RPC port, and Cassandra partitioner to `PIG_INITIAL_ADDRESS`, `PIG_RPC_PORT`, and `PIG_PARTITIONER` respectively.

You may write a simple shell script that does this for you. Here is a shell script that accommodates the four steps (assuming $CASSANDRA_HOME points to the Cassandra installation directory):

```
export CASSANDRA_HOME=/home/nishant/apps/cassandra11


for cassandra_jar in $CASSANDRA_HOME/lib/*.jar; do
CLASSPATH=$CLASSPATH:$cassandra_jar
done


export PIG_CLASSPATH=$PIG_CLASSPATH:$CLASSPATH;


export PIG_OPTS="$PIG_OPTS -Dudf.import.list=org.apache.cassandra.
hadoop.pig";


export HADOOP_PREFIX=/home/nishant/apps/hadoop
export PIG_INITIAL_ADDRESS=localhost;
export PIG_RPC_PORT=9160;
export PIG_PARTITIONER=org.apache.cassandra.dht.RandomPartitioner;
```

If everything goes OK and Cassandra and Hadoop are up, you may access the Pig console to execute queries in an interactive mode.

```
pig$ bin/pig
2013-07-22 13:32:22,709 [main] INFO  org.apache.pig.Main - Apache Pig
version 0.11.1 (r1459641) compiled Mar 22 2013, 02:13:53
2013-07-22 13:32:22,710 [main] INFO  org.apache.pig.Main - Logging error
messages to: /home/nishant/apps/pig-0.11.1/pig_1374480142703.log
2013-07-22 13:32:22,757 [main] INFO  org.apache.pig.impl.util.Utils -
Default bootup file /home/nishant/.pigbootup not found
2013-07-22 13:32:23,080 [main] INFO  org.apache.pig.backend.hadoop.
executionengine.HExecutionEngine - Connecting to hadoop file system at:
hdfs://localhost:9000
2013-07-22 13:32:24,133 [main] INFO  org.apache.pig.backend.hadoop.
executionengine.HExecutionEngine - Connecting to map-reduce job tracker
at: localhost:9001
grunt>
```

Let's copy some Hadoop XML files into HDFS and run a word count on it.

```
# Load all the files in $HADOOP_HOME/conf to pigdata in HDFS
$ bin/hadoop fs -put conf pigdata
```

```
# --- in pig console ---
# load all the files from HDFS
grunt> A = load './pigdata' ;

# loop line by line in all the input files from A split them into
words
grunt> B = foreach A generate flatten(TOKENIZE((chararray)$0)) as
word;

# Group the tokenized words into variable C, groub by attribute
â€œwordâ€
grunt> C = group B by word;

# Generare a map of number of terms in each group and group name
grunt> D = foreach C generate COUNT(B), group;

# print this map to console
grunt> dump D;
```

If it works, you will see an output something like this:

```
. . .
(31,for)
(2,get)
(4,jks)
(12,job)
(1,log)
(1,map)
(2,max)
(1,pid)
(8,set)
(1,sig)
(1,ssh)
(83,the)
(1,two)
(6,use)
(3,via)
(3,who)
. . .
```

Integrating Pig and Cassandra

By getting Hadoop working with Cassandra, we are almost done and ready to use the Pig console to get data from Cassandra and store results back to Cassandra. One thing that you need to know is what storage method is used to store and retrieve data from Cassandra. It is `CassandraStorage()` that you will be using in your Pig Latin to transfer data to and from Cassandra. Usage is exactly the same as you would use `PigStorage()`.

In Pig, the data structure that is used to store/get data to/from Cassandra is a tuple of row key and a bag of tuples, where each tuple is a column name and column value pair, such as this:

```
(ROW_KEY, { (COL1, VAL1), (COL2, VAL2), (COL3, VAL3), ...})
```

Here is an example of word count from the Cassandra table. This example uses the same data ("Alice in Wonderland" book) as we did when we showed the MapReduce example with Cassandra. The book is split into lines and each row contains 500 lines in 500 columns. There are a total of six rows.

```
# Pull Data from dataCF column family under testks Keyspace
grunt> rows = LOAD 'cassandra://testks/dataCF' USING
CassandraStorage();
grunt> cols = FOREACH rows GENERATE flatten(columns);
grunt> vals = FOREACH cols GENERATE flatten(TOKENIZE((chararray)$1))
as word;
grunt> grps = group vals by word;
grunt> cnt = foreach grps generate group, COUNT(vals), 'count' as
ccnt;
grunt> grp_by_word = group cnt by $0;
grunt> cagg = foreach grp_by_word generate group, cnt.(ccnt, $1);


# Put Data into result1CF column family under testks Keyspace
grunt> STORE cagg into 'cassandra://testks/result1CF' USING
CassandraStorage();

2013-07-22 14:12:45,144 [main] INFO  org.apache.pig.tools.pigstats.
ScriptState - Pig features used in the script: GROUP_BY
[-- snip --]
2013-07-22 14:12:50,464 [main] INFO  org.apache.pig.backend.hadoop.
executionengine.mapReduceLayer.MapReduceLauncher - Processing aliases
cnt,cols,grps,rows,vals
2013-07-22 14:12:50,464 [main] INFO  org.apache.pig.backend.
hadoop.executionengine.mapReduceLayer.MapReduceLauncher - detailed
locations: M: rows[6,7],cols[7,7],vals[8,7],cnt[10,6],grps[9,7] C:
cnt[10,6],grps[9,7] R: cnt[10,6]
```

```
[-- snip --]
2013-07-22 14:13:45,626 [main] INFO  org.apache.pig.backend.hadoop.
executionengine.mapReduceLayer.MapReduceLauncher - 97% complete
2013-07-22 14:13:49,669 [main] INFO  org.apache.pig.backend.hadoop.
executionengine.mapReduceLayer.MapReduceLauncher - 100% complete
[-- snip --]

Input(s):
Successfully read 6 records (360 bytes) from: "cassandra://testks/
dataCF"

Output(s):
Successfully stored 4440 records in: "cassandra://testks/result1CF"
[-- snip --]
2013-07-22 14:13:49,693 [main] INFO  org.apache.pig.backend.hadoop.
executionengine.mapReduceLayer.MapReduceLauncher - Success!
```

Let's look at the result that is stored in `result1CF` and compare it with the previous result.

```
cqlsh> use testks;
cqlsh:testks> select * from result1CF where key = 'the';
 KEY | count
-----+-------
 the |  1666

cqlsh:testks> select * from resultCF where key = 'Alice';
 KEY   | count
-------+-------
 Alice |   377

cqlsh:testks> select * from resultCF where key = 'Hatter';
 KEY    | count
--------+-------
 Hatter |    54

cqlsh:testks> select * from resultCF where key = 'Cat';
 KEY | count
-----+-------
 Cat |    23
```

There is a small difference in the counting of `the`, but that's likely due to the split that I use and the split function that Pig uses.

Please note that the Pig Latin that we have used here may be very inefficient. The purpose of this example is to show Cassandra and Pig integration. To learn about Pig Latin, look into the Pig documentation. Apache Pig's official tutorial (`http://pig.apache.org/docs/r0.11.1/start.html#tutorial`) is recommended reading to know more about it.

Cassandra and Solr

Apache Solr is a text search platform written on top of Apache Lucene. Solr uses the Lucene search library and provides a simpler interface to manage indexes and perform search over a variety of sources such as RDBMS, text, and rich documents, for example, PDF and Word. Solr can be started as an independent Java web service on any application container such as Tomcat or Jetty.

Lucene, Solr, and search mechanism/indexing each require a separate book of their own. We will keep this section brief. You may learn about Solr from the Apache Solr wiki page (`http://wiki.apache.org/solr/`).

In this section we will see how we can use Cassandra to serve as a database backend of Solr. So, we will have Solr running on top of Cassandra. Please note that this does not give us the ability to text search in Cassandra.

Solandra (`https://github.com/tjake/Solandra`) is an open source project that allows you to set up Cassandra to be used as storage for Solr. To configure Solandra, you need to follow the steps mentioned:

```
$ git clone https://github.com/tjake/Solandra.git
Cloning into 'Solandra'...
[-- snip --]
$ cd Solandra
$ ant  -Dcassandra=/opt/cassandra11cassandra-dist
$ $CASSANDRA_HOME/bin/solandra
INFO 11:41:52,784 Starting Messaging Service on port 7000
[-- snip --]
INFO 11:41:53,063 Bootstrap/Replace/Move completed! Now serving reads.
INFO 11:41:53,116 Binding thrift service to localhost/127.0.0.1:9160
[-- snip --]
INFO 11:41:54,547 QuerySenderListener done.
INFO 11:41:54,547 [] Registered new searcher Searcher@63ab3977 main
INFO 11:41:54,548 user.dir=/home/nishant/apps/solandra/Solandra
INFO 11:41:54,548 SolrDispatchFilter.init() done
INFO 11:41:54,551 Started SocketConnector@0.0.0.0:8983
```

Now Solr is ready to serve. You can post data to it to index. For a large-scale data search in a cluster environment, you will need to have embedded Solandra running on each node of the ring. This way Solandra makes Solr as scalable as Cassandra. Let's check Solr with Cassandra by executing one of the built-in examples.

```
$ cd $SOLANDRA_HOME/reuters-demo/

$ ./1-download-data.sh

[-- snip --]

Data downloaded, now run ./2-import-data.sh

$ ./2-import-data.sh

Posted schema.xml to http://localhost:8983/solandra/schema/reuters

Loading data to solandra, note: this importer uses a slow xml parser

READING FILE: /home/nishant/apps/solandra/Solandra/reuters-demo/data/
reut2-002.sgm

 - reut2-002.sgm(0) title(1.0)={JAGUAR SEES STRONG GROWTH IN NEW MODEL
SALES}

 - reut2-002.sgm(1) title(1.0)={OCCIDENTAL PETROLEUM COMMON STOCK
OFFERING RAISED TO 36 MLN SHARES

}

 - reut2-002.sgm(2) title(1.0)={CCC ACCEPTS BONUS BID ON WHEAT FLOUR TO
IRAQ}

 - reut2-002.sgm(3) title(1.0)={DIAMOND SHAMROCK RAISES CRUDE POSTED
PRICES ONE DLR, EFFECTIVE MARCH 4, WTI NOW 17.00 DLRS/BBL

}

 - reut2-002.sgm(4) title(1.0)={NORD RESOURCES CORP <NRD> 4TH QTR NET}


[-- snip --]


Data loaded, now open ./website/index.html in your favorite browser!
```

If you observe, all this does is it downloads some data and posts it to Solr the same way you would do for regular Solr. You can open `./website/index.html` to play with Solr (see the next figure).

It is sometimes confusing to someone who first learns about Solandra; it seems that it provides a text search facility to Cassandra. If you want to achieve something like that, you will have to make two calls: one to update Solr by posting appropriate changes to it and the other to make those changes in Cassandra. The good thing is you do not need to run two Cassandra instances for Solr and your application.

Development note on Solandra

Solandra is a pretty impressive project. One of the saddening things about this project is that it is no longer actively developed. At the time of writing, the Solandra project was last updated a year ago. The owner of the project has moved to DataStax to provide more efficient integration of Solr with Cassandra and a text search capability to Cassandra that one always wished for (we will discuss briefly about this in the next section).

The project seems to be in a decent working condition, but it may not be recommended for production-ready deployments. If you are planning to use Solandra, test it rigorously.

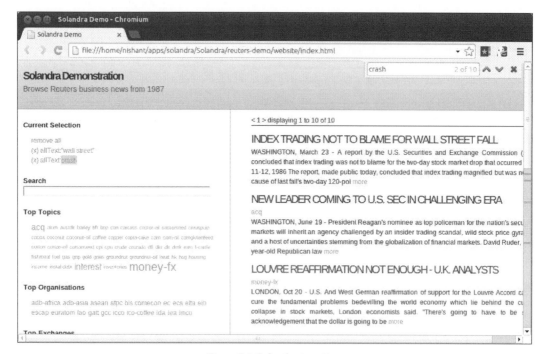

Figure 8.6: Solandra in action

DataStax Enterprise – the next level Solr integration

DataStax Enterprise solution for Cassandra comes with built-in Solr integration to provide a text search facility directly from column families. DataStax documentation says that its Solr implementation is two to four folds faster than Solandra.

To learn more about Solr in the DataStax offering, you may visit their blog on the URL http://www.datastax.com/dev/blog/cassandra-with-solr-integration-details.

Summary

So, we can store large data and run MapReduce on them to analyze the data. We can also set up Hadoop in such a manner that it does not impact the transactional part of Cassandra in a negative way. We also know how to set up Pig for those who want to quickly assemble an analysis instead of writing lengthy Java code. We can also power Solr searches by Cassandra, making Solr more scalable than it already is.

With a plethora of analytical tooling available in the market, you may or may not choose Cassandra. Maybe you could perform stream analysis that does not require data to be stored and analyzed later; for example, if you decide to apply multiple operations on live streaming tweets and show the result immediately, you would likely use a tool such as Twitter Storm. Although there is no explicit project to guide you on how to do that, it is pretty simple to configure Twitter as Storm Spout, which will emit the tweet stream to the next Bolt, get it processed and forwarded to the next Bolt, and finally you can use the Cassandra Java driver to simply store the result. It is as simple as that. You may want to put a queue between Bolt and Cassandra as a buffer if you find Tweets are too fast for Cassandra. But normally, you wouldn't need that.

Some distributed computation tools such as Spark have people developing nice integration tools such as Calliope (`http://tuplejump.github.io/calliope/`). In general, you wouldn't be disappointed for choosing Cassandra because there is no documentation available to integrate it with a relatively popular framework.

Cassandra is a rapidly developing project. The changes and feature additions in this open source project takes place once in six months and doesn't happen in many big label proprietary applications. You get faster, stronger, and better Cassandra for free (obviously, there are technical debts) every half year. While this is a great thing, it comes with a pain point—new learning. To be able to upgrade, you will need to know new ways to do things. There may be changes that require you to change things at code level to keep pace with Cassandra. Most times, you could just upgrade Cassandra and things will work as expected. But you may not be taking benefit of new features. The next chapter is about the current edition of Cassandra, Cassandra 1.2.x. It has many new features, new ways to do things, and new ways to visualize the data.

Introduction to CQL 3 and Cassandra 1.2

Cassandra is a rapidly developing project. Massive improvements, features, supports, and extensions are added with every release. At the start of this book, Cassandra 1.1.x was the most stable version. At the time of writing this chapter, 1.2.x has been well matured and thoroughly tested. CQL is becoming a de facto Cassandra language, and Thrift API, although promised to be supported indefinitely, is dying slowly.

It is nice to see Cassandra from Thrift lenses, because it transparently shows what the underlying storage structure is. However, it requires lots of mind bending to get the picture. CQL on the other hand is feature laden, terse, and an SQL-like language. This chapter will generally dive into an informal introduction to CQL 3. We will see some of the most impacting features of Cassandra 1.2.x. It will also have some assorted topics remotely related to Cassandra.

CQL – the Cassandra Query Language

CQL is an SQL-like querying language for Cassandra. This book concentrates on Cassandra version 1.1.x, which is a sort of transition version from a querying perspective. It has Thrift API fully functional and well tested. It has CQL version 2, which does not give a lot of leverage against Thrift version. It also has CQL 3 beta version.

CQL 3 is a big step foward compared to Thrift or CQL 2. It has a lot of usability features and it is less verbose than Thrift. The main thing that distinguishes CQL 3 from the other two is it is the future. Thrift is not going to get abandoned, but it is not going to get any updates either. CQL 2 is likely to be removed. CQL 3 will be the most preferred way to interact with Cassandra going forward.

You need to use **CQL shell (cqlsh)** to be able to execute CQL queries. In Cassandra 1.1.x, the default cqlsh console provides support to CQL 2. In order to use CQL 3 via cqlsh, use:

`$CASSANDRA_HOME/bin/cqlsh -3`

In all the places in this chapter, CQL refers to CQL 3. If there is a discussion about CQL 2, it is mentioned explicitly.

A little history on CQL:

Thrift RPC has been the primary way to communicate with Cassandra. But Thrift has a couple of issues, namely, being verbose and hard to digest for people migrating from SQL. CQL 2 was an effort to fix these issues and bring it closer to SQL. It had its own problems—wide-row insertion was unintuitive, client code needed to decompose the composite columns, count does not count columns but rows, and a few more issues. Ultimately, CQL 2 was just a good syntactic sugar for Thrift with some inefficiency. Cassandra 1.1 comes with CQL 3-beta that uses the learning from CQL 2. It is much easier than CQL 2, but if you are coming from a Thrift world, it may require a little learning to understand how CQL 3 represents the same underlying column family differently.

CQL 3 for Thrift refugees

This section gives a quick overview on CQL 3. It is possible that new features get added as Cassandra evolves. Someone experienced working with Thrift API will have a hard time getting their head around the CQL 3 representation. Let's see a couple of changes when going from Thrift API to CQL 3.

Wide rows

Wide rows in Thrift are transposed in CQL 3—columns are treated as rows. So, a wide row in the Thrift world is just a table with three columns, namely `key`, which is the row key, `column1`, which is the column name in Thrift realm, and a column named `value`, which is the value stored in the column. Here is an example:

```
# Create a wide row column family in Thrift (cassandra-cli)
[default@cqltest] CREATE COLUMN FAMILY WideRowThrift
WITH
KEY_VALIDATION_CLASS = UUIDType AND
COMPARATOR = DateType AND
DEFAULT_VALIDATION_CLASS = UTF8Type;
```

```
# Insert some rows
[default@cqltest] SET WideRowThrift[fa408aff-a55b-4a52-b4b7-
2314bb5bb86f][1374742812] = 'New chat session';

# View the wide row in Thrift-way
[default@cqltest] list WideRowThrift;
[-- snip --]
RowKey: 72da9d1a-4802-47b4-ab50-249a8ea00038
=> (column=1970-01-17 03:22:20+0530, value=some text1,
timestamp=1374740832800000)
=> (column=1970-01-17 03:22:20+0530, value=some text2,
timestamp=1374740870667000)
=> (column=1970-01-17 03:22:20+0530, value=some text3,
timestamp=1374740893446000)
-------------------
RowKey: fa408aff-a55b-4a52-b4b7-2314bb5bb86f
=> (column=1970-01-02 19:41:14+0530, value=Message #2,
timestamp=1374742875637000)
=> (column=1970-01-17 03:22:22+0530, value=New chat session,
timestamp=1374742833147000)
=> (column=1970-01-17 03:22:22+0530, value=Message #1,
timestamp=1374742854154000)
[-- snip --]
```

This is the old way of looking at wide rows. CQL 3 treats it this way (in cqlsh, see the following figure):

```
cqlsh:cqltest> select * from "WideRowThrift";
 key                                  | column1                    | value
--------------------------------------+----------------------------+------------------
 72da9d1a-4802-47b4-ab50-249a8ea00038 | 1970-01-17 03:22:20+0530 |        some text1
 72da9d1a-4802-47b4-ab50-249a8ea00038 | 1970-01-17 03:22:20+0530 |        some text2
 72da9d1a-4802-47b4-ab50-249a8ea00038 | 1970-01-17 03:22:20+0530 |        some text3
 fa408aff-a55b-4a52-b4b7-2314bb5bb86f | 1970-01-02 19:41:14+0530 |        Message #2
 fa408aff-a55b-4a52-b4b7-2314bb5bb86f | 1970-01-17 03:22:22+0530 | New chat session
 fa408aff-a55b-4a52-b4b7-2314bb5bb86f | 1970-01-17 03:22:22+0530 |        Message #1
```

Figure 9.1: Wide row gets transposed in CQL 3

If you are from a relational database world, it will be easier for you to see that it seems like a table that has a non-unique key. Also, a unique key can be created by combining `key` and `column1`. In Thrift terms, if we assume a thrift column value as a cell, each cell in a row can be uniquely identified by using a compound key, a row key, and a column name. This leads us to the difference in terminology between Thrift and CQL 3.

To avoid confusion between Thrift and CQL 3 representation of the same underlying data, people use a different terminology for CQL 3. A row in CQL 3 means a row in a static column family, but in a dynamic column family, such as the one above a row in CQL, it means a row with columns row key, column name, and column value. Note that the underlying representation is unchanged. It is still a wide row in Thrift terms. A row key in a wide row works as a partition in CQL 3 representation. A column in the Thrift world is just a cell in CQL 3—the same way you see a cell in a spreadsheet.

Composite columns

We have seen how a dynamic column is transposed. When you use a composite column name in Thrift, you are basically composing two or more columns into one, in terms of an RDBMS. This means a composite column name in Thrift is two or more columns in CQL 3. Let's see an example:

```
# Thrift - composite column
[default@cqltest] CREATE COLUMN FAMILY CompositeCol
WITH
KEY_VALIDATION_CLASS = UUIDType
AND
COMPARATOR = 'CompositeType(DateType, IntegerType)'
AND
DEFAULT_VALIDATION_CLASS = UTF8Type;

# Insert some values
[default@cqltest] SET CompositeCol[6606f5b4-c536-4413-8d3d-
63fa6f22a876]['1374774648000:1'] = '10.110.6.4';
[ -- snip --]

# View column family in Thrift
[default@cqltest] list CompositeCol;
[-- snip --]
RowKey: 6606f5b4-c536-4413-8d3d-63fa6f22a876
=> (column=1974-05-11 08\:48\:11+0530:3, value=10.110.6.30,
timestamp=1374774565946000)
=> (column=2013-07-25 23\:20\:48+0530:1, value=10.110.6.4,
timestamp=1374774694423000)
=> (column=2013-07-25 23\:21\:08+0530:3, value=10.110.6.4,
timestamp=1374774771822000)

1 Row Returned.
Elapsed time: 4.35 msec(s).
```

This represents a column family that tracks users' login with composite key as timestamp and an integer role that the user uses to log in to the system. The value is the IP of the machine used to access the system. CQL 3 breaks composite column names into its components—each component represents a column. The same column family looks like this in CQL 3:

```
cqlsh:cqltest> select * from "CompositeCol";

key                          | column1                   | column2 | value
-----------------------------+---------------------------+---------+------------
6606f5b4-c536-4413-8d3... | 1974-05-11 08:48:11+0530 |       3 | 10.110.6.30
6606f5b4-c536-4413-8d3... | 2013-07-25 23:20:48+0530 |       1 | 10.110.6.4
6606f5b4-c536-4413-8d3... | 2013-07-25 23:21:08+0530 |       3 | 10.110.6.4
```

It may require some focus to understand the presentations in Thrift and CQL 3, but once you get the idea of transpose, you can easily see both the pictures and justify it.

We will see some more stuff like compact storage and collections in CQL 3 in the next section. In general, CQL 3 is an effort to make RDBMS/table-minded people understand the storage. One may argue that the actual data storage structure differs from what CQL 3 shows, while Thrift has a much more accurate representation. But CQL 3 is the future. It restricts users to avoid anti-patterns and it is much more brain-friendly to a new person.

CQL 3 basics

This section is a brief introduction to CQL 3 on Cassandra 1.1.x. We will see queries and discuss options available. For more formal query definitions, please refer to the Cassandra CQL 3 documentation that is appropriate for the Cassandra version that you are using. One of the good sources for this is the Apache CQL 3 documentation and the DataStax Cassandra documentation. Most of the queries that are mentioned here should work in 1.1.x as well as in 1.2.x versions, but the queries are not tested against 1.2.x and further versions.

Apache CQL 3 documentation at http://cassandra.apache.org/doc/cql3/CQL.html.

Cassandra CQL documentation at http://www.datastax.com/docs/1.1/references/cql/index.

The CREATE KEYSPACE query

Creating keyspace just requires keyspace name, strategy class, and options for the specific strategy class as mandatory elements. Keyspace name has the same restrictions as Java variable naming has. Keyspace names should be alpha-numeric and they must start with an alphabet.

```
CREATE KEYSPACE "MyKeyspace1"
with
STRATEGY_CLASS = SimpleStrategy
and
STRATEGY_OPTIONS:REPLICATION_FACTOR = 2;
```

Double quotes around the keyspace name are not mandatory. If you do not use quotes, the casing will be ignored and the name will be stored in lowercase.

STRATEGY_CLASS has two options: SimpleStrategy and NetworkTopologyStrategy. Refer to section *Replica placement strategies* from *Chapter 4, Deploying a Cluster,* for details.

If you use SimpleStrategy, all you need to specify is REPLICATION_FACTOR as a part of STRATEGY_OPTIONS.

If you use NetworkTopologyStrategy, you will need to specify the replication factor for each data center. Something like this:

```
CREATE KEYSPACE "MyKeyspace1"
with
STRATEGY_CLASS = NetworkTopologyStrategy
and
STRATEGY_OPTIONS:DC1 = 2
and
STRATEGY_OPTIONS:DC2 = 1;
```

The preceding statement basically says to set the replication factor to 2 in the data center DC1 and the replication factor to 1 in the data center DC2.

Apart from this there is another optional parameter called DURABLE_WRITES. Its value can be true or false, depending on your need.

The CREATE TABLE query

A table is the way CQL 3 chooses to call a column family. Always translate a table to a column family, if you are used to seeing things the Thrift way.

In the simplest form creating a table is just like an SQL table creation
(except, obviously, for foreign keys and some other constraints).
The other settings are for the column family and are set to a sensible default.

```
# create table with default settings
CREATE TABLE simpletable
    (
id UUID PRIMARY KEY,
name VARCHAR,
age INT,
aboutMe TEXT
);


# let's see what are the default assignments
cqlsh:MyKeyspace>DESC TABLE simpletable;

CREATE TABLE simpletable (
id uuid PRIMARY KEY,
aboutme text,
age int,
name text
) WITH
comment='' AND
caching='KEYS_ONLY' AND
read_repair_chance=0.100000 AND
gc_grace_seconds=864000 AND
replicate_on_write='true' AND
compaction_strategy_class='SizeTieredCompactionStrategy' AND
compression_parameters:sstable_compression='SnappyCompressor';
```

The latter CREATE TABLE command in the previous snippet is interesting.
Apart from describing everything that constitutes that column family/table,
it also prints the command to create this table with all the optional parameters.
Let's see the optional parameters quickly.

1. comment: It is used to store any comment or information that anyone might
    be interested in while looking at the table.

2. caching: As we know from section *Cache settings, Chapter 5, Performance
    Tuning*, there are four caching options available to a column family. These
    options can be KEYS_ONLY, ROWS_ONLY, ALL, and NONE. The default option
    is KEYS_ONLY. If you have no idea about caching, leave it to the default.
    It is generally a good option.

3. read_repair_chance: It denotes the chance to query extra nodes than
    what the consistency level dictates for read-repairs. Refer to section *Read
    repair and Anti-entropy* from *Chapter 2, Cassandra Architecture* for read-repairs.

4. `gc_grace_seconds`: It determines the duration to wait after deletion to remove the tombstones.

5. `replicate_on_write`: This is a boolean variable that can be set to true or false based on whether you want to replicate the data on write. This can be set to false only for column families/tables with counter column values. It is not advisable to turn this to false.

6. `compaction_strategy_class`: The approach that you wanted to take on SSTable compression for this column family. Refer section *Choosing the right compaction strategy, Chapter 5, Performance Tuning,* for details. There are two options available: `SizeTieredCompactionStrategy` and `LeveledCompactionStrategy`. The former option is the default option.

7. `compression_parameters:sstable_compression`: This command sets the type of compressor you wanted to use for a column family. There are two compressors available out of the box: `SnappyCompressor` and `DeflateCompressor`. `SnappyCompressor` is the default compressor.

8. To disable compression, use an empty string '' (two single quotes without anything in between).

9. `compression_parameters:chunk_length_kb`: SSTable unit block size to be compressed by the specified compressor. The larger the chunk length, the better the compression. But a large block size affects the amount of the data read negatively. Read more on compression in section *Enabling compression* from *Chapter 5, Performance Tuning,* The default value is 64, which implies 64 kilobytes.

10. `compression_parameters:crc_check_chance`: The probability of validating checksums during reads. Always check that by default this parameter is 1. It helps avoid corrupted data to move across replicas. It can be set to any value between 0 and 1, both included. To disable CRC, set it to zero, but this is not a good idea.

Here is an example of a completely customized CREATE TABLE command with all the anti-default settings:

```
CREATE TABLE non_default_table (
id uuid PRIMARY KEY,
aboutme text,
age int,
name text
 ) WITH
comment='test c' AND
caching='ALL' AND
read_repair_chance=0.900000 AND
gc_grace_seconds=432000 AND
replicate_on_write='false' AND
compaction_strategy_class='LeveledCompactionStrategy' AND
```

```
compression_parameters:chunk_length_kb='128' AND
compression_parameters:sstable_compression='DeflateCompressor' AND
compression_parameters:crc_check_chance=0.5;
```

Compact storage

Compact storage is a true representation of wide rows. Have a look at the following statement:

```
# Wide row definition in CQL 3 with compact storage
CREATE TABLE compact_cf
(key BIGINT, column1 VARCHAR, column2 varchar, PRIMARY KEY(key,
column1))
WITH COMPACT STORAGE;
```

In a case where you want to have a row key, a column name—it may be of composite type, and a column value, the preceding statement is exactly the same as the following:

```
# Wide row definition in cassandra-cli
CREATE COLUMN FAMILY compact_cf
WITH
KEY_VALIDATION_CLASS = LongType
AND COMPARATOR = UTF8Type
AND DEFAULT_VALIDATION_CLASS = UTF8Type;
```

Compact storage is generally discouraged, especially if you are starting with CQL 3. There are a couple of reasons for this. First, like wide rows in Thrift, you can have just one value per column name. Speaking in terms of CQL 3, if you declare a compact storage, you will have all but one column that is not a part of the primary key. It is because compact storage takes all the first components of primary keys to be column names (in THE Thrift realm) and the first component is treated as a row key. It makes the structure rigid. A non-compact table does this by representing the column name as a static slice of a wide row. So, a non-compact wide row in CQL looks like this:

```
cqlsh:MyKeyspace> CREATE TABLE non_compact_cf
(key BIGINT, column1 VARCHAR, column2 varchar, value VARCHAR, PRIMARY
KEY(key, column1));

cqlsh:MyKeyspace> INSERT INTO non_compact_cf (key, column1, column2,
value)
VALUES (1, 'text1', 'text2', 'val1' );

cqlsh:MyKeyspace> SELECT * FROM non_compact_cf;
 key | column1 | column2 | value
-----+---------+---------+-------
   1 |   text1 |   text2 |   val1
```

This is basically a smartly sliced materialized row sort of thing when you see it from the Thrift perspective:

```
[default@MyKeyspace] LIST non_compact_cf;
[-- snip --]
RowKey: 1
=> (column=text1:column2, value=text2, timestamp=1375074891655000)
=> (column=text1:value, value=val1, timestamp=1375074891655001)
```

You can see that non-key columns just create a static slice for a given column name.

The second reason to discourage compact storage is static tables with collections (please note that collections are introduced in Cassandra 1.2.x, so this is not valid in older versions). Static tables, as one would expect, should have no dynamic parts. So, the column names should be simple UTF8Type, but that is not true. It uses CompositeType internally, the reason being a new feature to support—collections. We will see collections support later in this chapter under the *Collections support* section. A collection provides the ability to store sets, lists, and maps as column values, and to get them working you need to have composite column names. So, the following code snippet will fail:

```
cqlsh:my_keyspace> CREATE TABLE compact_with_set
(id INT PRIMARY KEY, name VARCHAR, emails SET<VARCHAR>)
WITH COMPACT STORAGE;
Bad Request: Collection types are not supported with COMPACT STORAGE
```

The bottom line is unless you are sure that you are not going to modify a table, do not use compact storage. It provides a little storage benefit at the cost of major impairment in flexibility.

Creating a secondary index

Secondary indexes can be created on a static column family, on named columns. You can create a secondary index only after defining the table. It is a good practice to provide a name to the index, but it is optional.

```
 CREATE INDEX
index_name ON
table_name(column_name );
```

The previous query creates an index named index_name on a table named table_name for a column named column_name.

The INSERT query

The insert query looks exactly the same as SQL, except there are a few extra optional parameters that you can set, such as TTL (**Time To Live**), TIMESTAMP, and obviously, CONSISTENCY. These three have their usual meaning.

```
INSERT INTO
simpletable (id, name, age)
VALUES
('f7a1cb71-50b4-4128-a805-fc3cd0c1623c', 'Foo Bar', '42')
USING
CONSISTENCY QUORUM
and
TTL 864000
and
TIMESTAMP 1374893426000;
```

A few things worth noting:

- Did you notice how there is no equal sign after the TTL or TIMESTAMP keywords?

- Although Cassandra is a schema-optional database, CQL 3 does not allow you to add any random column without declaring it during table creation. If you try to insert an unknown column, you will get an error.

- Cassandra 1.2.x and onward does not have the CONSISTENCY setting.

To view the remaining TTL and write TIMESTAMP, you can always query using special functions for each column. Here is an example:

```
cqlsh:MyKeyspace> select name, age, WRITETIME(name), TTL(age) from
simpletable;

   name   | age | writetime(name) | ttl(age)
----------+-----+-----------------+----------
 Leon Kik |  59 |   1374893123000 |   853426
  Foo Bar |  42 |   1374893426000 |   855792
```

Note that insert is basically upsert (update or insert). Insertion on an existing key will overwrite the contents.

The SELECT query

The select statement has pseudo SQL select like pattern. There are fine prints while using select, if you are coming from SQL development. The caveats are due to the difference between the underlying storage mechanisms. The Cassandra storage model is different from a fixed tabular or B-tree-like structure. The general structure looks like this:

```
SELECT <select expression>
FROM <column family name>
USING CONSISTENCY <consistency level>          //OPTIONAL
WHERE <AND separated where clauses>            //OPTIONAL
ORDER BY <orderable field>                     //OPTIONAL SUBCLAUSE
LIMIT <limit number>                           //OPTIONAL
```

The simplest select query is just pulling all the columns from a column family. Since we do not specify a limit, it returns 10,000 records as default. Here's what it looks like:

```
SELECT * FROM select_test;
 id                                   | age | location | name
--------------------------------------+-----+----------+-------
 5bc25ea7-1636-4a54-b292-bc0877653d24 |  15 |       LA | name4
 367d2c7e-d878-4211-8021-3e92cb2a45f5 |  13 |       VA | name2
 ae64284b-5413-41b8-a446-fdcd373c8fc0 |  14 |       NY | name3
 98cf99b9-8c93-4b64-bd06-a3c91f57e5b9 |  12 |       TX | name1
```

Notice that the rows are unordered. They are not ordered by key. They are not in the order of insertion. Basically, an order is not preserved since we use `RandomPartitioner` in `cassandra.yaml`. For more on partitioners, read section Partitioner from *Chapter 2, Cassandra Architecture*.

Let's see what all those terms within angled brackets in the previous snippet mean.

select expression

`select expression` can be a `*` to select all the columns of a CQL row. To select specific columns, use comma-separated column names to be fetched. One can apply `WRITETIME` and `TTL` functions on column names to retrieve the timestamp that was set during the latest write of that column and `TTL` tells about the remaining time of that particular cell after which it will be deleted and marked as a tombstone.

`COUNT(*)` is another function that can be used to fetch a number of CQL columns for a particular query. It looks exactly the same as an SQL count function.

```
select count(*) from select_test;
count
-------
    4
```

The WHERE clause

This clause is used to narrow down the result set by specifying constraints. The WHERE clause in CQL is not as fancy as it is in the SQL world and it is where you need to understand what you can or cannot do with Cassandra.

The WHERE clause supports only the AND conjunction. There is no OR conjunction. You can only use the columns that compose PRIMARY KEY or have a secondary index created on them. But you cannot use a partition key (or a row key in Thrift terms) with an inequality. Here are a few examples on the data we inserted in the previous example:

```
# WHERE clause with equality sign on partitioning key
cqlsh:MyKeyspace> select * from select_test where
id = 'ae64284b-5413-41b8-a446-fdcd373c8fc0';

 id                                   | age | location | name
--------------------------------------+-----+----------+-------
 ae64284b-5413-41b8-a446-fdcd373c8fc0 |  14 |       NY | name3

# Inequality is not supported
cqlsh:MyKeyspace> select * from select_test where
id >= 'ae64284b-5413-41b8-a446-fdcd373c8fc0';

Bad Request: Only EQ and IN relation are supported on first component
of the PRIMARY KEY for RandomPartitioner (unless you use the token()
function)


#If you have to use inequality you may use token comparison, it may or
may not serve your purpose.
cqlsh:MyKeyspace1> select * from select_test where
token(id) >= token('ae64284b-5413-41b8-a446-fdcd373c8fc0');

 id                                   | age | location | name
--------------------------------------+-----+----------+-------
 ae64284b-5413-41b8-a446-fdcd373c8fc0 |  14 |       NY | name3
 98cf99b9-8c93-4b64-bd06-a3c91f57e5b9 |  12 |       TX | name1
```

The trick to use inequality with partition keys is to use the token function. However, it may not help you. What it does is it creates a token of the partition key based on the partitioner that you are using (RandomPartitioner, ByteOrderPartitioner, and so on) and uses it to fetch the rows with matching tokens. It may not make sense to use tokens for rows in case of RandomPartitioner, but be aware that in ByteOrderPartitioner case, the tokens are ordered by bytes, so it may or may not be lexicographically ordered.

You can, however, use the IN keyword to provide a comma-separated list of partition keys to pull the rows for them. IN follows the same format as in SQL.

There is another caveat with compound keys. If you use compound keys, the selection is limited to contiguous CQL 3 rows. It is much easier to think in terms of SLICE from Thrift. The Thrift columns or CQL 3 cells are ordered entities. You can apply SLICE only to continuous regions. This example will clarify why this happens:

```
# Create table
cqlsh:MyKeyspace> CREATE TABLE where_clause_test
(id int, name varchar, role int, message text, PRIMARY KEY (id, name,
role) );

# Insert some data
cqlsh:MyKeyspace> INSERT INTO where_clause_test (id, name, role,
message)
VALUES (1, 'A Smith', 3, 'Hi! everyone');
cqlsh:MyKeyspace> INSERT INTO where_clause_test (id, name, role,
message)
VALUES (2, 'B Washington', 2, 'Logging out');
cqlsh:MyKeyspace> INSERT INTO where_clause_test (id, name, role,
message)
VALUES (2, 'B Washington', 3, 'Logging in');
cqlsh:MyKeyspace> INSERT INTO where_clause_test (id, name, role,
message)
VALUES (2, 'A Smith', 1, 'Creating new tickets');
cqlsh:MyKeyspace> INSERT INTO where_clause_test (id, name, role,
message)
VALUES (2, 'B Washington', 4, 'Added new employees');


# How it looks in CQL point of view
cqlsh:MyKeyspace> SELECT * FROM where_clause_test;

id | name         | role | message
----+--------------+------+----------------------
```

```
1 |         A Smith |   3 |          Hi! everyone
2 |         A Smith |   1 |  Creating new tickets
2 |  B Washington |   2 |           Logging out
2 |  B Washington |   3 |            Logging in
2 |  B Washington |   4 |   Added new employees
```

Let's experiment with a few select queries:

```
# Get all users logged via machine id = 2, named 'B Washington' as a
# role less than equal 3 (3 = manager priviledge, say).
cqlsh:MyKeyspace> SELECT * FROM where_clause_test WHERE id = 2 AND
name = 'B Washington' AND role <= 3;
```

```
 id | name            | role | message
----+---------------+------+-------------
  2 |  B Washington |    2 |  Logging out
  2 |  B Washington |    3 |   Logging in
```

```
# get all the users logged in from machine is = 2 as manager (role =
# 3) and name anything lexically greater than 'A'
cqlsh:MyKeyspace> SELECT * FROM where_clause_test WHERE id = 2 AND
name > 'A' AND role = 3;
Bad Request: PRIMARY KEY part role cannot be restricted (preceding
part name is either not restricted or by a non-EQ relation)
```

```
# get all the users logged into the system from machine id = 2 as a
# manager (role =3) irrespective of their names.
cqlsh:MyKeyspace> SELECT * FROM where_clause_test WHERE id = 2 AND
role = 3;
Bad Request: PRIMARY KEY part role cannot be restricted (preceding
part name is either not restricted or by a non-EQ relation)
```

It is a bit frustrating for a beginner that you can see the columns just like in an RDBMS; you can run some of the queries but you cannot run some others that look closely similar. The answer lies in the underlying representation. When we defined the composite key, the data for each composite key does not actually go in separate rows. Instead, the first part of the compound key is the row key and the rest is just secondary keys creating partitions in a wide row. This view can be seen using Thrift.

```
# incassandra-cli
[default@MyKeyspace1] list where_clause_test;
Using default limit of 100
Using default column limit of 100
-------------------
RowKey: 1
```

```
=> (column=A Smith:3:message, value=Hi! everyone,
timestamp=1374934726143000)
------------------
RowKey: 2
=> (column=A Smith:1:message, value=Creating new tickets,
timestamp=1374934870771000)
=> (column=B Washington:2:message, value=Logging out,
timestamp=1374934807710000)
=> (column=B Washington:3:message, value=Logging in,
timestamp=1374934836937000)
=> (column=B Washington:4:message, value=Added new employees,
timestamp=1374934915607000)

2 Rows Returned.
Elapsed time: 84 msec(s).
```

Now, you can see why we cannot use inequality in any of the primary keys but the last one.

The ORDER BY clause

ORDER BY enables ordering of the rows by the second component of the primary key, even if your primary key contains more than two components. The reason again is the same as we discussed in the previous section, when discussing the WHERE clause for tables with compound keys. ORDER BY can order only one column and there must be a valid WHERE clause before it. Here is an example:

```
cqlsh:MyKeyspace> SELECT * FROM where_clause_test WHERE id = 2 ORDER
BY name DESC;
```

id	name	role	message
2	B Washington	4	Added new employees
2	B Washington	3	Logging in
2	B Washington	2	Logging out
2	A Smith	1	Creating new tickets

You can sort in a descending order by specifying the DESC keyword. The ascending column value is default if nothing is mentioned. To explicitly mention ascending, use the ASC keyword.

The LIMIT clause

The limit clause works the same way as in an RDBMS. It limits the number of rows to be returned to the user. It can be used to perform pagination. If nothing is mentioned, CQL limits the results to 10,000 rows. Use `limit` to fetch either more or fewer results than the default `limit` value.

```
# limiting resulting rows to 2 of total 4 rows
cqlsh:MyKeyspace1> SELECT * FROM where_clause_test LIMIT 2;

id  | name     | role | message
----+----------+------+----------------------
  1 | A Smith  |    3 |           Hi! everyone
  2 | A Smith  |    1 | Creating new tickets
```

The USING CONSISTENCY clause

In Cassandra 1.1.x, you can specify the consistency level for a read request. For example:

```
# Consistency clause in Cassandra 1.1.x select query
cqlsh:MyKeyspace> SELECT * FROM where_clause_test USING CONSISTENCY
QUORUM LIMIT 2;

id  | name     | role | message
----+----------+------+----------------------
  1 | A Smith  |    3 |           Hi! everyone
  2 | A Smith  |    1 | Creating new tickets
```

The UPDATE query

The UPDATE query is basically an upsert query, which means that it will update the specified column for the given row or rows in existence, else it will create the column and/or the row. It is the same thing as insert except it has a different syntax.

In its simplest form, UPDATE is the same as an SQL update:

```
# Updating a column requires complete information about PRIMARY KEY
cqlsh:MyKeyspace> UPDATE where_clause_test SET message = 'Deleting old
tickets' WHERE id = 2 AND name = 'A Smith' AND role = 1;

# Column is updated
cqlsh:MyKeyspace> SELECT * FROM where_clause_test;
id  | name         | role | message
----+--------------+------+----------------------
```

```
1 |       A Smith |   3 |           Hi! everyone
2 |       A Smith |   1 | Deleting old tickets
2 | B Washington |   2 |           Logging out
2 | B Washington |   3 |            Logging in
2 | B Washington |   4 | Added new employees
```

```
# A non-existing column in UPDATE statement can lead to new column or
# row row creation
cqlsh:MyKeyspace1> UPDATE where_clause_test SET message = 'This row
will be inserted' WHERE id = 3 AND name = 'W Smith' AND role = 1;
```

```
# New row is created!
cqlsh:MyKeyspace1> SELECT * FROM where_clause_test;
 id | name         | role | message
----+--------------+------+--------------------------
  1 |       A Smith |   3 |           Hi! everyone
  2 |       A Smith |   1 |   Deleting old tickets
  2 | B Washington |   2 |           Logging out
  2 | B Washington |   3 |            Logging in
  2 | B Washington |   4 |     Added new employees
  3 |       W Smith |   1 | This row will be inserted
```

There are a few optional elements for the UPDATE statement and they are the same as the optional elements for the SELECT statement. These are TTL, write TIMESTAMP, and CONSISTENCY level. These must be specified before the SET keyword:

```
UPDATE where_clause_test
USING
  CONSISTENCY QUORUM AND
  TIMESTAMP 1374945623000 AND
  TTL 84600
SET
  MESSAGE = 'Fixing bugs.'
WHERE
  id = 2 AND
  name = 'A Smith' AND
  role = 1;
```

The DELETE query

The DELETE query deletes columns by marking them with a tombstone and a timestamp. These columns are deleted after gc_grace_period ends. Refer to the *Tombstones* section in *Chapter 2, Cassandra Architecture,* for more details.

Unlike SQL, in CQL, you can delete specified columns from a row. A simple query looks like an SQL delete query with the columns to be deleted mentioned before the FROM keyword.

```
# before deletion
cqlsh:MyKeyspace> SELECT * FROM my_table;
id | address                | age | name
----+------------------------+-----+----------
  1 |      36, Keyye Blvd, NJ |  42 | John Doe
  2 | 277, Block 4, James St |  31 | Sam Woe

# Delete the address for id = 1
cqlsh:MyKeyspace> DELETE address FROM my_table WHERE id = 1;

# Deleted column is shown as null
cqlsh:MyKeyspace> SELECT * FROM my_table;
id | address                | age | name
----+------------------------+-----+----------
  1 |                   null |  42 | John Doe
  2 | 277, Block 4, James St |  31 | Sam Woe
```

There are two optional parameters: CONSISTENCY and tombstone creation TIMESTAMP. These can be specified before the WHERE keyword like this:

```
DELETE address FROM my_table
USING
CONSISTENCY ALL AND
TIMESTAMP 1374945623000
WHERE id = 2;
```

The TRUNCATE query

Truncate is like the DELETE FROM TABLE_NAME query in SQL without any WHERE clause. It deletes all the data in the column family. The syntax is like this:

```
TRUNCATE my_table;
```

The ALTER TABLE query

The ALTER TABLE query performs four tasks: adding a new column, dropping an existing column, altering the type of a column, and changing the table options.

Adding a new column

Adding a new column follows a syntax like this:

```
ALTER TABLE my_table ADD email varchar;
```

Existing data is not validated, so there may or may not be an existing column in the rows.

Dropping an existing column

Dropping an existing column is not the same as deleting data and removing the column name from the metadata. It is just the latter. On the DROP query execution, the column family metadata loses the column definition that is being dropped but the data in the existing rows still stays. Let's delete the address column from the my_table column family and see what happens:

```
# Existind data in my_table
cqlsh:MyKeyspace> SELECT * FROM my_table;
 id | address                | age | email | name
----+------------------------+-----+-------+----------
  1 |     36, Keyye Blvd, NJ |  42 |  null | John Doe
  2 | 277, Block 4, James St |  31 |  null |  Sam Woe

# Drop the address column
cqlsh:MyKeyspace> ALTER TABLE my_table DROP address;

# CQL does not show it.
cqlsh:MyKeyspace> SELECT * FROM my_table;
 id | age | email | name
----+-----+-------+----------
  1 |  42 |  null | John Doe
  2 |  31 |  null |  Sam Woe

# But it exists, let's use Thrift call (cassandra-cli console)
[default@MyKeyspace] list my_table;
[-- snip --]
RowKey: 1
=>(column=address, value=36, Keyye Blvd, NJ,
timestamp=1374948385939000)
=> (column=age, value=42, timestamp=1374948385939001)
=> (column=name, value=John Doe, timestamp=1374948385939002)
-------------------
RowKey: 2
```

```
=>(column=address, value=277, Block 4, James St,
timestamp=1374948401402000)
=> (column=age, value=31, timestamp=1374948401402001)
=> (column=name, value=Sam Woe, timestamp=1374948401402002)
```

Modifying the data type of an existing column

The syntax to change the data type of an existing column looks like this:

```
ALTER TABLE my_table1 ALTER name TYPE int;
```

The bad thing about this is it does not check the data type of the underlying existing cells. This may lead to a problem if you modify a column to a type that is not compatible to the existing data. It may cause problems during deserialization.

```
# Exisiting data - name is a varchar type
cqlsh:MyKeyspace> SELECT * FROM my_table;
id  | age | email | name
----+-----+-------+----------
  1 |  42 |  null | John Doe
  2 |  31 |  null |  Sam Woe

# altered the name column to an incompatible type
cqlsh:MyKeyspace> ALTER TABLE my_table ALTER name TYPE int;

# accessing the columns throws deserialization exception
cqlsh:MyKeyspace> SELECT * FROM my_table;
id  | age | email | name
----+-----+-------+------------
  1 |  42 |  null | 'John Doe'
  2 |  31 |  null |  'Sam Woe'

Failed to decode value 'John Doe' (for column 'name') as int: unpack
requires a string argument of length 4
Failed to decode value 'Sam Woe' (for column 'name') as int: unpack
requires a string argument of length 4
```

Altering table options

The table's options that were used during the table creation can be altered using this command. Here is a sample of that:

```
cqlsh:MyKeyspace> ALTER TABLE my_table WITH comment = 'updated caching
to none' and caching = NONE;

cqlsh:MyKeyspace>DESC TABLE my_table;

CREATE TABLE my_table (
id int PRIMARY KEY,
age int,
email text,
name int
) WITH
comment='updated caching to none' AND
caching='NONE' AND
read_repair_chance=0.100000 AND
gc_grace_seconds=864000 AND
replicate_on_write='true' AND
compaction_strategy_class='SizeTieredCompactionStrategy' AND
compression_parameters:sstable_compression='SnappyCompressor';
```

The ALTER KEYSPACE query

ALTER KEYSPACE lets you change all the aspects of a keyspace that are available during keyspace creation. The query looks very similar to CREATE KEYSPACE specifications. Here is an example:

```
CREATE KEYSPACE "MyKespace"
    WITH strategy_class = NetworkTopologyStrategy
    AND strategy_options:DC1 = 2
    AND strategy_options:DC2 = 2
    AND durable_writes=false;
```

This updates the placement strategy and sets durable writes as false.

> CQL is a case-insensitive query language. This means the query is toLowerCase and processed. If you have created a column family or keyspaces that contains uppercase letters using the Thrift interface or using double quotes to preserve case in CQL, you would not be able to access it in CQL without putting double quotes around it as we did in the previous query.

BATCH querying

BATCH enables users to execute a set of data modification operations such as INSERT, UPDATE, and DELETE, to club into a single logical execution. CONSISTENCY level and TIMESTAMP may be provided at the batch level that is applied to all the statements under the batch. An example of a batch is as follows:

```
BEGIN BATCH USING CONSISTENCY ALL TIMESTAMP 1374983889000
   INSERT INTO my_table1 (id, name, age, email) VALUES (42, 'Cameleon
Woe', 59, 'email not available')
   UPDATE my_table1 SET name = 'Leon Woe' WHERE id = 42
   DELETE email FROM my_table1 WHERE id = 42
APPLY BATCH;
```

Note that there is no semicolon after the individual statements inside the batch. Semicolon is the delimiter, so it should be applied at the end of BATCH. Execution will break if you place a semicolon within the BATCH statement.

The DROP INDEX query

DROP INDEX drops secondary indexes from a table. The syntax is like this:

```
DROP INDEX index_name;
```

index_name is the name of the index that you provided during index creation. If you haven't provided a name for the index during creation, the index_name can be replaced with <table_name>_<column_name>_idx. For example, an unnamed index for a column name in a table named users will be referred to as users_name_idx in the DROP INDEX statement.

The DROP TABLE query

It deletes the table and all its contents. The syntax follows an SQL pattern.

```
DROP TABLE my_table;
```

The DROP KEYSPACE query

It deletes the keyspace and all the tables that it contains.

```
DROP KEYSPACE my_keyspace;
```

The USE statement

The USE statement tells the client to connect to a specified keyspace. After this statement is issued, the client's current session gets authorized to use tables and indexes in the current keyspace. The syntax is like this:

```
USE my_keyspace;
```

What's new in Cassandra 1.2?

At the time of writing this book, Cassandra 1.2 is released with massive improvements over its precursor. Cassandra version 2.0 is set to release in August 2013, which is Cassandra 1.2 plus a few major features such as improvements in repair and compaction, triggers (as an RDBMS provides), eager retries, and **compare and set (CAS)** features. Version 1.2, with all its disruptive changes, can be thought of as a step to version 2.0. However, by the time this book is available to you, you might want to use Cassandra 2.0 or Cassandra 1.1.x for your production setup. This section will briefly cover new features in 1.2. It does not break the concepts that we learned throughout this book; it adds some more to that.

Virtual Nodes

Virtual Nodes (VNodes) are introduced to solve two major problems of previous versions:

- **Change in cluster leads to heavy load on some nodes**: The addition, removal, or restoration of a node causes heavy data transfer on the nodes that share the replica for the node in question. That is, if a node is added, for instance, it will be streamed in data from the nodes that contain that data. It is likely that the majority of the nodes are not involved in pushing data to this new node. So, some nodes are very busy and some are not. VNodes solves this problem by making nodes to be responsible for more than one range. See Figure 9.2.

- **Manual load balancing**: Whenever a new node is added or a node is removed, the cluster gets imbalanced. This is not a desired state. It leads to recalculation of tokens and balancing nodes by nodes. It is time consuming and error prone. VNodes solves this issue.

The idea behind VNodes is simple. In a situation of a 30-node cluster with a replication factor of 3, imagine a case where one of the nodes dies and we add a new replacement node for it. In Cassandra versions before 1.2.0, we would have lost one replica for each three ranges that lived on the dead nodes. We still have six replicas for the three ranges that the dead node held, spread in the remaining 29 nodes. When we replace the dead node, three of those six replicas will stream the data to a new node. We are heavy-loading three nodes, but the remaining 26 nodes are not contributing in bootstrapping of the new node. This is inefficient.

VNodes makes a node responsible for multiple ranges. As if each of their physical node hosts multiple virtual nodes, and each virtual node is responsible for a slice of data. For the sake of argument, assume each node as 32 virtual nodes. In a cluster of 30 machines, you have 960 VNodes. If a physical node dies, and you launch a new machine, this machine will require 32 ranges. If VNodes are distributed homogeneously, it is likely that all the remaining 29 nodes will be used to stream data to the new node. You get faster restoration, because you are streaming the data in a more parallelized way than before. See Figure 9.3.

VNodes is not activated by default. So, if you are upgrading from an older version, do not worry about compatibility. To enable VNodes, you need to edit `cassandra.yaml` to uncomment and set `num_tokens` to some value. A decent default is 256 for a mid-sized cluster. Here is the snippet from `cassandra.yaml`:

```
# If you already have a cluster with 1 token per node,
and wish to migrate to
# multiple tokens per node,
see http://wiki.apache.org/cassandra/Operations
num_tokens: 256
```

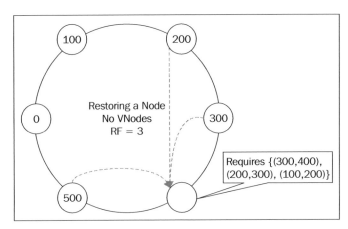

Figure 9.2: Restoring a node in Cassandra without virtual nodes enabled, assuming partitioner ranges from 0 to 599

The higher the virtual nodes, the more the token slices. This means there will be more uniform distribution of ranges across the cluster. However, a large number of slices will also make it hard to keep track of the slices. It will cost more to calculate which key lives where. So, a general rule of thumb is 256 `num_tokens` per node.

Off-heap Bloom filters

In Cassandra 1.2, Bloom filters and compaction metadata is moved to native memory. This is done to help reduce frequent garbage collection to some extent. Please note that off-heap operations require you to install JNA. Please read the section *Installing the Java Native Access (JNA) library* from *Chapter 4, Deploying a Cluster*.

JBOD improvements

Just a bunch of disks (JBOD) has the potential to make the node go down even if one of the disks go down. Cassandra version 1.2's new configurations tackle this issue. There is a new option, `disk_failure_policy`, to handle it differently.

 Refer to JBOD at `http://en.wikipedia.org/wiki/Non-RAID_drive_architectures#JBOD`.

There are three settings to this configuration:

1. `stop`: On a disk error, the node will be available. One may still connect via JMX to troubleshoot.

2. `best_effort`: Cassandra will try its best to get things working as much as possible. Due to its inability to write, it will blacklist this node for writes but serve reads. If there is a read problem, it will just serve the data from the SSTables that are still in a readable state. This can be a problem if you are using consistency level ONE. If the data is not updated on the broken node, you might be serving stale data.

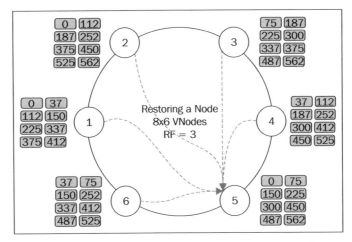

Figure 9.3: Replacing a dead node with VNodes enabled uses all nodes to stream data, assuming partitioner ranges from 0 to 599 and num_tokens = 8 on each serverImage

3. `ignore`: This retains the same behavior of JBOD as in previous versions of Cassandra. It is suggested to not use this option. Use `stop` or `best_effort` options.

Parallel leveled compaction

Leveled compaction has been upgraded to run multiple compaction processes in parallel. The number of compactors can be controlled by tweaking the `concurrent_compactors` setting in `cassandra.yaml`:

```
# concurrent_compactors defaults to the number of cores.
# Uncomment to make compaction mono-threaded, the pre-0.8 default.
concurrent_compactors: 8
```

Earlier, only one leveled compactor could run at a time for a given table.

Murmur3 partitioner

Murmur3 partitioner is available in 1.2. It is not compatible with `RandomPartitioner` from previous releases. This partitioner is claimed to provide a three- to five-time performance gain compared to `RandomPartitioner`.

Please note Murmur3Partitioner is the default partitioner for version 1.2 onward. If you are upgrading from an older version, make sure you change this setting back to what you had in the previous Cassandra setup. Not changing partitioners to the appropriate settings will cause Cassandra to not start up.

Atomic batches

Atomic batches in version 1.2 guarantee that if one part of a batch succeeds, all of it will. The improvement here is the fact that the batch is first written to the system table. It is removed once the batch is executed. This has some performance penalty. So, in case you wanted to use super-fast, but relatively risky batch updates, you may use the UNLOGGED keyword in the BATCH statement like BEGIN UNLOGGED BATCH.

Replaying failed batches are usually safe in general except for the counter cases as they are not idempotent. Replaying counter queries will have side effects. For a batched counter updated, use BEGIN COUNTER BATCH.

Query profiling

Cassandra 1.2 provides a query profiling tool that lets you analyze the performance of queries and view which action is taking how much time; a detailed overview much like EXPLAIN from the RDBMS world.

In cqlsh, you can turn on profiling by executing tracing on before running a statement to trace.

Collections support

In CQL 3 there is either a static family or a dynamic family. In case you wanted to store multiple shipping addresses or multiple credit card details or multiple e-mail IDs in the users table, you will need to have a static column family for static entities user_name, age, passwords, and so on. You will need to have a dynamic column family that can store any number of shipping records. But it is a pain. In Thrift, you would have just created a tag-like column name in the same column family. CQL 3 provides a very nice extension of this approach, instead of you managing the tags; it gives you three collections based on the same idea that work pretty neatly. CQL 3 supports list, set, and map collections.

Sets

Here are some examples of operations on a set:

```
# Creating a table with shipping_addr as set of text type
cqlsh:my_keyspace> CREATE TABLE users
(id int primary key, name varchar, shipping_addr set<text>);

# Inserting values to as set
cqlsh:my_keyspace> INSERT INTO users (id, name, shipping_addr)
VALUES (1, 'John Doe', {'some addr1', 'some addr2'});

# CQL interprets it as a single entity
cqlsh:my_keyspace> SELECT * FROM users;

id  | name      | shipping_addr
----+-----------+-------------------------
  1 | John Doe  | {some addr1, some addr2}

# Adding more elements to set. Set does not allow duplicates
cqlsh:my_keyspace> UPDATE users SET
shipping_addr = shipping_addr + {'new addr1', 'new addr2', 'some
addr1'}
WHERE id = 1;

# No terms are repeated
cqlsh:my_keyspace> SELECT * FROM users;

id  | name      | shipping_addr
----+-----------+----------------------------------------------------
  1 | John Doe  | {new addr1, new addr2, some addr1, some addr2}

# Removing elements from set
cqlsh:my_keyspace> UPDATE users SET
shipping_addr = shipping_addr - { 'someaddr1'}
WHERE id = 1;
```

Set is denoted by a set of curly brackets.

Lists

Lists follow the same patterns for creating, inserting, adding, and removing entities. There are two differences. First, list is denoted with square brackets — []; and second, a list can have duplicate items. Removal of items from a list will remove all instances of it.

```
cqlsh:my_keyspace> CREATE TABLE session_record
(id uuid primary key, user varchar, activity list<text>);

cqlsh:my_keyspace> INSERT INTO session_record (id, user, activity)
VALUES (3c71c50a-9686-4313-a045-3bdc908b9816, 'Jack P', ['logged
in']);

cqlsh:my_keyspace> UPDATE session_record SET
activity = activity + ['closed open bug']
WHERE id = 3c71c50a-9686-4313-a045-3bdc908b9816;

[-- snip --]
cqlsh:my_keyspace> UPDATE session_record SET
activity = activity + ['closed open bug']
WHERE id = 3c71c50a-9686-4313-a045-3bdc908b9816;

[-- snip --]

cqlsh:my_keyspace> SELECT * FROM session_record;

id       | activity        | user
---------+-----------------+--------
3c..16   | [logged in, closed open bug, added bug, closed open bug,
logged out] | Jack P
```

Maps

Maps are dictionaries-like structures. Maps have unique keys. Here are some typical usages of map in CQL:

```
# Creating map column is pretty similar to set or list
cqlsh:my_keyspace> CREATE TABLE map_test
(id int primary key, txt varchar, some_map map<int, varchar>);

# elements in map follow Python dictionary or JSON like structure
cqlsh:my_keyspace> INSERT INTO map_test (id, txt, some_map)
values (1, 'txt 1', {42: 'hello world'});
```

```
# adding is a bit different than that for set or list
cqlsh:my_keyspace> UPDATE map_test SET
some_map[314] = 'pi is a lie'
WHERE id = 1;

# updating a record requires its unique key to be known
cqlsh:my_keyspace> UPDATE map_test SET some_map[42] = 'Hello
Cassandra' WHERE id = 1;

cqlsh:my_keyspace> select * from map_test;

id  | some_map                                | txt
----+-----------------------------------------+-------
  1 | {42: Hello Cassandra, 314: pi is a lie} | txt 1

# Element deletion is done by key.
cqlsh:my_keyspace> delete some_map[314] from map_test where id = 1;
```

Collections in Cassandra 1.2 greatly enhance the user experience. It is probably the most motivating feature to upgrade from the previous version to Cassandra 1.2. Note that collections look deceptively similar to Java collections with generics. However, unlike Java, you cannot nest elements to have multiple-level collections.

Support for programming languages

Cassandra is supported by most of the major programming languages. Most of these libraries are open source, and rigorously tested. The libraries provide fail-over support and connection pooling ability. The latest driver lists can be viewed at http://wiki.apache.org/cassandra/ClientOptions. Here is a list of some drivers that support CQL 3:

- **Java**: You can find the DataStax Java driver at https://github.com/datastax/java-driver and the Hector Java client at http://hector-client.github.io/hector/build/html/index.html

- **Python**: You can download the drivers for Pythons such as Pycassa at http://github.com/pycassa/pycassa and the DataStax Python CQL driver at https://github.com/datastax/python-driver

- **Node.js**: You can find the Node.js driver Helenus at https://github.com/simplereach/helenus

- **PHP**: You can find the Cassandra PDO driver at http://code.google.com/a/apache-extras.org/p/cassandra-pdo/

- **C++**: You can find the LibCQL C++ driver at `https://github.com/mstump/libcql`

- **NET**: Find the DataStax C# driver at `http://github.com/datastax/csharp-driver`

- **Ruby**: Find the cql-rb Ruby driver at `https://github.com/iconara/cql-rb`

- **Closure**: Find the Alia driver at `https://github.com/mpenet/alia`

The Cassandra community wiki advises to use CQL 3 driver for new projects. If you are using an old version or wanted to use Thrift API, you may look into a list of drivers supporting Thrift for various languages at this web page: `http://wiki.apache.org/cassandra/ClientOptionsThrift`.

Here is a quick example of CQL with the DataStax CQL driver:

```
$ python
Python 2.7.4 (default, Apr 19 2013, 18:28:01)
[GCC 4.7.3] on linux2
Type "help", "copyright", "credits" or "license" for more information.

>>>from cassandra.cluster import Cluster
>>>cluster = Cluster(['localhost'])
>>>session = cluster.connect()
No handlers could be found for logger "cassandra.metadata"

>>>session.execute("DROP KEYSPACEcql_test")
>>>session.execute("CREATE KEYSPACEcql_test WITH replication =
{'class':'SimpleStrategy', 'replication_factor':1}")

>>>session.execute("USE cql_test")
>>>session.execute("CREATE TABLE users (id VARCHAR PRIMARY KEY, name
VARCHAR, email VARCHAR, passwdVARCHAR, subscription_typeINT)")

>>>session.execute("insert into users (id, name, email, passwd,
subscription_type) values ('james@fargo.com', 'James Gray', 'james@
fargo.com', 'p@sswd123', 3)")

>>>session.execute("select * from users")
[Row(id=u'james@fargo.com', email=u'james@fargo.com', name=u'James
Gray', passwd=u'p@sswd123', subscription_type=3)]

>>>session.execute("insert into users (id, name, email, passwd,
subscription_type) values ('jane@fargo.com', 'Jane Jessy', 'jane@
fargo.com', 's3crate', 1)")
>>>session.execute("select * from users")
```

```
[Row(id=u'jane@fargo.com', email=u'jane@fargo.com', name=u'JaneJessy',
passwd=u's3crate', subscription_type=1), Row(id=u'james@fargo.com',
email=u'james@fargo.com', name=u'James Gray', passwd=u'p@sswd123',
subscription_type=3)]

>>>session.execute("DELETE FROM users where id = 'james@fargo.com'")
>>>session.execute("select * from users")
[Row(id=u'jane@fargo.com', email=u'jane@fargo.com', name=u'JaneJessy',
passwd=u's3crate', subscription_type=1)]

>>>cluster.shutdown()
```

This is just a quick example to show you how easy it is to use CQL 3 with Python. However, for a real project, you might want to use connection pooling, prepared statement, and batches. Please read the full documentation for details at `http://datastax.github.io/python-driver/api/index.html`.

Summary

We have seen CQL 3 add big leaps in Cassandra usability. It is easier to understand for someone moving from SQL development to Cassandra. At the same time, to a Thrift developer, it is again a rework to rewire the map-of-maps schema-free structure of Cassandra to the transposed version of that.

Cassandra 1.2 has been a nice upgrade. It strengthens CQL 3 by adding syntactic sugar to storage techniques to provide collections support. CQL 3 is laconic and supported by all leading programming languages. Apart from CQL, VNodes are the other major development. VNodes is extremely useful for mid-to-large Cassandra setup. VNodes alleviates the load generated by ring alteration by distributing responsibility to stream out across a larger number of nodes and by making the bootstrap process more parallel. A side effect of this load balancing task gets solved automatically. There are other smaller performance boosts for version 1.2.

Cassandra 2.0 is proposed in the latter half of 2013. It will have some improvements, and legacy systems might not be supported. Some of the exciting features of version 2.x are the ability to provide JAR files as triggers, so one can send a registration mail as soon as a new row is inserted in the `users` table. Compare and Set (CAS) enables clients to update a column by checking if its value matches the provided value. For example, `UPDATE  loans SET debt = debt + 10000 WHERE user_id = 6f757ca0-dd32-4149-b46d-8f2b744cab02 IF DEBT = 31415`.

Index

R

S

tunable 49

U

ulimit -a command 114
update-alternatives utility 120
update-dependencies utility 118
UPDATE query 287, 288
upgradesstable command 201
userName column 68
user object 92
users column family 68, 80
USE statement 294
USING CONSISTENCY clause 287
UTF8Type comparator 81, 83
UTF8Type text 74

V

validators
  about 75
  setting 76
Virtual Nodes. *See* VNodes
VisualVM
  about 191
  URL 191
VNodes 294, 296

W

WHERE clause 283, 284, 285
wide column family. *See* dynamic column
      family
wide-row index 80
wide-row time series
  about 95-97
  issues 98
  solution 98
write performance 153

Y

Yahoo! Cloud Serving Benchmark. *See*
      YCSB 152
Yet Another Resource Negotiator (YARN)
  URL 243

Z

ZkMultiLock class 104
ZkTransaction class 104

Thank you for buying
Mastering Apache Cassandra

About Packt Publishing

Packt, pronounced 'packed', published its first book "*Mastering phpMyAdmin for Effective MySQL Management*" in April 2004 and subsequently continued to specialize in publishing highly focused books on specific technologies and solutions.

Our books and publications share the experiences of your fellow IT professionals in adapting and customizing today's systems, applications, and frameworks. Our solution based books give you the knowledge and power to customize the software and technologies you're using to get the job done. Packt books are more specific and less general than the IT books you have seen in the past. Our unique business model allows us to bring you more focused information, giving you more of what you need to know, and less of what you don't.

Packt is a modern, yet unique publishing company, which focuses on producing quality, cutting-edge books for communities of developers, administrators, and newbies alike. For more information, please visit our website: www.packtpub.com.

About Packt Open Source

In 2010, Packt launched two new brands, Packt Open Source and Packt Enterprise, in order to continue its focus on specialization. This book is part of the Packt Open Source brand, home to books published on software built around Open Source licences, and offering information to anybody from advanced developers to budding web designers. The Open Source brand also runs Packt's Open Source Royalty Scheme, by which Packt gives a royalty to each Open Source project about whose software a book is sold.

Writing for Packt

We welcome all inquiries from people who are interested in authoring. Book proposals should be sent to author@packtpub.com. If your book idea is still at an early stage and you would like to discuss it first before writing a formal book proposal, contact us; one of our commissioning editors will get in touch with you.

We're not just looking for published authors; if you have strong technical skills but no writing experience, our experienced editors can help you develop a writing career, or simply get some additional reward for your expertise.

Cassandra High Performance Cookbook

ISBN: 978-1-84951-512-2   Paperback: 310 pages

Over 150 recipes to design and optimize large-scale Apache Cassandra deployments

1. Get the best out of Cassandra using this efficient recipe bank

2. Configure and tune Cassandra components to enhance performance

3. Deploy Cassandra in various environments and monitor its performance

4. Well illustrated, step-by-step recipes to make all tasks look easy!

Instant Apache Cassandra for Developers Starter

ISBN: 978-1-78216-390-9   Paperback: 50 pages

Start developing with Cassandra and learn how to handle big data

1. Learn something new in an Instant! A short, fast, focused guide delivering immediate results

2. Tune and optimize Cassandra to handle big data

3. Learn all about the Cassandra Query Language and Cassandra-CLI

4. Practical examples of Cassandra's Java APIs

Please check **www.PacktPub.com** for information on our titles

[PACKT] open source �✲
PUBLISHING   community experience distilled

Scaling Big Data with Hadoop and Solr

ISBN: 978-1-78328-137-4   Paperback: 144 pages

Learn exciting new ways to build efficient, high performance enterprise search repositories for Big Data using Hadoop and Solr

1. Understand the different approaches of making Solr work on Big Data as well as the benefits and drawbacks

2. Learn from interesting, real-life use cases for Big Data search along with sample code

3. Work with the Distributed Enterprise Search without prior knowledge of Hadoop and Solr

Instant Cassandra Query Language

ISBN: 978-1-78328-271-5   Paperback: 54 pages

A practical, step-by-step guide for quickly getting started with Cassandra Query Language

1. Learn something new in an Instant! A short, fast, focused guide delivering immediate results

2. Covers the most frequently used constructs using practical examples

3. Dive deeper into CQL, TTL, batch operations, and more

4. Learn how to shed Thrift and adopt a CQL-based binary protocol

Please check **www.PacktPub.com** for information on our titles